*Victorian Writing and
Working Women*

Victorian Writing and Working Women,

The Other Side of Silence

Julia Swindells

University of Minnesota Press, Minneapolis

Copyright © 1985, by Julia Swindells

Published by the University of Minnesota Press
2037 University Avenue Southeast, Minneapolis MN 554414.
Published simultaneously in Canada by Fitzhenry & Whiteside Limited, Markham.

Printed in Great Britain.
Typeset by Saxon Ltd., Derby. England.

Library of Congress Cataloging-in Publication Data
Swindells, Julia
   Victorian writing and working women

   Bibliography: p.
   1. English prose literature – 19th century – History and
criticism.   2. Women in literature.   3. Work in
literature.   4. English fiction – 19th century – History
and criticism.   5. Autobiography – Women authors.
6. Laboring class writings, English – History and
criticism.   7. Women – Employment – Great Britain –
History – 19th century. I. Title
   PR 788.W65S9   1985   828'.808'09352042   85-20821
   ISBN 0-8166-1476-8
   ISBN 0-8166-1477-6 (pbk.)

The University of Minnesota is an equal-opportunity educator and employer.

If we had a keen vision and feeling of all ordinary human life, it would be like hearing the grass grow and the squirrel's heart beat, and we should die of that roar which lies on the other side of silence.

George Eliot, *Middlemarch*, 1872

Contents

Acknowledgements

This book was possible because of the emotional, moral, intellectual and political support of Lisa Jardine, Su Kappeler and Ben Bradnack. Many thanks as well, for help past and present, to Margaret Coleman, Ros Morpeth, Morag Shiach, Joan Swindells, Jane Thompson and Jill Walker.

I am also indebted to Cambridge Women's Resources' Centre, especially to Kath Gordon and Anna O'Connor; and also to the Southampton Women Writers' Workshops of 1979, especially to Chris Kent and Karen Wyatt.

I would like to thank Michelle Stanworth for her work on the manuscript, Shirley Barry for typing it, Jack Swindells for help with proofs, Jesus College, Cambridge, for affording me some resources and time for the book's research, and, not to be forgotten, the LTP Cambridge cowboys for being consistently provoking.

For solidarity in these times of crisis I would like to add my thanks to old allies: Lynda Rogers, Linda Turner, Rachel Wyndham, and to Judy Cooke, Nick Alexander and Jim Hornsby.

The author and publisher are grateful to the following organizations and individuals for permission to reproduce previously published material in this volume:

J. M. Dent and Sons Ltd for extracts reprinted from *A Fire in the Kitchen: The Autobiography of a Cook* by Florence White.

Europa Publications Limited for extracts reprinted from *Bread, Knowledge and Freedom* by David Vincent.

Oxford University Press for extracts reprinted from *Miss Weeton's Journal of a Governess* edited by Edward Hall, vols

1 (1936) and 2 (1939).

Adrienne Rich and W. W. Norton and Company Inc for stanza 12 of 'Natural Resources' in *The Dream of a Common Language,* 1974-77.

Virago Press Ltd for extracts from *Tea and Tranquillisers* by Diane Harpwood, © Diane Harpwood 1981, and from *Life as We Know It* edited by Margaret Llewelyn Davies, published by Virago 1977, © 1931 Quentin Bell and Angelica Garnett.

Michelene Wandor for 'Some Male Poets' first published in *UpBeat.*

Hail! natural desire! Hail! happiness! divine happiness! and pleasure of all sorts, flowers and wine, though one fades and the other intoxicates; and half-crown tickets out of London on Sundays, and singing in a dark chapel hymns about death, and anything, anything that interrupts and confounds the tapping of typewriters and filing of letters and forging of links and chains, binding the Empire together.

Virginia Woolf, *Orlando*, 1928

Introduction

I could say that this book is about writing. I could also say that it is about some problems of men and writing. It is indeed about something to do with the forging of power and the binding of Empire through the tapping of typewriters. It may also be, in the great scale of things, about the search for flowers and wine.

I prefer, though, to say that its primary concerns relate to women *now*, to our experiences and our perceptions of the world. This emphasis on women *now* may seem a strange one in relation to a book which announces itself as being about *Victorian* writing, but it is an emphasis which I make strongly. This concern with women now, with being a woman now, was and is the chief informant of two specific aspects of the book's content: women's recent history – how women's experiences are constituted in what is here described as 'the past-present relation' – and the position of women in the division of labour.

To bring these matters – women now, women in history, women in the division of labour – together, I have written about gender, class and labour relations in the nineteenth-century novel, with particular reference to the writings of Dickens, Eliot, Gaskell and Thackeray, and I have written about a number of autobiographies by working women. The book is in two mutually informing parts, taking fiction and autobiography as separate types or genres of writing, but important in their relations for Victorian writing and the professional, literary production process.

The first chapter, 'Outrageous Claims', is important because it is an introduction to the close readings of nineteenth-century novels which immediately follow, and to the book as

a whole. It makes use of theories of professionalism in
relation to the position of the writer, and in particular to the
position in gender and class of the writer. Before giving more
detail of the concerns of that chapter, however, I shall make
reference again to the autobiographies of working women.
The significance I am giving to the description 'working
women' is important throughout the book, carrying, as the
phrase does, a particular load in the 'working'.

The book is not a survey of women's labour in Victorian
writing or society: not, at least, unless the definition of
'labour' is one in which some of the conventional terms of
social class are revised and reconstituted for women. My
concern is with an experience and an experience of work
which is inseparable from subjectivity and self-perception. In
other words, the book is at pains to resist both the notion that
'work' is that which is defined exclusively and exhaustively
according to the capitalist production process as it is understood now, and the belief that 'self', the gendered self, is
defined exclusively and exhaustively according to some
separate set of operations called patriarchy.

> It seems to me that the construction of gender difference and
> hierarchy is created at work as well as at home – and that the
> effect on women (less physical and technical capability, lack of
> confidence, lower pay) may well cast a shadow on the
> sex-relations of domestic life.
>
> In socialist-feminist thought there has been a clear divide
> between production (privileged site of class domination) and
> the family (privileged site of sexual domination). The patriar-
> chal family is recognized as adapted to the interests of capital
> and the capitalist division of labour as being imprinted with
> the patterns of domestic life. They are conceded to be
> mutually effective, but are nonetheless still largely conceived
> as two separate spheres, capitalism holding sway in one,
> patriarchy in the other.[1]

My writing about working women autobiographers is about
subjectivities constructed 'at work as well as at home'. And I
have taken autobiographies from the nineteenth century in
the main, because this is the crucial history in which the

gender attitudes and practices we have inherited in the twentieth century were formed. It is the relationship of these attitudes and practices to the division of labour with which I am concerned in the first chapter, as it raises the whole issue of professionalism.

> The point I wish to make is that any sociological analysis of the profession has to take seriously the view that many of the dominant categories of thought which permeate our common-sense attitudes – as well as the power to enforce them - are to some extent traceable to the political organization of particular occupations.[2]

'Outrageous Claims' should not be thought of as a 'sociological analysis', but it does make what I take to be very important connections between the writer and professional organization.

The nineteenth century is the series of historical moments which structured and restructured the professions in a growth of that work seeking to describe itself as professional. It is the nineteenth century, then, which saw the development of the professions as the powerful groups and 'reality definers' (in a phrase of Geoff Esland's) which they are now. My argument in that chapter, and in the book as a whole, is that *literary* professionalism in the nineteenth century is an important part of this process.

I do not intend, however, to isolate the professions as the source and sole origin of social inequity, gender restriction and dominant categories of thought. In criticizing professionalism and certain kinds of professional organization, the book is taking issue with the structure of labour as a whole, and with the values, philosophies and modes of thinking which articulate the politics sustaining that structure.

The chapter 'Outrageous Claims' starts from ideas about professionalism and proceeds to chart a set of connections which are needed before beginning to explore the gender, class and labour relations of women's writing and women's experiences: the placing of that writing and those experiences in, and in relation to, literary professionalism. It is worth saying more precisely what those connections are.

The nineteenth century was formative in the development of the professional structures and practices that we now experience as highly significant in the division of labour. These structures and practices grew up with industrial capitalism which is sustained by a hierarchical, sexual division of labour. This hierarchy is also one of class, and involves rewarding 'mental' more highly than 'manual' labour. For women workers in that hierarchy, class and gender act as mutual mediators and mutually restricting categories. For this reason, the terms needed to describe women's labour, and the position of women in relation to capitalism, need to call upon and create broader definitions of class than those available for men.

The arguments I am putting in this chapter are not isolated to one particular profession or organization of work. They are, more generally, about what the professions share and what common interests they have as 'reality definers' and organizers of dominant thought, from their position in the division of labour. The brief study of medicine, as an example of one type of nineteenth-century professional organization, sets up some of the terms and ways of thinking about literary professionalism. It has implications for some of the connections and inter-relations of the professions in the structure of labour. If all professions had different and competing or conflicting interests, they might represent less of a cohesive political force.

The logic of the connections that the chapter makes incorporates a consideration of women in relation to professionalism, and of women writers. I ought to emphasize, though, that my argument about women and about women writers is *not* an argument about biological determinism. It is not an argument which says that women's biology predisposes us women or limits us to writing only in certain ways. The case I am making is about culture, not nature. It is about the dispositions and predispositions, socially organized, particularly in the division of labour, of gender prejudices and gender relations. It is about the implications of these dispositions and predispositions for writing, and about their organization in writing. Culture allows the possibility, though not the likelihood, that some individual women will escape the restrictions of gender and gender history and that some individual men will avoid perpetuating patriarchal and masculinist practices. It is because culture grants permission in this way, albeit in limited conditions, and within certain constraints and to subserve particular interests, that not all nineteenth-century women were victims of their biology and not all nineteenth-century men were sexist oppressors. The culturally mediating factors of class and other social influences on individual experience are important challenges to any determinations of biology.

The argument about women writers would be simpler, though more depressing in its implications, if it *were* about biology. It would also be simpler if it were not complicated by questions of class. The difficulty and the issue is in puzzling out how and in what circumstances and conditions, gender, with and in class, functions as restriction: and the circumstances and conditions in which liberation from restriction (real liberation – not a token cross-gendering to subserve dominant interests) does or can occur.

I reiterate, though, that chapter 1 'Outrageous Claims', is not a sociological study or a comprehensive theory of professionalism, even of literary professionalism. Rather, it calls upon some of that sociology and some of that theory to make a political and politicized case for reading texts and understanding culture.

The three chapters following 'Outrageous Claims', from 'George Eliot' to 'The Gentleman's Club, Literature', are about some nineteenth-century novelists and some of their novels. There is also some reference, particularly in relation to Gaskell and Thackeray in chapter 4, to autobiographical and biographical writings. These three chapters might be read as a self-contained study of some nineteenth-century fiction and its writers: as, say, some thoughts about literary professionalism as presented or articulated by the four writers concerned, or as a study of gender, class and labour relations in particular nineteenth-century novels of a certain fame and continuing influence. To take these three chapters as only a self-contained study, however, would not be quite the point.

The more particular purpose is to set some readings of Victorian fiction, particularly of canonical texts or that which has been selected from Victorian fiction as special (and which continues to reproduce cultural influence), alongside some readings of working women's autobiographies.

The book, indeed, states my reasons for a commitment to this comparison of autobiography and novel. For all the complexity of representation by and of women in Victorian fiction, there remains something to be said, something missing by and of and about women. It is this belief, or rather discovery, which largely informs my reading of working women's autobiographies.

In finding 'something missing' in the nineteenth-century novel, though, I already betray a high expectation of that genre. Indeed, I take the novel, in its history and in the past-present relation, to be crucial to the construction of gender relations and sexual ideology as we experience them now. To tease this out a bit further, I should say that I take *the nineteenth century* to be crucial to the formation of present-day gender attitudes and practices, *and* that I take nineteenth-century *fiction* to be crucial. In other words, there are two aspects to the argument, and I shall comment now on the fiction.

The importance of the fiction is in the way that our readings and our culture have selected and incorporated certain books and certain artists as special. Those books and artists have, in that process, become influential in and have reproduced influence on the construction of socio-sexual ideologies. Certain nineteenth-century writers of fictional narrative are particularly powerful in their effects on contemporaries such as the working women autobiographers, and, I maintain, on twentieth-century readers.

My response to each of the four novelists is, though, different in kind. In taking Eliot first of the four 'great writers', the book gives a particular load to her representations of class and gender. The chapter is about the division of labour as Eliot presents and represents it, and the significance she gives in her earlier fiction to the artisan, and in her later fiction to members of the professional classes. It is about what can be made of how she writes about 'mental' and 'manual' work: of how this distinction features in her (re)presentation of a fictional world. It is particularly about how the women in her novels 'fit' the division of labour, and what follows for the gender relations internal to the fiction.

The chapter carries a load in another way. It is the first in the sequence of those about fiction and it is the only one which deals exclusively with a woman who is 'successful' in terms of the literary production process. There is a slight danger that what I write may be asking a woman writer to take responsibility for what I argue elsewhere is a masculinist tradition, characterized, that is, by certain kinds of gender prejudice which derive from a male history. Alternatively, putting this burden on Eliot might be read as an appropriate approach to the whole question of what pressures there are on women to function as men when an entry into the professional, literary production process is being, or has been, made. It might also be read as a way into that other whole question about the nature of that literary production process: what kind of process it is that requires women to function as men within certain constraints and what the gender relations, gender attitudes and prejudices, sexual ideologies of such a process might be.

In the chapter about representational responsibilities in Dickens, these questions about the professional literary production process and its gender attitudes and practices are, in one sense, more simply approached than they are in relation to Eliot. Dickens, a man, articulates various kinds of gender prejudice unambivalently. It would be wrong and reductive, however, to imply that a reading of his novels, and of the gender, class and labour relations of his fictional representations, finds him simply ideologically unsound or erroneous. His own class position is such that there are significant and complex mediating factors in his representation of gender. The chief aspect of the argument is, though, that his fiction or some of his fiction maintains a systematic and rigorous attack on certain normative operations of the

division of labour, an attack which includes a response to the
sexual division of labour that cannot simply be dismissed as,
in itself, normative.

His representation of women does, however, pose distinct
limitations on his exploration of gender relations as social
relations. It was this sense of restriction or lack which made
me use a particular strategy to take the measure of some of his
writing about sexuality. From outside his fiction I call on
histories, biographies and letters of Florence Nightingale, to
present an example, from history and text, of a powerful
counter-possibility to those constructions of womanhood and
of woman's labour most congenial to Dickens.

The chapter about Gaskell and Thackeray, 'The Gentleman's Club, Literature', relies much more heavily than the
previous two on polemical and autobiographical utterances
about literary professionalism. That is also to say that it relies
less heavily on readings of novels, on the internal detail of
fiction. In that sense, it represents a median point between
the chapters about autobiography and those about fiction. (I
would not, however, wish to overestimate the importance of
this connection. The important strategy is in the invitation to
set a reading of fiction alongside that of autobiography
producing some comparisons between working women's
autobiographies and the nineteenth-century novel, in the
literary production process.) I speculate, for instance, on the
different class and gender routes whch have their determinations in the lives of the two writers – Gaskell and Thackeray –
which dispose and predispose them towards different types of
writing career and to different types of writing, which yet
have their shared aspects. The play of comparison between
different kinds of novelist, different kinds of literary professional, as with the central idea of comparing nineteenth-
century novelist with working woman autobiographer, comments on the whole business of writing, of the literary
production process, of the writer. It is my belief that this is the
area – writing, the writer – where professional ideologies and
practices are most firmly encoded as norms of taste, morality
and subjectivity; and that all texts, and perhaps most of all the
canonical text, are involved and implicated in this process of

encoding. This is not to imply culpability – no text is innocent – but is a starting-point and a framework for a productive, politicized reading, which recognizes that dominant discourse carries certain kinds of inescapable and unavoidable influence.

It is from chapter 4 to chapter 5 that the shift occurs from novel to autobiography, from famous writer to working woman. 'Working Women Autobiographers' begins to describe and establish the social group of 'working women', and the individuals and individualities within that group. Certain class alignments are made, but without finding the terms of definition of the social group 'working women' identical with or symmetrical to those of 'working-class men'. This chapter also establishes a working method for a gender- and class-conscious history, as well as introducing the particular autobiographies which are the chief subject(s) of chapters 5 to 8, and presenting some of those restrictions which, I argue, the women autobiographers share with working-class men in their initial and formative experience.

'Women's Issues' argues that the adult experience of working people begins to diversify according to gender and that there is a special, differentiated case to be made for and about women. This chapter concentrates in detail on close readings of the autobiographies, paying particular attention to women's sexuality and women's politics.

It is the chapter 'An Itch for Scribbling' that specifically maps some of the ways in which working women autobiographers perceive 'work', and perceive themselves in relation to work. It traces some of the ways in which these self-perceptions influence the kinds of work the women autobiographers do, the kinds of work they might elect to do, and their attitudes to working lives. It is this chapter too that develops from some thoughts about how writing (and 'the literary') enters, with work and alongside work, into the ways in which the women autobiographers see, construct, and write about themselves.

The final chapter, in which I consider the effects of the professional production of history and art on our readings of the working women's autobiographies, shows my method of reading and understanding textuality at its most explicit. It traces some effects of editors, editorial processes, commentators and critics on the autobiographies and our readings of them. The method, though, is not confined to this chapter, but is an informing principle in the book as a whole. The final chapter also draws together some thoughts about professionalism and supposed amateurism, in the writing process and in relation to critical judgement.

POLITICIZED READINGS

Some of the terms used in the chapter, 'Outrageous Claims', are important to the book as a whole. My concern has been with utilizing these terms for the purposes of critical readings, and the test of their validity is in the coherence or incoherence of those textual readings rather than in extant definitions. It may help, though, if I make some reference here to some of the terminology that I have incorporated into the ways I think about and read texts. I use 'ideology', for instance, a lot. Without wishing to induce groans by producing or reproducing yet another definition of that term, I will refer to two extracts which have influenced and ought to serve as indicators of how I am using it. It is not accidental that they are both from cultural/literary studies.

> Finally there is an obvious need for a general term to describe not only the products but the processes of all signification, including the signification of values. It is interesting that 'ideology' and 'ideological' have been widely used in this sense. Volosinov, for example, uses 'ideological' to describe the process of the production of meaning through signs, and 'ideology' is taken as the dimension of social experience in which meanings and values are produced.

In the second extract, 'ideology' is:

> the sum of the ways in which people both live and represent to themselves their relationship to the conditions of existence. Ideology is *inscribed in signifying practices* – in discourses,

myths, presentations and re-presentations of the way 'things are' [author's emphasis].

In taking 'ideology' to be 'inscribed in signifying practices' and as 'the dimension of social experience in which meanings and values are produced', I subscribe to neutral senses of the term. It is difficult, though, to avoid giving the word more loaded, adversely critical connotations, especially in the territory of sexual ideology where the common signifying practices and social experience are ones of which it is difficult to approve. In the book, this critical use of the term, in which 'ideology' may have suggestions of unwelcome dominance and even of coercion, is in tension with more neutral senses.

The second extract above is also useful for understanding the way in which I use 'representation', and the way in which I use 'discourse', which Catherine Belsey, in the same work, elaborates as follows: 'Ideology, I have gone on to argue, is *inscribed in* specific *discourses*. A *discourse* is a domain of language-use, a particuar way of talking (and writing and thinking)' (her emphases). As for my use of 'representation', I tend to assume a common and understood meaning in certain kinds of cultural/literary studies, frequently in the domain of 'representation' in fiction. I do, however, also try to give that use additional resonance by picking up uses in other disciplines and particularly in polemic. This is what I do later when I make connections between different professions and different subject disciplines - between, for instance, Medicine and Literature in chapter 1. It is important that these terms should retain and acquire an inter-disciplinary, cross-cultural power, and not be confined to special subject disciplines where their meanings may well be politically neutered.

For understandings of other terms such as 'the literary', I shall have to rely on the reader's patience with the main body of the text, on the principle that oaks cannot be shrunk into acorns, except perhaps by some demoniacal being - the omniscient critic – who can invert the process of creation.

My concern with inter-disciplinary approaches and politi-cized readings is also a concern with feminist criticism. As with 'ideology' and 'professionalism', it would be inappropriate to explain the theory (that would require three additional books), but it is important to make reference to feminist criticism as another of the influences on the mode of reading texts presented here. The mention of that commitment or influence does, however, raise problems immediately.

It will be clear from a glance at the chapter titles and footnotes of the book that it is concerned to some extent with male writers as well as female, and with representations of men as well as women. It will also be clear that this concern has been informed by and constructed out of readings of male theorists as well as female. Such a type of criticism or critique might be thought revisionist by those who believe that men have no part, even as objects, in feminist discourse. However, a feminist analysis which concerns itself solely, say, with women writers, or solely with representations of women in texts, or even with both of those, is, paradoxically, in greater danger of placing us women as *objects* in the discourse than the type of analysis offered here, in which women are the key subjects in a study of gender relations as social relations.

There is, though, a sense in which texts have nasty habits of turning subjects into objects. For instance, while I am convinced that I am a woman writing, you, reading, may see only a writer writing about women. It is not always possible to discern where the object ends and the subject begins. Leaving that set of relations for the moment under-theorized (though the work is being done), I leave the issue with a reiteration of my commitment to exploring the position in gender and class of the writer, with the intention of perceiving and understanding women now, as a woman now.

Part I
Literature and the Professions

Literature cannot be the business of a woman's life, and it ought not to be.

Robert Southey, letter to Charlotte Brontë, 1837

Literature has become a profession . . . like the army of Xerxes, swelled and encumbered by women, children, and ill-trained troops.

Fraser's Magazine, 1847

Ah! ye knights of the pen! May honour be your shield and truth tip your lances! Be gentle to all gentle people. Be modest to women. Be tender to children . . .
W.M. Thackeray, *The Chances of the Literary Profession*,
1850

America is now wholly given over to a d———d mob of scribbling women.

Nathaniel Hawthorne, letter to publisher, 1855

Man is more courageous, pugnacious, and energetic than woman, and has a more inventive genius.
Charles Darwin, *The Descent of Man*, and *Selection in Relation to Sex*, 1871

The crowning evil which arises from the system of lionism is, that it cuts off the retreat of literary persons into the great body of human beings. They are marked out as a class, and can no longer take refuge from their toils and their publicity in ordinary life. This is a hardship shared by authors who are far above being directly injured by the prevalent practice . . .
I had heard all my life of the vanity of women as a subject of pity to men: but when I went to London, lo! I saw vanity in high places which was never transcended by that of women in their lowlier rank. There was Brougham, wincing under a newspaper criticism, and playing the fool among silly women. There was Jeffrey, flirting with clever women, in long succession. There was Bulwer, on a sofa, sparkling and languishing among a set of female votaries, – he and they dizened out, perfumed, and presenting the nearest picture to a seraglio to be seen on British ground – only the indifference or hauteur of the lord of the harem being absent.

Harriet Martineau, *Autobiography*, 1877

1

Outrageous Claims

The contemporary attack on professionals is gaining momentum. Critics have reversed the arguments which legitimate professional status to assert that professionals, far from existing to meet service demands made by the public, exist to create those demands.[1] The same argument more darkly shaded claims that the demands which professionals set out to create for their services are largely unnecessary, and that professionals play 'on public fears of disorder and disease', 'deliberately' mystifying the public with jargon.[2]

One version of the argument has even gone so far as to equate professionals with racists. Professionalism, like racism, finds the client 'deficient', proceeds to support this finding with scientific/biological evidence, and finishes by substituting a prescription for a prejudice. That act of diagnosis, neatly bypassing the client, inscribes the professional's claim to special knowledge and special privilege.[3] The professional, ever more solipsistic in this special knowledge, proceeds to pronounce the client efficient for having submitted to the act of diagnosis.

The analogy with racism quickly extends to gender:

The professional and the racist ethos converge. They are both based, albeit with different subtleties, on the same assumption: biological diagnosis entitles the biocracy to social grading. Nowhere can this convergence of professional ethos with biological discrimination be seen more clearly than through the history of gynecology.[4]

The 'history of gynecology' mentioned here is a particular creature connecting professional medics with female parts, but a glimpse at the *OED* extends 'gynecology' to: 'That branch of medical science which treats of the functions and diseases peculiar to women' and also to '*loosely*, the science of womankind' – and in that emphasis on 'loosely' is more than one story from gender history.

It is not yet time, though, to take on in this account the full implications of gender for professionalism. The priority is to pose some questions about why the attack on professionals has been such a long time in coming, and why it constitutes a still small voice. It may just happen that in answering these questions, some gender terms will emerge. In beginning the process of answering, a significant recent history beckons.

From 1841 to 1881, there was a massive expansion of the professions, of work describing itself and seeking to describe itself as professional. This expansion and redefinition of professional work was part of that change in the labour process and in the organization of labour which has been historicized and dramatized as the Industrial Revolution. In emphasizing the change from agricultural to industrial work, elaborated as the Industrial Revolution, historians have, until recently, neglected to account for the extent to which both agriculture and industry were being subsumed in an increasingly *professional* society.[5] The common term in Victorian Britain to describe the newly emerging power group (1840s to 1880s) was precisely 'the professional classes', more frequently used than later terms such as 'bourgeoisie', 'middle class'.[6] Commentaries selected to illustrate the development of the terms 'professional' and 'professionalism' for the *OED* are significantly from this same period:

Under 'professional':
'that raises his trade to the dignity of a learned profession' (1860)
'there has been a great upward movement of the p. class' (1888)

Under 'professionalism':
'the class of professionals' (1884)
'New professions have come into existence, and the old professions are more esteemed. It was formerly a poor and beggarly thing to belong to any other than the three learned professions.' (1888)

Reference to 'the three learned professions' reminds us that professional work is not peculiar to the nineteenth and twentieth centuries. The professions have been influential since the sixteenth century in Britain (and it is not accidental that that century also saw the rise of capitalism) in the way in which wealth organizes culture. The *OED* dates 'the learned professions' from the sixteenth century. It is however the nineteenth century which is definitive for 'professional' and for 'professionalism' and for the formative development of the professional structures and values which we in the twentieth century have inherited. While it is in the nineteenth century that the term 'industry' acquires factory work as its special meaning, and while critics of the labour process have focused on that shift from field to factory, it is also in the nineteenth century that the terms 'professional' and 'professionalism' acquire definitive and common usages. These usages signify important changes both in the division of labour and in the broader territory of the cultural practice within which the division of labour exists.

Recent historians have begun to articulate the Industrial Revolution as additional kinds of revolution and additional kinds of problem, about something more than factory work and the introduction of new machines. 'The exact nature of the relationship between the bourgeois and the scientific revolutions in England is undecided. But they were clearly a good deal more than just good friends.'[7] This account will not attempt, at this stage, to do more than shift the problematic terms 'bourgeois' and 'scientific' from their different subtleties towards the concept of 'professionalism'. It is to be hoped that the hint of this movement will be enough, for the moment, to retain the sense of an intimate friendship.

'All men are intellectuals', says Gramsci, shifting the debate in his turn to the division of labour as a whole and to the ways in which ideology is enshrined in that structure. Thus the socialist struggle to appropriate the terms of 'intelligence' receives its important inflection.[8] Do not see a gentleman and think you see an intellectual![9] We could extend the thought. Do not see a professional and think you see an intellectual![10] This terrain of struggle – mental labour in the manual/mental distinction – has been further articulated as ideology (after Althusser) and as cultural capital (after Bourdieu). Now, radical scientists (bless their feminist inclusions) have entered the scenario to write about their own sphere of work: 'There is something faintly ludicrous about a group of people who teach and do research talking largely about industrial 'point of production' politics and not about struggles in their own places of work and in their own lives.'[11] What emerges from studying the division of labour – as distinct from an aspect of the labour process, or an element within that division, such as factory work - is a Gramscian emphasis on 'men', not only as the utilizers or victims of the production process, but for 'the entire social complex which they express'.[12]

> It should no longer be permissible for politicians, civil servants, lawyers, bankers, accountants, scientists and other professional people to persuade themselves that their function is to deal with one particular facet of society's problems in an abstract manner from outside. They themselves are part of these problems; in fact, it is they who constitute the most important problem that we have to tackle today. The idea that clever people, climbing to strategic peaks in the structure of society and thence surveying social and economic questions from a great height, can make objective assessments of costs and benefits, right and wrong, true and false, that will be valid for us all - that is one of the biggest lies in the soul of institutional man.[13]

'The most important problem' is the professionals, 'they themselves' and what emerges further, not least in the connections *Power, Money and Sex* (the title of the book from which the extract above is taken), are gender terms and gender relations and the entire social complex which *they* express. These are the terms needed to enquire into 'the soul of institutional man', not only to find out what kind of man he is, but also because we cannot know for certain whether Gramsci's 'men' who are going to be 'intellectuals' are also women (non-generic men), nor indeed whether Gramsci's men are going to want 'their' women to be intellectuals.

At this moment, feminist theory intervenes to begin the

work of clarification. 'Studies of professional socialization', by Virginia Olesen and Elvi W. Whittaker, shifts closer to the direct concerns of this account.[14] The authors, not least, are women. Professions, they argue, are not only about particular processes of occupational development (professionalization) and about institutions (the sites in which professions occur, exist, are enacted), but about adult socialization. Acquiring sex roles, they perceive, is also about adult socialization. Good! It is the gender question and we have arrived. What then – and this is the significant question that their essay seeks to pose - do the two processes of sex and professionalism make of each other? How, in short, do they relate?

WOMEN AND THE PROFESSIONS

> People, when they draw an ideal picture of woman, especially poets, transport her from all contact with material life. A lover, a virgin, an angel, a young and beautiful woman – these terms, so diverse, all unite in representing a being who scarce touches the earth with the tip of her wings; whose feet do not walk; whose hands do not work . . . And what is it to ask an opening for woman in a professional career, but to pluck off those angel wings, and put her to hazard in the foul streets of the city; to make the virgin descend from her pedestal, to expose her to the miscellaneous gaze, to burden her with the fatigues of life, to mix the wife in the rude strifes of reality; to take thus from the one her grace, from the other her purity, from both the ideal charm of modesty?[15]

In nineteenth-century representation, the construction of woman sets up, for the most part, an antithesis with the construction of the professions. Woman is 'lover', 'virgin', 'angel', 'young and beautiful'. If she is virgin, she is 'pure'. If she is wife, she is 'modest'. The professions, in contrast, are 'the foul streets of the city', 'the miscellaneous gaze', 'the fatigues of life', 'the rude strifes of reality'. Nineteenth-century sexual ideology thus inscribes the incompatibility of women and a professional career.

This commentator of the 1850s locates the central problem with such an inscription: 'People, when they draw an ideal picture of woman, especially poets, transport her from all contact with material life.' The problem at the centre of representation – the 'picture of woman' drawn 'especially by poets' - is the polarizing of 'the ideal' and of 'the material'. Woman is posited as the ideal, whose 'angel wings . . . scarce touch the earth'. A professional career is posited as 'material life'. If this is a general problem about much nineteenth-century sexual ideology (in which the representation of woman has no bearing on that which can be realized: femininity as impossibility[16]), it is a specific problem of the relationship between woman and work, which is a problem about how woman in action challenges dominant representations. In negating material existence, this type of construction of woman relies upon separating woman from work; 'feet do *not* walk . . . hands do *not* work'.

Nineteenth-century capitalism however, in its 'material life', relies on a different notion of woman which does not separate woman and work.

> Woman lives upon the earth. Wealth may occasionally allow her this poetic leisure, and youth, or beauty may confer on her a grace; but wealth, beauty, youth, belong only to a select few, or last but a few short years; and for three-fourths of the life of woman the sovereign law of labour is demanded by her as a boon, or is submitted to by her as a necessity.[17]

Nineteenth-century capitalism, here, does not appear to have much to do with the poets. Rather, woman is required to submit to 'the sovereign law of labour', either as boon or necessity.

The representation of woman as 'ideal' is, it must seem, a construction of 'wealth' and 'poetic leisure'. It is thus a construction to legitimate a particular practice in the name of a particular ideology. Nineteenth-century sexual ideology of this kind, that is, separates woman from work in representation, not to separate woman from work in practice but to separate woman from power – as we have seen, capitalism requires that the separation of woman from the work-force does not occur. The inscription of incompatibility (of women and professional careers) is thus an inscription by governing men (including, it seems, poets) to legitimate the exclusion of women from professional power. The inscription of incompatibility masks the reality of exclusion.

From the 1850s again: 'the practical intelligence of man is, for the most part, attributable to the training he has received in preparation for, or in the practice of his industrial profession, and to the social intercourse into which it has necessarily led him.'[18] The 'training' and 'practice' of the profession (particular processes of occupational development (professionalization) and institutions (sites in which professions occur, exist, are enacted)) confer 'intelligence' and 'social intercourse' of particular kinds: these are the terms of power which the profession confers on man. Nineteenth-century professionalization involves the crystallizing of certain forms of power as new kinds of class allegiance in masculinity (in male hands). The socio-political organization of institutions proceeds to consolidate that power in ways which are exclusive of women, and to deploy that power against women. The history of gynaecology is a potent example of this. Nineteenth-century experts declared, for instance, that the uterus worked in opposition to the brain.[19]

For a long time in the nineteenth century (and afterwards), the debate about women and the professions was about exclusion, masked in incompatibility, versus entry. That debate, for as long as women were kept in ignorance of the experience of professional work, could go no further.

Moving away from the 1850s and through the individual and feminist struggles (without diminishing the significance and difficulty of those struggles) which resulted in the first woman professionals, we arrive at the 1919 Sex Disqualification (Removal) Act which, nominally at least, removed all formal barriers to women's entry into the professions. By the 1920s and 1930s, women's entry into the professions in some numbers is being celebrated.

> The whole position, as I see it – here in this hall surrounded by women practising for the first time in history I know not how many different professions – is one of extraordinary interest

and importance. You have won rooms of your own in the house hitherto exclusively owned by men. You are able, though not without great labour and effort, to pay the rent. You are earning your five hundred pounds a year. But this freedom is only a beginning; the room is your own, but it is still bare. It has to be furnished; it has to be decorated; it has to be shared. How are you going to furnish it, how are you going to decorate it? With whom are you going to share it, and upon what terms? These, I think are questions of the utmost importance and interest. For the first time in history you are able to ask them; for the first time you are able to decide for yourselves what the answers should be.[20]

In making an entry into the professions, women win that material requirement - a room of one's own and five hundred pounds a year – which Virginia Woolf sees as essential to 'freedom'. To that extent, women's entry into the professions is 'of extraordinary interest and importance'. The mistake occurs, though, in transferring the metaphor 'room' to the institution of work. Professional work, that 'house hitherto exclusively owned by men', does not leave room. That house does not leave its rooms bare and empty. 'Ownership' is not axiomatically acquired by entry, and work is a difficult commodity. The 'freedom' of having made an entry into the professions is indeed 'a beginning', but 'the room' is not 'still bare'. The 'freedom' to furnish, to decorate, to share is severely constrained. The choice of whom to share with is severely constrained. These questions *are* 'of the utmost importance and interest', but they are not open questions.

When Virginia Woolf transfers her attention to her own profession, Literature, she begins to perceive some of the problems which are not solved by the fact of entry.

Outwardly, what obstacles are there for a woman rather than for a man? Inwardly, I think, the case is very different; she has still many ghosts to fight, many prejudices to overcome. Indeed it will be a long time still, I think, before a woman can sit down to write a book without finding a phantom to be slain, a rock to be dashed against. And if this is so in literature, the freest of all professions for women, how is it in the new professions which you are now for the first time entering?

Those are the questions that I should like, had I time, to ask you. And indeed, if I had laid stress upon these professional experiences of mine, it is because I believe that they are, though in different forms, yours also. Even when the path is nominally open – when there is nothing to prevent a woman from being a doctor, a lawyer, a civil servant – there are many phantoms and obstacles, as I believe, looming in her way. To discuss and define them is I think of great value and importance; for thus only can the labour be shared, the difficulties be solved. But besides this, it is necessary also to discuss the ends and the aims for which we are fighting, for which we are doing battle with these formidable obstacles. Those aims cannot be taken for granted; they must be perpetually questioned and examined.[21]

Even in Literature, 'the freest of all professions for women', there are 'obstacles'. There are 'ghosts to fight'. There are 'prejudices'. (Remember how in 'Outrageous Claims' professional prejudices had subtly passed as prescriptions.) There are phantoms and rocks. The problems might be 'inward' rather than 'outward', although we might now want to challenge that separation, but they are common to the professions ('I believe that they are, though in different forms, yours also.') The path is 'nominally' open, but the room is cluttered with phantoms and obstacles; bringing the 'inward' phantom and the 'outward' obstacle together. It is not 'bare'. Important questions must still be asked and we are still 'for the first time in history' in a position to ask them, but the questions are not open. We must 'discuss', and place great value and importance on that discussion, but it must be addressed not only to open questions of freedom – which must be recognized as *necessarily* utopian, but nevertheless utopian – but to the 'phantom' and 'obstacles' of ideology. 'For thus only can the labour be shared, the difficulties be solved.'

This may leave us still with a utopian faith in discussion, in questioning, in freedom, but it begins to acknowledge, however ghostly the form, some of the socio-political problems. Entry has not been synonymous with freedom. The path is only 'nominally' open. That ideal picture of the poets which put woman in opposition to the professions is being experienced again. The problems are indeed inward (*in* the professions) as well as outward. Professional socialization, which we now begin to glimpse working as a complex ideology, has inscribed masculine dominance against 'being female'.

For us now in the 1980s, the significant conflicts remain, though history has complicated the issue. It is no longer possible – perhaps it never was – to argue a simple matter against exclusion of women from the professions. Nor is it as simple as it may have been at one time to argue a whole-hearted strategy of entry. History has shown that, where the path is nominally open, ideological problems are not axiomatically solved. Indeed, ideological problems may deepen. In any case, history prevents our motives in wishing to enter the professions from being as pure as those motives of the 1920s and 1930s which saw in the future of the professions the ideal formation of democracy.[22] If Virginia Woolf shared some of that idealism, she had also begun to ask searching questions about professional aims.

> It is necessary also to discuss the ends and aims for which we are fighting, for which we are doing battle with these formidable obstacles. Those aims cannot be taken for granted; they must be perpetually questioned and examined.[23]

In experiencing phantoms and obstacles, Virginia Woolf had begun to perceive what we now begin to perceive: that the history of the professions is predominantly and pervasively a history of gentlemen, with all the differing and accumulative meanings that the history of that term has, and that the nineteenth-century history of the professions is largely about safeguarding careers for gentlemen, and defining and redefining (the bourgeois revolution?) structures of work in relation to male power. Is the medical man a gentleman? Is the literary man a gentleman? These are the nervous Victorian questions about those professions expanding to challenge or reformulate 'the learned professions'. In being a history of gentlemen (the gender connotation must not escape us) and aspiring gentlemen, that history is not only one of male dominance, but of masculinity (male socialization, being male). The structures of professional work have, in that history, enshrined masculinity as status and generated a range of class-related forms of masculinity, reproducing with greater subtleties than before, for instance, distinctions and gradations between mental and manual work. The entry of women into the professions is not therefore the beginning of freedom, but, in being in the gift of gentlemen, the beginning of a courtship, in *its* gender and class terms, or a less ambivalent power struggle. And perhaps it is as well at this stage to remind ourselves that even a large entry of female professionals does not make a sexually egalitarian summer.

This had become a familiar theme by the end of the 1970s. Newspapers regularly celebrated female pioneers: the first 'girl' on a building site, the plucky young thing in the stock exchange, the 'lady' in the lorry cab . . . all living, breathing proof that women were winning equality at work. But the pioneers can be numbered in their hundreds. For the remaining ten million women workers, the story has been different altogether. Far from making progress towards equality, they have found it slipping away from them . . . Between 1911 and 1971, women's share of skilled (higher-paid) manual work dropped by nearly *half*, from 24 to 13.5 per cent. Over the same span of years, their share of unskilled manual jobs more than *doubled* – from 15.5 to 37.2 per cent. This astonishing trend, which amounts to a 'breakthough' of men into a near-monopoly of skilled work, continued during the 1970s.[24]

Women's entry into the professions is the beginning 'again' of particular kinds of gender restriction.

One feature of this restriction is that it privileges, or excepts, certain kinds of individual escape. It is important to begin to tease out some of the ways in which professionalism permits certain kinds of common subjectivity to the sexes – with class frequently existing as a mediating factor, and resting on the assumption crucial to this account: that gender

behaviour can be learned. It is a popular idea, indeed, that
women in certain circumstances are 'allowed' to 'become'
men.[25] It is also clear, though, that while such adaptability
may be cited for its importance in defying notions of gender
fixity, it is only permitted to operate in limited circumstances.
In constructing subjectivity, professional ideology requires
on occasion to extinguish gender difference, and can celebrate women simulating men. On other occasions, the
interests of professional power depend on separating those
subjectivities previously supposed as common. We women at
such times may well be replaced in our gender-specificity, and
not always courteously. But the argument must proceed with
caution, because this does not mean that gender difference is
always a punishment. Professional ideology prefers to reward, even more than those women who know when to be
men and when to be women (and when to be the lady to the
gentleman), those women who accept traditional femininities
within the convoluted ritual of professional courtship. It is for
this reason that there is a phenomenon even more dangerous
to our cause than individual escape from gender restriction ('*I*
made it'). This is the requirement for women to adopt within
the professions the secondary and servicing positions for
which we are famous (or not).

The relationship of women to the professions has been and
is problematic in ways not simply solved by entry, nominal
and otherwise. The solution is not, of course, to stage a mass
departure from the professions – would they even notice? –
but to challenge the practice of that work which results in such
exclusions. To begin to make that challenge, it is necessary to
look more closely at some of the detail of the history of the
professions in its construction of professional ideology and of
subjectivities in gender and class.

NINETEENTH-CENTURY MEDICINE – A CASE STUDY OF PROFESSIONAL POWER

Sociological analysis of professions has shifted from attempts
to characterize professions according to attributes (expertise,

autonomy) in terms which tended to flatter the professional self-image, to two other kinds of method. Recently, professions have been studied as occupational groups analogous, for instance, to craft unions with certain occupational interests. More recently still, there has been a concern to analyse professions as class-related and gender-related power blocks involved in structuring reality and subjectivity.

The nineteenth-century history of Medicine is peculiarly and usefully representative of certain important aspects of professional power, in its bearing on gender and class.

The period 1840 to 1855 is one of the most significant eras in the history of Medicine. Between these dates, the British Medical Association was founded, Florence Nightingale discovered her vocation to reform the hospital service, and seventeen medical reform bills were discussed in Parliament.

The issues which made this a turbulent and significant time for developments in Medicine are evident both in the history of the medical profession itself and in the politics, at home and abroad, of mid-Victorian England. Arguments within the medical profession, focusing on the need to consolidate professional expertise (through opposing quackery) and establish a system of medical training, were part of a larger movement towards a new ordering of labour relations. This movement, sometimes described as the rise of the middle class, gave to the newly defining professional classes of the Industrial Revolution, particular types of political and cultural dominance.[26]

In 1853, the Provincial Medical and Surgical Association invited London practitioners to participate as members, and changed its name to the British Medical Association (BMA). The process which led to this change indicates a significant sacrifice of the values of provincialism, with its concomitant emphasis on differentiation and diversity of need, in favour of a centralized and national consolidation of professional power. There followed a certain, nominal at least, levelling within the medical profession. From a highly stratified profession consisting of a tripartite division into physicians, surgeons and apothecaries, there was a move towards establishing a Medical Register of Doctors (achieved in the Medical Act of 1858 which also introduced the term 'general practitioner') united in their interests by specific notions of professional conduct.[27] 'The traditional tripartite structure of Medicine was breaking down.'[28]

These, at least, are the judgements presented and moments selected in most medical histories, often culminating in a celebration of the democratization of Medicine and the advent of an expert and caring profession. It is important to recognize these directions in the nineteenth-century history of Medicine.

What is less widely recognized in these histories is the extent to which the professions, in particular Medicine, were in the process of acquiring that power traditionally given to Government. 'The learned professions' in previous history had worked as Government.[29] The particular conditions of this power in the case of Medicine are those conditions outside the control of Government. Two instances of social developments requiring increasing medical intervention in the nineteenth century are war and the growth of cities.

With reference to the Crimea:

> The catastrophe which destroyed the British Army was a catastrophe of sickness, not of losses in battle. There were two different sicknesses. The troops on the heights before Sebastopol fell sick of diseases resulting from starvation and exposure. When they were brought down to Scutari and entered the Barrack Hospital, they died of fevers resulting from the unsanitary construction of the Barrack Hospital assisted by insufficient food, filth and overcrowding. The second sickness was the more fatal. When the war was over, it was found that the mortality in each regiment depended on the number of men which that regiment had been able to send to Scutari.[30]

The issue is war, the responsibility of Government. The Government is found wanting. A *Punch* cartoon of April 1855, shows Queen Victoria visiting the 'imbeciles of the Crimea', the various war departments. *Punch* comments on their 'disgraceful failures'. The issue appears as its symptoms: as sickness; sickness resulting from the disgraceful failures of war departments (lack of food supplies, lack of sanitary hospitals), but within the specific province of Medicine.

Over-crowding and inadequate sanitation in the industrial cities had similar consequences in shifting the responsibility from Government to Medicine. If Government could not prevent, Medicine must cure – an acknowledgement that the social problem could be faced only at the level of symptom. Apothecaries were increasingly and desperately needed in the cities to respond to epidemics, cholera and influenza in particular, beyond the control of Government. By 1834, there were 12,000 apothecaries and only 1,500 physicians – some indication of the scale of the city problem. A *Punch* cartoon of 1848 shows a fat, rich alderman visiting a poor apothecary in a London slum. *Punch* comments on the 'shamefully underpaid city medical officers'.

Blue books and hospital reports of the 1840s manifest a similar accumulating reliance on Medicine to solve social and political problems, and an increasing intervention by the medical profession in criticisms of the state. A *Lancet* report of 1855 records how a surgeon, George Dawson, spoke to a meeting: 'Now we demand that the whole system of England should be altered (Cheers). Not the Army only, not the Navy only, but all the Government affairs, all the Government offices.'[31] The rhetoric is of revolution, but Dawson proceeds to argue that the chief means to improvement is the 'approved ability' of professional qualification.[32]

And here in the mention of professional qualification (remember 'the practical intelligence of man' on p.21 above) is an invocation of the friendly, connecting revolutions, scientific and bourgeois. The medical profession accumulates special knowledge, medical science, in assuming responsibility for problems beyond the solution of Government. The adequacy of that special knowledge is then tested, not in solving the problem (after all, the problem is not of medical but governmental making), but in treatment (of symptoms) substantiated by professional qualification; paper representations of the problem. We might begin to see medical knowledge as a kind of ideological capital.[33]

With the introduction of the idea of capital, it is appropriate to move on from nineteenth-century responses surrounding professionalism (the *Lancet* etc.) to recent critiques of nineteenth-century Medicine. For, if nineteenth-century Medicine as a profession was accumulating a power akin to that of Government, if it was responding in some measure to the problem both beyond and posed by Government, then it was doing so in the context of a particular stage of capitalism. Without forgetting that the important questions are about what gender and professionalism make of each other, it is time in this account to glimpse what money and professionalism make of each other.

> If society is organized by production, and if class ownership of the means of production entails domination, then medical knowledge as ideology will hide that domination, make a hierarchical stratification appear natural and conceal its own social roots.[34]

Here, the Marxian understandings of terms – production, class ownership, domination – transfer from their focus in *Capital* on finance capital and the commodity in its exchange relations to the ideological capital of knowledge ('medical knowledge') in its exchange relations. As the commodity is demonstrated in *Capital* to conceal the social and power relations between men[35] which produce it, so 'medical knowledge as ideology' conceals the relations or 'domination' which produce it.

In, existing within the capitalist mode of production, Medicine is the terrain both of profit-making material production (now the drugs industry producing its medical commodities) and of ideological production (medical knowledge). The commodity produced (medicine as pills in bottles) conceals the ideology produced (medicine as medical knowledge), which conceals the capitalist relations which produced it. Ideology and commodity thus act to conceal the domination of Medicine. Medical concepts (which we now begin to see as complicated, perhaps devious, 'symbolic systems')[36] thus appear in society as 'natural', failing to come clean about their 'social roots'. In appearing 'natural', medical knowledge thus confers upon itself the status of common sense or truth. Medical knowledge, in other words, signals its own objectivity at the moment when it is necessary for it to make an entry into society. The profession, Medicine, prepares the ground for that entry.

Medicine, as profession, thus begins to be revealed in some of its power relations. To substitute 'ideology' for 'commodity' in a theory of exchange relations, though, does not necessarily mean a parity of terms. It begins to seem, indeed, that ideology begins to win the day over commodity. For the profession, Medicine, accumulates the power not only to establish itself as 'natural' through medical knowledge, but to construct allegiances with capitalist sites of commodity production, like the factory (primarily the drugs industry); though Medicine, as a profession, is not so far in allegiance with other capitalist producers that it is above, or perhaps beneath, directing their 'intelligence'.

> The importance of the professions and the professional classes can hardly be overrated, they form the head of the great English middle class, maintain its tone of independence, keep up to the mark its standard of morality, and direct its intelligence[7]

That there are problems, though, in a critique which meshes knowledge with capitalism in these ways, can be seen precisely in relation to Medicine. Unless we believe that disease will disappear under socialism (and that is not such a bad plan[38]) and that pre-capitalist medical knowledge was 'natural' and free from ideological blemish, there is reason to suppose that there is something other than deviousness about the way in which medical knowledge functions in society. There may even be something like a reciprocity of certain interests, not a simple issue of dominance. (Let us for the moment eschew the 'outrageous claims' that professionals are simple racists and misogynists.) If we are looking towards a reciprocity of interests, we could do worse than employ the mediating term 'representation', one increasingly utilized in analysing the way knowledge functions in society and a term which has accumulated usefully specific meanings in relation to Literature.

> I also use the term *representation* e.g. the press 'represents' the opinions of the people to the state. These opinions do not, however, exist outside the process and the means of representation. Representation is a two-way process. For example, in the process of articulating public opinion, the press and broadcasting help to *form* 'public opinion' – in the simplest sense, by *formulating* it. We know better what we think, and have a clearer sense of our interests, when we see them formulated in the public domain, in a public language, on our behalf. The process of representation *forms* groups into social subjects, publics, social forces. They *become* the authors of the viewpoints attributed to them, their agents in practical action. An 'interest group' is often inert and fragmented until, through the process of representation, it becomes the collective subject of a particular position, opinion or policy.[39]

The argument about representation, as applied to medical knowledge, might look something like the following description.

Medical knowledge appears in society as 'symbolic concepts' or representations. Medical representation, through the ideological capital it is accumulating in the nineteenth century (in being called upon to take responsibilities for aspects of government), intervenes between the people and the state. In making this intervention, it both represents the people to the state (assessing for the state what the 'condition' of the people is) and constructs, in its own discourse or process of representation, the 'condition' of the people, in doing so representing the people to themselves. The professional process is the central means by which this reciprocating representation is constituted and validated.

The problem of medical knowledge thus becomes the problem of medical representation itself. Medical knowledge no longer needs to act as a conspirator – concealing its own social roots – but functions to constitute, through representation, relations between the people and the state.

It might be tempting to emphasize 'the people' as the medical profession's key subject. But gender intervenes to complicate the issue, for some of us are more subject than others. Medical representation, forming an increasingly dominant discourse in the nineteenth century for the reasons mentioned, thus constitutes woman in particular ways. Medical professionals, like the poets, invest their representational interests in perceiving woman in particular ways. They too, though in pathology, derive woman from 'poetic leisure' as 'lover', 'virgin', 'angel', 'young and beautiful'. The history of gynaecology, described 'loosely' as the science of womankind, is the pathological construction of these terms.

We now see that professionalism is the significant process whereby medical representation legitimates itself as mediator between state and people. We also know that the history of professionalism as occupational development has been a history of men, masculinity, being male. What professionalism and sex make of each other extends with this consideration of the gender terms of nineteenth-century medical representation. For we are still concerned with 'entry' (so often a male concern). Women, it hardly needs to be said, did becomes doctors in the nineteenth century, did enter into the profession, Medicine. But it does need to be said, without underestimating the achievements of individual women in becoming doctors, nor the achievements of their sisters in that struggle, that nineteenth-century Medicine remained intensely stratified sexually and that it has been no historical accident that the professional status of nursing has been constantly uneasy.

In terms of representation, then, women in the nineteenth century remain the subjects rather than producers of representation. Entry into professional work is thus not only an entry into a history of representation and a discourse of medical representation which constitutes woman as chief subject. It is also a case (apt term) of woman doctor engaging with a subjectivity existing somewhere between that of producer (medical professional) and subject (medical representation). The terms which clarify distinctions and differentiations for the male professional (doctor, patient) cannot be so easily extracted from gender for the female professional, who is in many ways that very construction of difference, of 'patient'.

This account does not of course presume to detail medical history. The important connections are in the key terms: representation, ideological capital, professional processes. The important inference to be drawn is that, although the connections and elaborations are not fully stated here, and the account is consequently vulnerable, there are generalizations which must be made across the field of work to discover whether sexual ideology in professional work functions in unilateral or differentiated ways or in both, and if so, to what degree.

WOMEN WRITERS

When nineteenth-century women entered into a process of literary representation as writers, they did not (for we must avoid being literal about this) enter with a blank sheet of paper – cheap though it may have been – and a mind (in its solitude) unmarked as a clean slate. They entered, as writers, into a particular process and means of representation. That process and means of representation, like the professional process and like all social processes, has its own gender and class terms. More specifically, when women enter the representational process as writers, they enter, as we now know, a history of myth which inscribes women in particular ways. There has been a great weight of mythology, from Fall forward, inscribing woman as culpable: 'At stake in the myth of the Fall was not merely female culpability for the exile from Paradise but the issue of Eve's innate inferiority to Adam.'[40]

Women writers are inevitably part of a forceful history of representation which connects female culpability with female inferiority.

Women writers, like women doctors, thus enter into a history of representation allocating particular positions for women in myth and particular positions or lack of them for women as professionals. Women who make the entry to professional work are therefore required to negotiate conflicting and potentially conflicting subjectivities. Soon, we must look at individual writings and individual writers to see what is made of these conflicting subjectivities in action. That is the very important work of close reading. Before that, though, it is necessary to look back to the nineteenth century to glimpse some of its articulations of literary professionalism.

The case, as we women are always being told, is different for Literature. In making the transition from nineteenth-century Medicine to nineteenth-century Literature, the case is complicated in more than one way. Literature is different. Literature is special. There *are* women writers. There *are* nineteenth-century women writers. Women writers even made money in the nineteenth-century – male critics will not neglect to remind us of that.

But if we are looking toward some holistic theory of gender relations as social relations (which this account is), it will not do to exempt Literature from its residence, however complicated the terms of that residence may be, somewhere in the structure of work in all its power relations. The biggest concession we ought therefore to make to the differentiated mystique of Literature, is to reserve concluding that Literature is a profession, leaving that question open, without being dissuaded from using the terms of professionalism as a methodology by which to scrutinize Literature. We women owe it to each other to ask questions about the place of Literature in the structure of work. This is the way to begin to understand the manner of the entry of women to Literature, supposedly so liberal.

If we were thinking of *l*iterature rather than *L*iterature, we should not now need to be reminded of what Virginia Woolf discovered (or did not discover) in the British Museum: that a huge part of the world's literature, including nineteenth-century English literature (despite cheap paper and writing as a solitary task), has been produced by men.[41] We resume, because of not needing that reminder, with *L*iterature rather than *l*iterature, taking the term now to signify that which has been judged (by a particular process) a special kind of symbolic writing: in the nineteenth century particularly fiction. With the introduction of 'special' and of 'fiction', the promised complication of Literature's place in a gendered structure of work begins. For, however much the male world has required and continues to require the last word about what is 'special', what that world has tended to grant to women has been a certain capacity for telling stories, from gossip to lies to writing best-selling novels. The male world, it seems, has sanctioned a certain relationship between women and fiction.

Women write fiction. Nineteenth-century women wrote fiction. Nineteenth-century women had access, as writers as well as readers, to that special fiction becoming Literature. Agreed.

Nineteenth-century women wrote Literature, but the assertion is immediately interrupted, disturbed by obvious questions of materialism. Who published that fiction? Who owned the publishing houses? Who governed and controlled the particular processes of occupational development (professionalization) and the institutions (sites in which professions occur, exist and are enacted) in which the literary production process took place? And even if we insist that, whether *l*iterature be a profession or no, *L*iterature is not a profession because it has been judged special, and that all the collective subjectivities of occupational development, sites, social enactments, are less important than sublime solitude (writing as solitary task) and woman's 'special' relationship with fiction, there still remains in less material form *representation* - in all its history of constituting gendered myth and gendered writer.

Before this account returns, however, to questions of representation and writer, it will turn more directly to 'the profession, Literature', in some of its nineteenth-century formulations, for whether we eschew the phrase or not, it was used then.

The phrase 'an author by profession' appears to emerge from as early as the mid-eighteenth century.[42] Histories of letters nominate the first professional author as, variously, Johnson, Pope, Southey, Scott.[43] In 1776, Johnson proclaimed that, 'No man but a blockhead ever wrote, except for money.'[44] We allow for hyperbole and for the knowledge that Coleridge at about the same time was insisting that Literature should never be pursued as a trade, but the remark indicates significant changes, from the mid-eighteenth century, in the social and political relations of book production.

Key events in the technological and legislative development of the book trade might be celebrated as follows: the advent of the mail coach in 1748, facilitating the circulation of books and the distribution of paper, the amendment of the copyright laws in the 1840s to give greater autonomy than had previously existed to authors, the abolition of the paper tax in 1861, and most significant of all, improvements in technology for the printing and publishing of books. The first thirty-five years of the nineteenth century saw more development in the technology of book production than did the previous 350 years, the chief development being the acceleration of paper production and improved printing processes.[45] The 'new' technology, that story continues, greatly affected the distribution of the written word and generated new formats (periodicals, serialized novels), thus producing a more literate and educated society.

This kind of literary progress, however faithful it may be to the development of the commodity (technology helping the mass production of the book), is not, though, the full story. That kind of literary history does, indeed, conceal the social relations of production, lending itself to a Marxist critique of 'the book' as blind. The key exploitation concealed in that kind of account is exposed by Marx.

Certain London firms where newspapers and books are printed have gained for themselves the honourable names of 'slaughter-houses'. Similar excesses occur in book-binding, where the victims are chiefly women, girls and children.

Worse still were the conditions endured in the first stage of paper production, the process of sorting the rags which were the raw material of paper. As late as 1866, a Public Health report examined the spread of smallpox in the London rag trade, and notes: One of the most shameful, dirtiest and worst paid jobs, a kind of labour on which women and young girls are by preference employed, is the sorting of rags . . . they themselves are the first victims (of smallpox).[46]

Here are the significant terms of the place of 'women and girls' in the literary production process. This is the significant material aspect.[47] And if this kind of restriction operates materially, it is at least likely that some version of gender-specific restriction will operate ideologically - especially if we remember that the sexual division of work cuts across the mental/manual distinction.

In 1847, *Fraser's Magazine* announced that

Literature has become a profession. It is a means of subsistence, almost as certain as the bar or the church. The number of aspirants increases daily, and daily the circle of readers grow wider. That there are some evils inherent in such a state of things it would be folly to deny; but still greater folly would it be to see nothing beyond these evils. Bad or good, there is no evading the 'great fact', now that it is so firmly established. We may deplore, but we cannot alter it. Declamation in such a cause is, therefore, worse than idle.[48]

With a short paragraph intervening, the argument resumes:

If we reflect upon the great aims of literature, we shall easily perceive how important it is that the lay teachers of the people should be men of an unmistakeable vocation. Literature should be a profession, just lucrative enough to furnish a decent subsistence to its members, but in no way lucrative enough to tempt speculators. As soon as its rewards are high enough and secure enough to tempt men to enter the lists for the sake of the reward, and parents think of it as an opening for their sons, from that moment it becomes vitiated. Then will the ranks, already so numerous, be swelled by an innumerable host of hungry pretenders. It will be – and, indeed, is, now fast approaching that state – like the army of Xerxes, swelled and encumbered by women, children, and ill-trained troops. It should be a Macedonian phalanx, chosen, compact and irresistible.

Literature has become a profession. That is a 'great fact'. The great fact is evidenced in Literature as 'a means of subsistence' and in numbers: growing numbers of 'aspirants' and of readers. Here are some of the pervasive fears of the 1840s of a capitalism and a democratic tendency which imply the entry (that term again) of 'new' groups (like 'women, children, and ill-trained troops') into interests and areas threatening to slip out of the control of the governing class. In Literature, this fear is formulated in relation to both writers (producers) and readers (consumers).

The *Fraser* author is enough of a professional himself, though, to recognize how the term can shift in his favour. 'Professionalism' like 'trade' may be a source of fear in its temporary signification of change in structures of work and government, but it also, in signifying an 'irresistible' change, begins to signify the future, where future work and future interests are invested. 'We may deplore, but we cannot alter it.' The *Fraser* author, as a good professional, thus naturalizes history – 'we cannot alter it' – and seizes the moment to move the term 'profession' in the direction of his own interests: 'Literature *should be* a profession.'

Literature should be a profession in that 'the lay teachers of the people' - connecting literary men to other governors, Church and State – should be 'men' - we must not forget that emphasis – of 'unmistakeable vocation'. That literary men are unmistakeable is no longer guaranteed since the aristocratic formation of the arts (the literary gentlemen in *Fraser's* account) has changed. We - the gentlemen and the 'new'

gentlemen, perhaps co-operating in the bourgeois revolution
– must ensure that we create 'men of an unmistakeable
vocation' by controlling the development of Literature as
profession. (The contradictions are embraced: Literature has
become a profession. We may deplore, but we cannot alter it.
Literature should be a profession.)

We – the gentlemen – must ensure that we define the terms
of professionalism. If we can no longer ensure that 'the lay
teachers of the people' are part of the governing class, we can
at least endeavour to confine the practice to gentlemen,
giving back to the term 'gentlemen' a gender and class
connotation which it no longer has now. The argument
extends. To ensure gentlemen as producers, we acknowledge
the inevitability of the capitalist market (writers of books will
have to handle money and Literature must be lucrative
enough 'to furnish a decent subsistence'), but there must be
scope to retain the connection with 'natural' governors, away
from 'speculators' and 'hungry pretenders'. That way, professional interests marry with 'men' (the term weakened from
'gentlemen', signifying a historical weakening) of 'unmistakeable vocation'.

The argument has moved us to the blatant connection with
gender. If professionalism denotes a safeguarding of careers
for men, now assimilating in men/gentlemen the various
interests of the various governing groups, it is about remind-
ing women and men of the 'wrong' class of our 'outsider'
status. Remember incompatibility and exclusion. For the
Fraser author, the greatest problem with literary professionalism, is not about entering the capitalist market place
(being a good professional, he sees that as inevitable and
'natural', not open to political change), nor is it about the
possibility of the access of 'the people' to political power via
readership. It is about the reorganization of work and a fear
that that reorganization will escape his control; and 'his'
control signifies male control of a particular kind.

> It will be – and, indeed, is, now fast approaching that state –
> like the army of Xerxes, swelled and encumbered by women,

children, and ill-trained troops. It should be a Macedonian phalanx, chosen, compact, and irresistible.

The *Fraser* account is thus to be taken not as a declaration of an absolute historical truth (Literature has become a profession by 1847), but as a usefully open account of some of the significant issues centring upon literary professionalism and its terms in the mid-nineteenth-century. It should not be taken to represent a complete cultural or political position, but nor should it be taken to be uselessly idiosyncratic, individualistic, or unrepresentative. It is its very openness which allows us to read out its gender terms (the remainder of the article continues to refer to literary producers as 'sons' and 'gentlemen') in ways which expose some of the assumptions, in their changing histories, affecting Literature as the structure and practice of work. From the twentieth century, Virginia Woolf's fictional Orlando invokes again this representation of nineteenth-century Literature in revealing opposing assumptions:

> Orlando was unaccountably disappointed. She had thought of literature all these years (her seclusion, her rank, her sex must be her excuse) as something wild as the wind, hot as fire, swift as lightning; something errant, incalculable, abrupt, and behold, literature was an elderly gentlemen in a grey suit talking about duchesses.[49]

Literature in the nineteenth century, like Medicine, was powerful. Each utilized factory production (paper, print, drugs). Each was in an important relationship to the capitalist market. Each, in its relative autonomy, was in a position to mediate the capitalist state. Each was particularly influential in the social and political problems of the nineteenth century. Each relied heavily on systems of representation. And there is another important gender argument which, while not developed in this account, unites nineteenth-century Medicine and Literature (respectively, the science and art of womankind) in particular perceptions and representations of woman as body.

The central gender argument, though, is about how women exist in a structure of work which relies upon woman as other and as powerless. But to continue with this kind of generalization is increasingly difficult. The time has arrived to look more directly at examples of individual writers, and at the ideological positioning which results from individual writers engaging with a history of professionalism and of representation which can do no other than construct the subjectivity of the writer.

The crucial memory to retain in what follows (and it is to this that this account in its parenthetic way has been leading) is that when women write in the nineteenth century, they do so against/within a structure of work in which the Macedonian phalanx and its 'chosen' men, though not 'irresistible', is dominantly valued. Women enter into writing, that is, against a complex (not least, for not always being what it seems) and powerful ideology of gender restriction.

Women are not likely, either, to make an entry against gender prejudice with the full weaponry of an oppositional mode searing in its purity. Gender is not nature. It is possible for women writers to become literary professionals in ways which are entirely accepting of the prevailing definitions which professionalism, in carrying strong elements of self-regulation, inscribes. This will not necessarily mean that women writers are accept*ed*, but the likelihood of being so is far greater for those who have understandings of professionalism which are compatible with its self-regulating mechanisms, than for those who do not carry prevailing definitions. Women writers will not necessarily articulate to themselves a perception of 'obstacles' as Woolf did, but may on occasions be so far in accordance with the gender and class terms of professionalism, its subjectivities, that little element of opposition comes into play.

To look at some aspects of this compatibility and of its limitations, I have given, in what follows, a particular place to fictional representations of professionals. I have also tried to explore the extent to which individual writers are compatible with the professional groups they represent in fiction, and to discover the gender and class terms which fracture compatibilities.

CONCLUSIONS

The outrageous claims that professionals are likely to be misogynists and racists, not to say elitist in their class politics, have prevailed, in some ways, in the argument. This chapter has shown how the Industrial Revolution, also a bourgeois and scientific revolution, had implications, beyond the restructuring of the relationship between industry and agriculture, for the division of labour. These implications were and remain in the territory of a development of professional power in ways which sustained and sustain invidious distinctions between manual and mental labour and between female and male labour, while structuring and consolidating certain class alliances as alliances between males.

The entry of women into professional work has not happened in significant numbers. Because professional power has the history it does, it would not be possible, anyway, to make the entry of women into professional work a matter of celebration. It is necessary, now, to scrutinize that history to see the kinds of power that professional work has accumulated and operates. This is what I have begun to do in writing, briefly, about nineteenth-century Medicine, and in writing about nineteenth-century Literature.

Nineteenth-century Medicine, through representation, accumulates and expresses an understanding of gender and class relations which extends beyond the immediate concerns of Medicine to the professions in general. Literature, far from being a free spirit, shares some of this history and this accumulation in ways which result in certain class and gender formulations and certain class and gender restrictions. For these reasons, the outrageous claims which criticize professionalism are important to an understanding of the sexual division of labour, and, more specifically here, to an understanding of women and men writers.

2

George Eliot: Man at Work and the Masculine Professional

THE ARTISAN

The restructuring of the occupational terrain which occurred in mid-Victorian England tended to polarize the terminology of labour. While previously the term 'artist' could have referred to any skilled worker, the nineteenth century saw the clear distinction that we have inherited between 'artist' and 'scientist'. More notable still in understanding the particular development of professional work is the further fragmentation of 'artist' into 'artist' and 'artisan'. The significant consolidation is of a division of labour (the artisan as the skilled manual labourer, the artist either seeking, or privileged above, professional status), which also operates and constructs distinctions in 'intelligence' (the artist being the intellectual, the artisan being the practical man) and in sensibility (the artist being imaginative and creative, the artisan being 'merely' skilled).[1]

This hierarchy of labour, as well as being a reinforcement of the maleness of paid work (for different reasons, neither 'artisan' nor 'artist' is easily applied to a woman worker), acts to distance certain sections of the occupational terrain from the operation of power, or to sanction in a different form a distance already existing.

In the 1840s and 1850s, there is something of a preoccupation, both in fiction and in social and political theory, with the artisan, his life, his work and his 'nature'. This concern denotes a political situation in which those bidding for control are interested in accommodating the potentially disruptive.

an operation of hegemony, in which power is operated both through dominance and through democratic responsibility. The construction of the artisan signifies the alienation of the dominant group from other groups of workers of presumed lower status, and also signifies the need to contain these other groups in a rhetoric of understanding and patronage.

The writer enters quite specifically into this exercise of hegemony as the powerful creator of the artisan, mediating his life and work through fiction, and through social and political theory. The writer thereby emerges as part of that occupational and power group bidding for control. This control is to be achieved through the writer's work, just as the artisan/skilled manual worker is to be contained through work and as worker.

The particular position of the fictional writer is to achieve cultural influence powerfully, through representation. The writer, privileged to create the life, work and feelings of the artisan, thus enters into the social control of the skilled manual worker, and becomes the cultural spokesperson of the controlling group. One section of the work-force is deprived of a language of feeling and another acquires an excess of feeling forms.

In this process, through culture, of political containment, the artisan therefore tends to be a construction of the ideal. Mid-Victorian writers are in the business of imagining and creating the artisan's way of life and his differentiated structure of feeling. In the late 1840s, Charles Kingsley reifies artisan 'nature' and endows it with special significance:

> Even our passionate artisan-nature, so sensitive and voluble in general, in comparison with the cold reserve of the field-labourer and the gentleman, was hushed in silent awe between the thought of the past and the thought of the future.[2]

The terms construct the sensibility: passionate, sensitive, voluble.

A decade later, George Eliot is preoccupied with a more elaborated version of artisan nature. *Adam Bede*, novel and protagonist, is a creation of the ideal type, the skilled manual worker for whom 'good carpentry' is 'God's will'. In *Felix Holt*, George Eliot presents a character who is a more self-conscious version of the same ideal. Felix Holt is more overtly politicized than is Adam Bede, in being 'the radical' who tries to enact his beliefs in work, disparaging the professional variety in favour of the manual. Protagonists Adam Bede and Felix Holt both, in the 1850s and 1860s respectively, are presentations of artisan-nature at its presumed best. While Felix Holt carries the more direct ideological inflection, Adam Bede is the more direct statement of physical ideal as nature.

> Such a voice could only come from a broad chest, and the broad chest belonged to a large-boned muscular man nearly six feet high, with a back so flat and a head so well poised that when he drew himself up to take a more distant survey of his work, he had the air of a soldier standing at ease. The sleeve rolled up above the elbow showed an arm that was likely to win the prize for feats of strength; yet the long supple hand, with its broad finger-tips, looked ready for works of skill. In his tall stalwartness Adam Bede was a Saxon, and justified his name: but the jet-black hair, made the more noticeable by its contrast with the light paper cap, and the keen glance of the dark eyes that shone from under strongly marked, prominent and mobile eyebrows, indicated a mixture of Celtic blood. The face was large and roughly hewn, and when in repose had no other beauty than such as belongs to an expression of good-humoured honest intelligence.[3]

Here is the ideal physical compendium of artisan man: the brawn (strong arm), the skill (supple hand), fine physique (good Saxon stock), fine feeling (Celtic blood), independent (well-poised head), yet subservient (air of a soldier). This celebration of British stock, with its nationalistic and genetic overtones, accumulates into the judgement, 'honest intelligence'. The parts of the bull who could win prizes are surveyed. The eye sees a dismemberment of a species type, a breed which is good stock, but not 'our' stock. That is Adam: a collection of compounded polarities called 'honest intelligence'. Brother Seth is the same species, but a reduced version – less tall, less old, less hair, less prominent eyebrows, less brawn, less skill. The qualification of 'intelligence' with 'honest' completes the condescension to a creature who is like us, but is not us (author/reader).

George Eliot proceeds to invest in Adam Bede the structural weight of the novel, the process of its writing, and her explication of the novel's basis in realism. The beginning of Book Second presents some of the contradictions to which this investment gives rise.

> Paint us an angel, if you can, with a floating violet robe, and a face paled by the celestial light; paint us yet oftener a Madonna, turning her mild face upward and opening her arms to welcome the divine glory; but do not impose on us any aesthetic rules which shall banish from the region of Art those old women, scraping carrots with their work-worn hands, those heavy clowns taking holiday in a dingy pot-house, those rounded backs and stupid weather-beaten faces that have bent over the spade and done the rough work of the world - those homes with their tin pans, their brown pitchers, their rough curs, and their clusters of onions. In this world there are so many of these common coarse people, who have no pictures-que sentimental wretchedness![4]

Here is the problem. Art must account for old women and heavy clowns, but old women and heavy clowns are reducible to pans, pitchers and curs. Art must present reality, but reality defines itself as not aesthetic. The logic is not that Art must change, but that Art must stoop. The attempt to avoid the banishing of Art's aesthetic rules from the region of old women and heavy clowns is thus an act of will in the face of a contradiction.

A further complicating movement is the characterization of Adam, ultimately precisely 'picturesque' and 'sentimental' in his 'wretchedness'. Adam himself, as representation and as structural load, fails to cohere, fragments, remains the problem. He does 'the rough work of the world', but he is also 'the painted angel', the first man, without sin. Adam is both a condescension and an over-construction. He is George

Eliot's attempt to resolve a problem which is both aesthetic and ideological.

Some of George Eliot's later novels avoid this problem by placing the artisan figure and his kind in less central positions than in *Adam Bede*. Chronologically, from *The Mill on the Floss*, the movement is more and more firmly into the region of the professional classes. *Felix Holt* is interesting in being at the juncture of artisan and professional. That the later novels are much more coherent than is *Adam Bede* should say something about this issue: about what is sacrificed, in terms of authorial intention and ideological difficulty, in settling for a realism which carries its own aesthetic.

It is not yet time, though, to move into the later novels, and into their more secure placement in the professional classes. The next duty of this account is to address the consequences for gender of the artisan ideal.

The account so far, in being about the artisan, has been searching also to be about the artist, or more specifically, the case of George Eliot, the writer. I have begun to place George Eliot as a member of the Victorian professional classes in her particular response to the artisan/manual worker: the endeavour to accommodate the latter in a charitable account which presents the conflicting terms of a realism which is forced to condescend. I have begun to explain or imply that it is not surprising that Adam Bede is more problematic to his creator than is Lydgate or Casaubon, who are rather problematic to their 'acquaintance'.

In beginning to trace these placements, my concern is also to indicate some of the ways the professional artist and the artisan/manual worker occupy their differentiated places in the division of labour, and, less obviously, to show how the artist is in a position to influence or compound the position of the artisan, to accommodate his 'honest' status, directly through her own work.

The argument must now begin to move towards the consequences for gender and in gender, of the artisan ideal. For, if artisan man is revealed as contradictory, if Adam Bede fails to cohere, what is happening to artisan woman? In beginning to answer this question, the argument also begins to be about the gendered position of the writer.

This 'new' argument is about a set of social (and literary) relations in which the mutually influencing categories of professionalism, sex, gender and individualism, are all important. No category can be subtracted, although it must be said that the over-emphasis in literary criticism has been on individualism.

It is important, therefore, to start complicating and qualifying the argument about the position of the writer. To assert George Eliot's position as a rather exceptional artist – with imaginative power, genius, etc. articulated for decades by critics as her subjectivity or individuality – is to neglect to mention her sex, and is to neglect to constitute the artist as a gendered subject and professionalism as a gendered category. The importance is not primarily that George Eliot is a woman (sex), but that *as* a woman, she is in a particular set of relations with man, with Literature, with culture, which perform a highly significant function in the constitution of subjectivity.

The argument begins to extend. George Eliot, in being an individual (of immense imaginative power, etc.) who is also a member of the professional classes, is also that very fraught thing, as yet under estimated, a woman negotiating with men and with masculinity and with masculine positions in a culture (and literary practice) now becoming well known for its masculine terms: paternalism, patriarchy, and their brothers.

Sex, gender, class, professionalism, subjectivity: the terms proliferate in their mutual dependencies. The account must now turn, as is so often the case with criticism, from the writer to the writing itself. The writing itself, it will be argued, not only reveals some of these gender and class terms, but can be better understood through that revelation. Criticism must continue to make such claims.

I return, therefore, to the artisan, and from the man, to the woman.

In constructing artisan woman, George Eliot has not only the problem of persuading Art to condescend, she has also set herself the task of giving the male reader what he wants, the point being that if gender prejudice is constructed in culture, the woman reader may also 'want' what the man reader wants. This is not the easy task it may sound, for what the male reader wants, particularly from woman, is not always free from contradiction. What George Eliot does, initially, is to construct a masculine persona for her own authorial and narrative position, in such a way that some of these contradictions can be explored. The persona is not axiomatically complicit with all things masculine, but it is complicit with the male view. 'We are apt to be kinder to the brutes that love us than the women that love us. Is it because the brutes are dumb?'[5] This setting-up of the 'us' as male carries over into representation and its accompanying judgements.

> Before you despise Adam as deficient in penetration, pray ask yourself if you were ever predisposed to believe evil of any pretty woman – if you ever *could*, without hard head breaking demonstration, believe evil of the *one* supremely pretty woman who has bewitched you. No: people who love downy peaches are apt not to think of the stone, and sometimes jar their teeth terribly against it.[6]

Woman looks as man wishes her to look: 'pretty', like a 'downy peach'; but she is also what man has taught himself to think she is: perversely 'evil' (against appearances), 'bewitching'. It is not then man, Adam, who is at fault (he cannot be blamed for being 'deficient in penetration' – incidentally, who but woman ever blames man for being 'deficient in penetration'?), but woman who is at fault for deceiving by appearance, for defying and perhaps corroborating the male view.

It is this masculine complicity which, elsewhere in the novel, prevents us (the female as well as male reader) from being able to judge whether misogyny, primarily in the representation of Bartle Massey, is a joke at his or our (women readers') expense.

> I tell you there isn't a thing under the sun that needs to be done at all, but what a man can do better than a woman, unless it's bearing children, and they do that in a poor make-shift way; it had better ha' been left to the men - it had better ha' been left to the men.[7]

Elsewhere in George Eliot's writing, misogyny is more carefully placed.[8]

The idealizing process which is reductive of the artisan male further reduces artisan woman because of this compacting with a masculine perspective. Dinah and Hetty, the two central female protagonists, are the binary form which signifies the even greater fragmentation of artisan woman than artisan man. To give the male reader what he wants from artisan womanhood, woman must separate into the physical and the moral, the sensual and the spiritual. In Adam, however ideally, the physical and moral beauty coexist, indeed, insist on signifying each other in the whole man. In Hetty Sorrel, beauty belies virtue. In Dinah, virtue subdues beauty. The two female characters are mutually dependent and mutually mediating. Each is needed to satisfy man. Dinah, the Methodist preacher, sublimely spiritual, would, without the presence of Hetty, supercharge the idea of artisan womanhood. Hetty, vibrantly erotic, would, without the presence of Dinah, undermine the artisan ideal with a temptation of Adam which is worse than Eve's.

The lie is given, again, to a notion of realism which can present the commonplace. In order to give the male reader what he wants, the artisan female must fragment into the moral and the physical; and it is a disintegration which, because of further intricacies in the male requirement of womanhood, also divides woman into saint and sinner, perfect and culpable.

'The Two Bed-Chambers' (chapter 15 of *Adam Bede*) encapsulates this force in the division of woman and the mutual mediation of the two central female protagonists. The chapter presents the two women in the respective bedrooms of a house (world, way of life) which they inhabit. Each is involved in a private ritual, which the reader is invited to observe, to act as voyeur (male reader?). One character is involved in her 'peculiar form of worship':

> Having taken off her gown and white kerchief, she drew a key from the large pocket that hung outside her petticoat, and, unlocking one of the lower drawers in the chest, reached from

it two short bits of wax candle – secretly bought at Treddleston
– and stuck them in the two brass sockets. Then she drew forth
a bundle of matches, and lighted the candles; and last of all, a
small red-framed shilling looking-glass, without blotches. It
was into this small glass that she chose to look first after
seating herself. She looked into it, smiling, and turning her
head on one side, for a minute, then laid it down and took out
her brush and comb from an upper drawer. She was going to
let down her hair, and make herself look like that picture of a
lady in Miss Lydia Donnithorne's dressing-room. It was soon
done, and the dark hyacinthine curves fell on her neck.[9]

She looks into the mirror. She reflects on self. Her activity
is furtive, secretive and full of sensuous vanity. She worships a
false goddess. She blasphemes. She emulates Miss Lydia
Donnithorne. She sins.

The other woman, in her bedroom, worships the right God.

Dinah delighted in her bedroom window. Being on the second
storey of that tall house, it gave her a wide view over the fields.
The thickness of the wall formed a broad step about a yard
below the window, where she could place her chair. And now
the first thing she did, on entering her room, was to seat
herself in this chair, and look out on the peaceful fields beyond
which the large moon was rising, just above the hedgerow
elms.[10]

She looks out of the window. She looks on to the world. She
reflects on God's nature, not her own. Her activity has private
meaning, but it is open, honest. She has nothing to hide. She
reflects on 'Love and Sympathy', God's love and God's
sympathy, the abstractions which make virtue, not the
sensualities which make vice.

Reflection (the mirror, the open window) carries a specific
connotation, declaring the moral imperative. Self-
absorption, in a woman, is a sin. Woman, the moral dictates,
must think not of self, but of others. Personal vanity, in a
woman, is a sin. Reflection on the wrong kind of love, on the
sensual or the sexual and not the spiritual, is a sin.

The ideological apparatus is familiar. Woman is sinner or

saint. The male reader gets what he wants. If beauty deceives it is not his fault. Not he, but the woman, is blamed for confusing the aesthetic with the moral, the sensual with the spiritual. Again, the male reader gets what he wants. Not he, but the woman, must be capable of being wholly good, wholly self-sacrificed. He is right to expect that.

What emerges here is a gender-differentiated idea of service which is also an idea of 'woman's work'. The direction of the argument is as follows. All women serve. That is the true place of woman. That it may be the inescapable social reality is a different argument. The bad woman aspires to serve above her social station (the lady, the aristocrat). The good woman aspires to serve God (and, later, the marital god). The material and spiritual are at odds: mirror bad . . . window good. Structurally, the bed-chambers' chapter moves artisan womanhood, its formations in work and in nature, forward firmly into its stereotype. Hetty fails to serve love or love service. Dinah succeeds in both.

Later, in *Middlemarch*, the types of sinner and saint reappear in more complicated representations: Rosamond and Dorothea. The move from artisan to professional classes is not enough (and this is important to the whole argument of this account) to disrupt the continuity of perception of what is woman's nature and what is woman's work. In *Middlemarch*, as in *Adam Bede*, woman must serve love and love service. This is woman's duty. Not only this, but woman must teach other women that duty. Again, the male reader gets what he wants. Teaching women their duty is not his responsibility.

Dinah is positioned to mediate between Hetty and her duty. Dorothea is positioned to mediate between Rosamond and her duty. Dinah reconciles Hetty to God. Dorothea reconciles Rosamond to Lydgate. Each is a mediation which abruptly changes the direction of each novel. Insurrection and challenge are replaced by an accommodating passivity. Dinah and Dorothea present Hetty and Rosamond with images of how they ought to be. To Hetty and Rosamond, the moral mirror reflects the discrepancy: rebellion and guilt, where there should be acceptance and harmony.

Woman mediating woman, powerful and complicated in its

formation in *Middlemarch*, is thus prefigured in the earlier novel, *Adam Bede*. Hetty, arrested for the murder of her child, intransigently silent under accusation, mutely resistant in imprisonment, awaits (as does the structure of the novel) Dinah's arrival.

> 'Dinah,' Hetty sobbed out, throwing her arms round Dinah's neck, 'I will speak . . . I will tell. . . I won't hide it any more.' But the tears and sobs were too violent. Dinah raised her gently from her knees, and seated her on the pallet again, sitting down by her side. It was a long time before the convulsed throat was quiet, and even then they sat some time in stillness and darkness, holding each other's hands. At last Hetty whispered – 'I did do it, Dinah . . . I buried it in the wood . . . the little baby . . . and it cried . . . I heard it cry . . . ever such a way off . . . all night . . . and I went back because it cried.'[11]

Hetty, who has been guilty, perverse, intractable, now confesses, is penitent, is redeemed. Woman is woman's confessor. Woman confers forgiveness on woman.

In *Middlemarch*, Dorothea's arrival to 'save' Rosamond repeats Dinah's catalytic entry. Rosamond has maintained an intransigent silence, mutely resistant to husband Lydgate. Dorothea enters, speaks. The silence breaks.

> Dorothea . . . had unconsciously laid her hand again on the little hand that she had pressed before. Rosamond, with an overmastering pang, as if a wound within her had been probed, burst into hysterical crying as she had done the day before when she clung to her husband.[12]

But to Lydgate, Rosamond had not been able to speak. It is left to Dorothea to transform domestic rebellion into recognition of marital responsibilities. The moral terms are less blatant than in *Adam Bede*. Confessor and criminal, saint and sinner, are less starkly present. Tears are not in themselves a sin (Hetty's tears had been 'too violent'). Dorothea, unlike Dinah, has her own problems. There is an element of reciprocity in the tears. The formulation, though, is essentially the same. Woman mediates woman for man. Womanhood must correct itself. We women, the inference is, should recognize our gender-specific responsibilities. Man does not have to worry. Man does not have to intervene. Woman will fix woman for him.

In loving service, the virtuous woman mediates the ideology of service in woman, for man. Thus George Eliot extends the authorial, masculine persona, in presenting woman as a problem *for* man, but a problem *of* woman.

The uniting of Dinah and Hetty, the uniting of Dorothea and Rosamond, are structured as powerful moments of redemption, of spiritual climax. Social taboos rightly collapse. Emotional honesty, ostensibly, rules. In contrary movement, though, is the complete capitulation of the supposed sinner, the utter complicity of the writer with the catalytic acceptance. What is absent is any space for woman to have grounds for challenging the accommodation, and any space for demanding of man a shared responsibility in constituting problem and solution. What is absent is a potentiality for change to the ground rules of domestic attitudes. What is absent is a potentiality for change in the relations between women and men.

Despite similarities and prefigurings, the move from *Adam Bede* to *Middlemarch* is also, as has been said, a move from the social and cultural world of the artisan to that of the professional classes. In this more fully developed world, fragmentation is not so acute. Woman of the professional classes is that much more realized and that much less culpable than her artisan counterpart. To understand is to forgive. Rosamond has her marginal virtues. Dorothea has her marginal vices, or weaknesses – for 'vice' is no longer appropriate. While this, as has been seen, is an indication of the extent to which George Eliot has 'given up' that other world of the artisan, the move to the professional classes thus usefully complicates gender. Woman of the professional classes is not reduced to sinner or saint . . . or, at least, not easily. The sinner or saint formulation is in itself challenged.

It is not in *Middlemarch*, but in *The Mill on the Floss*, where the challenge receives its keenest impetus. It is not accidental that where womanhood carries the structural load of the novel, as Maggie Tulliver does in *The Mill on the Floss*, the challenge to the fragmentation of womanhood is at its sharpest. In this novel, the judgement of the professional world (local community) that Maggie Tulliver is a sinner is set against an authorial construction which scrupulously refuses to reduce womanhood, or narrative process, to such simplistic terms. In *Adam Bede*, Hetty Sorrel is abandoned, not only by upper-class gent but also by author, to a miserable pregnancy, a lonely childbirth and transportation. These episodes are glimpsed, hinted, not written out, not narrated in feeling. The glancing approach allows Hetty to remain starkly the bad one. Such a piece of authorial indifference could not have occurred in the writing of *The Mill on the Floss*, nor so flagrantly in the writing of *Middlemarch*. With entry into the professional classes, the terms of responsibility have shifted. The author has challenged her own masculine persona. The experience of womanhood is too keen to resist. Man, at last, must take some responsibility. It is no longer possible to give the male reader, simply, what he wants. Man, at last, constitutes problem as well as solution.

This shift into the realm of a more keenly felt and developed gender politics thus constructs man, as well as woman, differently. The male reader is no longer going to be wholly satisfied, and the male representation is no longer going to be wholly satisfying. If there is no Adam Bede, there is no need, any longer, for a Hetty Sorrel.[13] Part of this is to state again that the terms of realism have changed. The move from the artisan, in which the idealizing processes attached to artisan man always gave the lie to realism, to the professional, is the move to a genre that works. (The class formation of realism and its aesthetic is thus accepted by George Eliot and revealed to us.)

As another crucial part of this settlement, in which man ceases to be unproblematically virtuous, is the increasing clarification that work itself is problematic. Professional work may carry its own elements of idealism (equivalent to carpentry being 'God's will'), but it also carries tensions and contradictions.

In *Middlemarch*, the relationship between work and man is

altogether more fraught than in *Adam Bede*. Surnames for
particular male characters (Casaubon, Lydgate) already
signify the change. Adam, the first man, harmonizes work
and nature in ideal relations. Lydgate and Casaubon are part
of a different formation. Work is in negotiating relationship
with man and the relationship is by no means ideal. The
mid-nineteenth century terms of Marx and his critique begin
to be appropriate. Work can be reifying, alienating, can
construct identity for ill rather than good, can cause deformi-
ty in the process of constructing identity. In these terms, work
does not constitute the means by which man harmonizes his
relationship with nature, but disturbs and distorts the harmo-
nizing tendencies of that relationship.

In George Eliot's fiction, professional work constitutes
some of these difficult relationships and therefore difficult
social relationships. Professional work is not simply celebrated as ideal, nor the professional man celebrated as a good
man. Professional work can carry elements of idealism, but at
a price, and anyway, idealism as part of professional work
begins to constitute the problem itself: image and reproduction of man's failure to secure satisfactory social relations.
Not least important in these social relations are the gender
relations constructed and disturbed by professional work. For
it is a particular kind of masculinity, in its professional
construction and connotations, which poses an acute problem
for sexual politics, for domestic relations, for relations
between woman and man, in its polarizing of man and
woman, of home and work, and of the thought and the felt.

Appropriately, in *Middlemarch*, we are out of bachelors
and courtship (Adam Bede, Felix Holt) and firmly into
marriage. Marriage is the site of sexual antagonisms. This is
where the tension between work and home, woman and man,
the thought and the felt, is enacted.

It is in Dr Lydgate that these tensions are centred.
Lydgate's social relations, from their inception, are problematic. For George Eliot, the professional world is immediately more problematic than that of the artisan. For the
best of us, it contains 'a pale shade of bribery which is
sometimes called prosperity'. In protagonist Adam Bede,

work supports and creates a coherent structure of feeling. If man's perception of woman in this world is misconceived, then it is the fault of artisan woman, not artisan man. But Lydgate's world is already tending towards corruption, signalled faintly in the twin attractions of money and material ease. The problems with professionalism, though, are only partially located in economics. The significant problems which George Eliot locates in and through Lydgate are of ideology in its particular ramifications for gender. The problem, to restate and reinstate it, is of the polarized terms which a particular kind of masculine professionalism inscribes; work and home, felt and thought, woman and man.

The oppositions are visited and revisited in their variants. It had already occurred to Lydgate, by the age of ten, that 'books were stuff, and that life was stupid.' The dichotomy recurs: books and life, thought and felt, work and home. Soon, the formulation is transposed directly into one of gender. Lydgate's is 'a strictly scientific view of women'. 'That distinction of mind which belonged to his intellectual ardour, did not penetrate his feeling and judgement about furniture, or women.'[14] Work separates from home in the material, 'furniture', and in the felt, 'feeling and judgement'. Man saves penetration for work. Man separates from woman.

George Eliot is specific in stating the separation, but it is often in tension with the contrary pull to blame woman, to construct woman as culpable. There is constant special pleading for Lydgate. This begins to be a reminder of Adam Bede. If Lydgate misunderstands his wife, it is because she invites misunderstanding. If he wants to assert 'despotic firmness' at home, it is because the woman provokes him. If he wants to assert further, 'brutally', that he is 'master', it is because the woman drives him to it. Rosamond is culpable (shades of Hetty). But George Eliot has moved the narrative into the telling impasse. The woman is culpable, but the man too is culpable, loaded as he is with a battery of contradictions, failing as he does to negotiate home and work, man and woman. Ultimately, George Eliot moves herself into a contradiction.

Rosamond's discontent in her marriage was due to the conditions of marriage itself, to its demand for self-suppression and tolerance, and not to the nature of her husband.[15]

Neither man nor woman, but marriage is the problem. In the anxiety to reclaim Lydgate, the polarizing terms of his masculinity are forgotten. Marriage is to blame. And marriage is a joint responsibility (or is it?). Marriage is home and not work. Home is not man's responsibility. Man evades the grasp again.

Lydgate does, indeed, remain 'morally lovable'. If Rosamond does not love him, it is not his fault. If Middlemarch does not love him, it is not his fault. He is a professional, a social reformer, an idealist, a good doctor. He is good at his work. He works well. He is a good man. He may not know much about life, furniture, women, but he does know about work, books, theoretical man.

George Eliot settles the complexity of sexual relations and of social relations on the professional classes, an arena which inscribes her own position as literary professional and the mode of realism which that position entails. It is on the professional that the inflection, in all its complications, falls.

'MENTAL' WORK: ACADEMICS, ARTISTS AND WRITERS

Of most obvious interest to George Eliot in the construction of masculinity in relation to the professional classes, to 'mental' workers, is the academic, and, in different ways, the artist. My account began with the distinction between artist and artisan in the division of labour and in sensibility, and it is to that division that I now return. For it becomes clear that George Eliot, despite her own significance as an artist, is as likely to idealize, as a masculine constriction, the artist as she is likely to idealize the artisan. The artist, within her fiction, signifies not simply another stratum in the division of labour, but, like the artisan, a mythologized version of that stratum which is 'the other'. The artist, more often than not in George Eliot's fiction, is a fine sensibility, surrounded, more often than not, by gentlemanly appurtenances, privileged above the professional and his banal need for income. Such figures are Will Ladislaw and Stephen Guest, with his 'diamond ring, attar of roses, and air of nonchalant leisure'. (Critics have commented on the way in which such figures are too slight to carry the resolution of a fraught sexual politics.)

The academic is different again, and tends to pose an antithetical masculinity to the idealized artisan and artist. Within the division of labour, the academic, scholar, pedant, has ever held an uncertain place, by virtue in a capitalist society of controlling not money (the prime indicator of high occupational status) but that troubled commodity, knowledge. George Eliot reserves for the academic her particular castigation of masculinity. Casaubon, not at all 'morally lovable', has completed the separation of home and work, thought and feeling, woman and man. His dreams are footnotes. He has 'no good red blood in his body'.

In the earlier novel, *Romola*, the relationship (or lack of it) between Casaubon and Dorothea has been prefigured in the blind scholar and his daughter. This prefiguring maps the gender terms centred on and latent in the pedant idea. The scholar, as we might expect, is metaphorically as well as literally blind. In particular, he cannot see his daughter, Romola, who works at his manuscripts by his side. He cannot see woman:

'If my son had not forsaken me, deluded by debasing fanatical dreams, worthy only of an energumen whose dwelling is among tombs, I might have gone on and seen my path broadening to the end of my life; for he was a youth of great promise . . . But it has closed in now,' the old man continued, after a short pause; 'it has closed in now – all but the narrow track he has left me to tread - *alone in my blindness*' [My emphasis].[16]

The consequences of the pedant's blindness are shaped, in both *Middlemarch* and *Romola*, in the reactions of woman. Living with Casaubon is for Dorothea a 'stifling depression'. She is 'a mere victim'. Romola is repeatedly 'stung' by her father's outbursts against 'the wandering, vagrant propensity of the feminine mind'. For the blind scholar, woman is the literal 'inferior gender' of his Latin. The gender collision is in knowledge. In this way, George Eliot brings the place of the academic in the division of labour, and the gender terms of his control of knowledge, into very direct bearing on sexual and social relationships.

These questions about knowledge can also be seen to have direct bearing on the whole question of experience in its gender terms, involving the collision, again, between thought and feeling in relation to that experience which is legitimated as 'knowledge'. In *Romola*, this struggle for the definition of knowledge centres, at one point, on experience recalled through memory. Romola remembers a time of 'far-off light' before she became embedded in 'dark mines of books'. Memory recalls the spring of her 'wintry life'. For her father, memory serves a different function:

> 'For when I was your age, words wrought themselves into my mind as if they had been fixed by the tool of the graver; wherefore I constantly marvel at the capriciousness of my daughter's memory, which grasps certain objects with tenacity, and lets fall all those minutiae whereon depends accuracy, the very soul of scholarship. But I apprehend no such danger with you, young man, if your will has seconded the advantages of your training.'[17]

Memory, about giving priority to value in relation to knowledge/experience, is clearly posed here as an issue of gender prejudice. In *Romola*, man (blind scholar) defines woman (Romola) as inherently faulty, incapable of 'accurate' memory, incapable of knowledge. But the authorial movement is against the scholar and his versions of masculinity. Casaubon and the blind scholar of *Romola* are the faulty ones. It is their version of knowledge which will not do. Man, at last, is blamed. Man must take responsibility for a definition of work and a definition of experience which destroys home and crucifies domestic relations and, of course, himself.

It seems from these kinds of representations that, although a professional writer herself, George Eliot does not privilege herself as 'artist' or 'thinker'. These representations, while critical, are constructions of *masculinity* in different class formations.

In making the movement back from representation more directly to writer, the direction is thus away from those representations more stereotypical in their castigations (Casaubon, etc.) and their idealizations (Will Ladislaw, Adam Bede), and towards the aspiring professional Lydgate who, despite confusing women with furniture, is enacting a sexual struggle whose terms are important and who shares, as a representation, some social attitudes with a woman, Dorothea. Before dealing directly with the writer as aspiring professional, it is necessary, however, to look at the representation of Dorothea, who is notable among George Eliot's women in *Middlemarch* in aspiring to perform professional work. Like Lydgate, she experiences the attraction of the professional ideal, and, like him, experiences a marriage which challenges this idealism. But unlike Lydgate (and this is where the differentiated terms of 'women's work' irresistibly assert themselves), Dorothea is firmly contained within a notion of womanhood which works against professionalism. Self-sacrifice, assimilation of self in man's purposes: these are the familiar significations of virtuous womanhood. The aspiration to professional work is thus subsumed or forgotten in the aspiration to marriage. Marriage is woman's work.

George Eliot, despite being a professional (writer) herself, thus allows the fiction to complete a containment of woman within the traditional terms of marriage and other issues domestic. What fails to come clear is a relationship of woman to man's work – defined by its practice. Perhaps in focusing on this lack of clarity, it is necessary to turn from the fiction to some of the more direct utterances made by George Eliot about the relationship between women and work, particularly the relationship of women to 'mental' work.

'The deepest disgrace', said George Eliot, is for women 'to insist on doing work for which we are unfit'. It is a woman's duty, she argued, to pursue unrewarded labour. Back we return to the mutually handicapping terms: woman's nature as woman's duty as woman's work. It is not surprising that, in

revisiting these formulations, we discover the culmination of
fear in the idea of the 'masculine woman'.

> She was keenly anxious to redress injustices to women, and to
> raise their general status in the community. This, she thought,
> could best be effected by women improving their work –
> ceasing to be amateurs. But it was one of the most distinctly
> marked traits in her character that she particularly disliked
> everything generally associated with the idea of a 'masculine
> woman'.[18]

So, 'ceasing to be amateurs' moves directly into the fear of
being 'masculine'. Professionalism moves into masculinity.
The work terms (professional/amateur) mesh with the gender
terms (masculine/feminine).

Finally, because prevarication is no longer necessary, I turn
directly to the writer: the writer disowning the academic,
distancing the artisan and the artist, aligning finally and in
complication with professional ideals and professional work,
but refusing to explicate fully the gender and class terms of
that alignment. Finally, this is a return to George Eliot and
subjectivity, to professional writer engaged with readership
in a complex exchange of gender terms and meanings,
positioning the reader as masculine, positioning the writer as
masculine. These terms and positions, regardless of the sex of
the reader, manoeuvre and negotiate the conditions of a
profession, which, while it permits the entry of women,
requires women to accept, however complicatedly, the
exchange relations of the masculine world.

3
Representational Responsibilities in Dickens

It is a significant speculation that while today Charles Dickens is a national monument, for *Fraser's Magazine* of the 1840s, before Dickens' reputation was irrevocably established, he might well have been numbered in that 'army of Xerxes' encumbering the profession, Literature. Certain elements in his personal history – his provincial birthplace, his father's occupation (clerk), his term of employment in the notorious blacking factory – signify a social and family placing of the kind likely to have brought him against the charge of 'hungry pretender' to the 'Macedonian phalanx'.[1] In becoming one of that phalanx's 'chosen men', Dickens' professional development is substantially indicative of what the *Fraser* author has illustrated: of the expansion of the professions and of the professional classes from the 1840s to the 1880s, of the access of new groups to professional power, and of the accompanying amelioration of the term 'professional'. Simultaneously, it is indicative of the development of the novel as the key genre of that Victorian history. It is of course a tribute to Dickens' uniqueness, but it is also a sign of the times, that he is able to surmount the obstacles of a 'vulgar' birth, to become the most successful Victorian novelist.[2]

Dickens is, characteristically, *not* disparaging of literary professionalism. As a member of the developing professional classes, he could respond less tortuously than did those literary gentlemen who, like the *Fraser* author, saw professionalism as inevitable but threatening to the idea of Literature as a secure profession.[3] 'Throughout his career he thought of himself as a professional writer, an identity which an older generation deplored.'[4] His faith in professional association can be likened to that of the early nineteenth-century medical reformers challenging, in discourse, the corruptions of Government.[5] There is, indeed, a historical continuity to this kind of utopian response to the professions: in different formations, it emerges, for instance, in 1930s writings about the socially reforming aspects of professional association.

In the 1860s, Dickens attempted to form an organization of professional writers, a Guild of Literature and Art, which would offer the opportunity for help and self-help to authors and would displace 'aristocratic patronage and amateurism'.[6] He had earlier written to Thackeray: 'I am always possessed with the hope of leaving the position of literary men in England, something better and more independent than I found it.'[7]

There is something of a discrepancy, however, between this faith in literary professionalism, reiterated in letters and speeches within literary circles, and the representations of other professions in Dickens' fiction. It is frequently in representations of professionals that Dickens' caricature emerges at its most sharp. Lawyers in *David Copperfield* are 'frozen-out old gardeners in the flower-beds of the heart'. In *Bleak House* they are similarly desiccated, having been 'squeezed dry years upon years ago'. Medical men, in the opening chapters of *Dombey and Son*, frame the wrong-headed and competitive assumptions of that household. In *Martin Chuzzlewit*, the medical man, John Jobling, enacts with the 'great capitalist' Montague Tigg, a similar apotheosis of a particularly close and corrupt relationship between capitalism and professionalism: wonderfully cemented in the Anglo-Bengalee Disinterested Loan and Life Insurance Company. Nor is such caricature reserved for 'the learned professions' or their nineteenth-century re-formations. The deplorable Mr Pecksniff, architect, is the empty 'sounds and forms' of professional behaviour. Educators, Gradgrind, Headstone, speak their own preoccupations as do civil servants . . . 'the Circumlocution Office went on mechanically, every day, keeping this wonderful, all-sufficient wheel of statemanship, How not to do it, in motion.'[8]

In *Martin Chuzzlewit*, the criticism is extended to a nation.

If that peculiarly transatlantic article, a moral sense, – for if native statesmen, orators, and pamphleteers, are to be believed, America quite monopolizes the commodity, – if that peculiarly transatlantic article be supposed to include a benevolent love of all mankind, certainly Martin's would have borne just then a deal of waking: for as he strode along the street, with Mark at his heels, his immoral sense was in active operation; prompting him to the utterance of some rather sanguinary remarks, which it was well for his own credit that nobody overheard. He had so far cooled down, however, that he had begun to laugh at the recollection of these incidents, when he heard another step behind him, and turning round encountered his friend Bevan, quite out of breath.

He drew his arm through Martin's, and entreating him to walk slowly, was silent for some minutes. At length he said:

'I hope you exonerate me in another sense?'

'How do you mean?' asked Martin.

'I hope you acquit me of intending or foreseeing the termination of your visit. But I scarcely need ask you that.'

'Scarcely indeed,' said Martin. 'I am the more beholden to you for your kindness, when I find what kind of stuff the good citizens here are made of.'

'I reckon,' his friend returned, 'that they are made of pretty much the same stuff as other folks, if they would but own it, and not set up on false pretences.'

'In good faith, that's true,' said Martin.

'I dare say,' resumed his friend, 'you might have such a scene as that in an English comedy, and not detect any gross improbability or anomaly in the matter of it?'

'Yes indeed!'

'Doubtless it is more ridiculous here than anywhere else,' said his companion; 'but our professions are to blame for that.'[9]

Bevan is the good American, exception to the case (exceptional 'kindness' compared with those other 'good citizens' who are set up on 'false pretences'). The voice of good America thus inscribes its citizens as like an English comedy, being 'pretty much the same stuff' as other nations. 'Our professions are to blame.' Professionalism displaces class as the means of social ranking. There are no 'masters' in America, but it is a nation of professionals.[10] 'There seemed to be no man there without a title: for those who had not attained to military honours were either doctors, professors, or reverends.[11]

Fictional America usefully places some of Dickens' concern with representations of professionals. The titles, ranks, pretensions of professionalism substitute, in their relations with capitalism and particular kinds of masculinity, for fictional England and its more complex social stratifications. The problem of fictional America is also its virtue as an example: the explicit simplicity of its attack on the professions as the signal problem of the social formation. We begin to be able to read out from the professionals of fictional England, with the help of the oversimplified America, some of the ideological and representational meanings of professionalism in Dicken's novels.

The particular sharpness in the caricature, John Jobling in *Martin Chuzzlewit*, for instance, is in the aping of the 'sounds and forms' of the gentleman (in its class and gender terms).

> 'Why, my dear Sir, with regard to the Anglo-Bengalee, my information, you see, is limited: very limited. I am the medical officer, in consideration of a certain monthly payment. The labourer is worthy of his hire; 'Bis dat qui cito dat' – ('Classical scholar, Jobling!' thinks the patient, 'well-read man!') - 'and I receive it regularly. Therefore I am bound, so far as my own knowledge goes, to speak well of the establishment.' ('Nothing can be fairer than Jobling's conduct,' thinks the patient, who has just paid Jobling's bill himself.) 'If you put any question to me, my dear friend,' says the doctor, 'touching the responsibility or capital of the company, there I am at fault: for I have no head for figures, and not being a shareholder, am delicate of showing any curiosity whatever on the subject. Delicacy – your amiable lady will agree with me I am sure – should be one of the first characteristics of a medical man.' ('Nothing can be finer or more gentlemanly than Jobling's feeling,' thinks the patient.)[12]

Here Dickens presents the pretension and the exposure: the accoutrements and appurtenances of 'the gentleman', played off by Jobling. The old and new versions of professionalism are exploited. Jobling is the hired 'labourer', but he is also the classical scholar (the learned professions). He is of the establishment ('I am bound to speak well' of it), but independent of it ('so far as my knowledge goes': uncompromising professional autonomy). He is not sullied by direct dealings with finance capital ('I have no head for figures') and is not a shareholder, for that would not be 'delicate' in a professional, and 'delicacy' is the mark of the gentleman ('a man of fine feeling', thinks the patient). Dickens makes the reader's task light, by initiating us (as distinct from the client) into the deception from the beginning.

The opening of *Dombey and Son* is a more complex framing of a similar set of devices. The 'genuine' article, Doctor Parker Peps, the court physician, attends with the family surgeon at the birth of young Paul Dombey. The weight of professional judgement, enacted with ritual obeisance from family surgeon to court physician, structures Dombey and the opening frames of the Dombey world. Time is of the essence. Dombey jingles and jingles his 'heavy gold watch-chain'. The idea is taken up again in the loud ticking of the court physician's watch (Jobling's gold watch-chain is also 'of the heaviest'). Time thus presides (capitalized, personified) over the birth of a son and the death of a mother. The ticking of Mr Dombey's watch and the ticking of Doctor Parker Pep's watch enter into a competition – 'seemed in the silence to be running a race' - bidding for control.

Despite the closing moment of the chapter, with mother and daughter for the last time together, and enough to invoke in the Doctor a human response ('The Doctor gently brushed the scattered ringlets of the child, aside from the face and mouth of the mother'), the prospect of Mrs Dombey's death has been satirically fractured in professional diagnosis:

'if our interesting friend the Countess of Dombey – I *beg* your pardon; Mrs Dombey – should not be -'
'Able,' said the family practitioner.
'To make,' said Doctor Parker Peps.
'That effort' said the family practitioner.
'Successfully,' said they both together.

'Then,' added Doctor Parker Peps, alone and very gravely,
'a crisis might arise, which we should both sincerely
deplore.'[13]

This is the professional world setting and inscribing the
priorities of the Dombey world. The death of the wife is not,
that is, of the same significance as the birth of a son. The dark,
masculine presences with their weighty tokens (gold watches,
sombre suits), enact the masculinist concerns of Dombey, of
capital.

The alignment of capital, professionalism and certain
characteristics of masculinity is at its most successfully
cohesive in *Dombey and Son*.[14] The court physician (high
rank . . . aristocracy) and the family surgeon (middle rank . . .
'bourgeois') cement the class alliance, which is also professional and masculine. When Dombey has to turn to a wet
nurse for the help that neither a surgeon nor a physician can
give, the satirical comment is of course one about class, but it
is also about gender, and gender in relation to work,
occupation. 'It was a rude shock to his sense of property in his
child, that these people – the mere dust of the earth, as he
thought them – should be necessary to him;'[15] which is most
forcefully realized in the reiteration of 'my son – my son'
during the eventual sacking of the wet nurse.

> 'The woman is discharged and paid. You leave this house,
> Richards, for taking my son – my son,' said Mr Dombey,
> emphatically repeating these two words, 'into haunts and into
> society which are not to be thought of without a shudder.'[16]

When Dickens makes these alignments – capital, professions, masculinity – the gender politics of his representations
are highly successful. The daughter and wives of the Dombey
household demonstrate these gender politics at their most
alive.

Other novels are less careful in the alignments they make,
which may only be to say that the equation of professionalism
with masculinity, and conversely, as Dickens makes the
equation of good work with femininity, has to be looked at
carefully.

We may be permitted these days – when sexual politics should no longer be separated from real politics (*realpolitik*) – to believe that Dickens is right to interpret the failure of professional values as essentially (we are down to essences) a failure of feeling: or, in his terms, a failure of 'heart'. Lawyers, as we have seen, are 'frozen-out', without 'heart', 'squeezed dry'. Civil servants and educators proceed 'mechanically'. Medical men, architects, operate the 'sounds and forms' only of fine feeling. Dombey reforms when he learns to feel. Gradgrind reforms when he learns the significance of feeling.

Problems occur when this commitment of Dickens to 'heart' is conflated with what he takes to be feminine values, thus taking gender terms too directly, instead of challenging the gender-linking of spheres: public, private; work, home; thought, feeling; personal, professional. Thus, we find when looking at Dickens' representations of virtuous professionals (if that is not already a contradiction in his terms), a representational sleight of hand which moves them away from one or more of the sources of indictment: away from masculinity (being male), or away from work itself, or, in some configurations, even almost out of the novel itself.

On occasions, this concern to displace the masculinist values of professionalism in order to inscribe virtue results in an emasculating sentimentality. Mr Chillip in *David Copperfield* is a significant figure in being the doctor who eschews (though he is barely capable of that much activity) 'professional' values in favour of community values. Being a good neighbour, a good family man, a dependable member of the community: these are the qualities which structure him in the work he does. His knowledge of patients is a knowledge of families, generations, neighbours and personal friends. This is the 'knowable community' of the village and small town of the provinces, where there is opportunity for continuity in relationships, and for the work to speak the man.[17] Professional experience is not delimited by category (physician, surgeon, apothecary) but is incorporating. The consequence, though, of the move away from these delimitations is representationally diminishing: 'being a mild, meek, calm little man'.

He was the meekest of his sex, the mildest of little men. He
sidled in and out of a room, to take up the less space. He
walked as softly as the Ghost in Hamlet, and more slowly. He
carried his head on one side, partly in modest depreciation of
himself, partly in modest propitiation of everybody else.[18]

And though Mr Chillip's judgement of other professionals
is morally appropriate (his response to giving 'professional
evidence' to a Commission of Lunacy in London is to say, 'It
would quite unman me.'[19]), the terms of that judgement
(unmanning) and of him as representational judgement
(meekest, mildest, littlest of his sex) is a problem in offering
(or failing to offer) a challenge to the more rigidly masculinist
versions of professionalism. A concern with putting the
'heart' back in work in this way becomes an overly direct
inscription of gender terms. The man with heart is unmanned.
(And this is one of the familiar separating taxonomies:
thought and feeling, work and home, preventing any other
than the sentimental investment in the 'man' who values heart
and home at work. Though perhaps this is an ungenerous
reading of Chillip who does at least challenge the notion that
to be professional is to be manly.)

Another virtuous professional presents us with similar
problems in a more complex form. Dickens' presentation of
Allan Woodcourt in *Bleak House* begins to show how, in the
attempt to construct that virtue, the terms of appraisal tend to
shift from work itself. Woodcourt is central to the idealizing
strains of the novel and these are frequently distanced from
the 'material life' of work.[20] Woodcourt is 'so cheery, so
fresh, so sensible, so earnest, so . . .' and again, 'so gentle, so
skilful, so unwearying . . .'; but these qualities are not tested
in representational action, as Woodcourt is absent for the
most morally problematic sections of the narrative. And
though he has absented himself for no more idealistic
purposes than 'a living' (surgeon on board ship), his absence
(in the land of light, the exotic East) and his return are
charged with a variety of idealistic narrative solutions and
resolutions. When he returns to the lands of darkness
(England, with Vholes as the epitome of deathly, black
professionalism), he brings 'enlightenment' to the narrative

('the place brightens whenever he comes, and darkens whenever he goes') in the form of sunny presence (repeated references to his 'sunburn') and other forms of narrative comfort. Simultaneously, unlike Chillip, he remains fully 'manned', satisfying in marrying Esther the sexual, as well as social, frustrations of the narrative.

If we begin to look closely at this load which Dickens puts on Woodcourt, there appear some narrative and ideological formations which become increasingly worrying with the looking. For the problems of Woodcourt as loaded narrative functionary – and the mode of that function – conceal other representational problems about him. Idealized rescuers – white (though with a suntan), Christian and, it hardly needs to be said, male – returning from the exotic East to resolve, albeit sunnily, the problems of the English class system, and through Medicine, should be more problematic for Dickens than sunshine. And if this is labouring the metaphoric point, it is possible to take the argument in a different direction to do with what occurs, what imaging is produced, when the social, sexual and professional ideals are required to mesh, to function for each other. Answering those questions may ultimately lead in the same direction: to the moral crusader (white, Christian, male), displaced curing persona of the white, male, Christian novelist himself.

This may begin to come clearer on looking at what kind of fantasy Woodcourt is. It is in this means of representation, and in the narrative responsibilities for Woodcourt as representation, that the problems appear candidly.

I believe – at least I know – that he was not rich. All his widowed mother could spare had been spent in qualifying him for his profession. It was not lucrative to be a young practitioner, with very little influence in London; and although he was, night and day, at the service of numbers of poor people, and did wonders of gentleness and skill for them, he gained very little by it in money. He was seven years older than I. Not that I need mention it, for it hardly seems to belong to anything.

I think – I mean he told us – that he had been in practice three or four years, and that if he could have hoped to contend through three or four more, he would not have made the voyage on which he was bound. But he had no fortune or private means, and so he was going away.[21]

The woman narrator, Esther Summerson, who has been thinking too much about the man ('I believe – at least I know . . . I think – I mean, he told us'), here presents, a touch apologetically, the rationale of our hero's movements. The woman takes responsibility for the rationale of the man. Woodcourt is 'not rich'. It is thereby legitimate for him to leave the poor (for whom he nevertheless 'did wonders of gentleness and skill') for he has no money. He has to live. What could be a comment on nineteenth-century professionalism (the rich paying the rich for their 'services') is the coy apologia of the woman for 'her man'. It is also the narrative apologia for Woodcourt's imminent disappearance from the narrative and a signal of the importance of his ultimate return. The woman takes the responsibility for the narrative and representational justification of the man. And this of course – Dickens producing the rationale through Esther Summerson rather than Woodcourt – is what sustains the exclusivity of the man, without flaw.

Mrs Woodcourt, fond motherhood, takes over the justification where Esther leaves it. Woodcourt is poor. He has 'no fortune or private means', but we learn from her that he is a gentleman. He has 'pedigree'. He has fine feeling.

Woodcourt as ideal begins to depend, we see, on the displacement of representational responsibilities on to women (and we must realize that, in this instance, it is not accidentally, nor incidentally, women). But the more important point moves us sideways to consider the construction of the women who are required to take these responsibilities, and we begin to see that taking responsibility is no equitable, collective act, but one which significantly diminishes, in other aspects of their representation, the women concerned. The fantasy of ideal man depends, that is, not only on abrogation of male reponsibility, but on the diminishing of women.

Esther Summerson *must* appear sentimental/besotted/coy

> He was seven years older than I. Not that I need mention it,
> for it hardly seems to belong to anything.

to give significance to Woodcourt and to the resolutionary
significance of the pattern of departure and return. Mrs
Woodcourt must be caricatured in her gender and class
interests

> Mrs Woodcourt, after expatiating to us on the fame of her
> great kinsman, said that, no doubt, wherever her son Allan
> went, he would remember his pedigree, and would on no
> account form an alliance below it.

to give Woodcourt the gender, class status of hero, which,
incidentally, even renders her rather than him suspect for that
previously apparent acute act of self-sacrifice:

> All his widowed mother could spare had been spent in
> qualifying him for his profession.

The gender formations of representation in Dickens begin
to be revealed. And at some point in the argument it is
necessary to invoke again the literary professional: Dickens'
celebration of that aspect of professionalism and his own
position as a professional writer. It has already been hinted
that the Woodcourtain ideal, though through medicine, may
speak some of the terms of the literary professional for
Dickens, in being the male, Christian, white, professional,
etc. ideal. (David Copperfield may be a less culpable version
of that same ideal, more directly related to literary professionalism.) The important point to make at this stage of the
argument is that Dickens' exemptions of 'the writer' from a
critical perspective (particularly clear in Copperfield) occur,
with important consequences, in fictional representation as
well as what may have been a necessary polemic. It is even
possible to begin to generalize about these consequences in
representation: that the woman is, at strategic points, required to take responsibility: that this is a requirement which
operates to woman's cost. It may be important to generalize

further: that woman, at least in representation, seems to be expected to take responsibility, strategic and moral, for man and man's work, whether it be directly or indirectly in the invocation of 'feminine' values. Ultimately, we can begin to say that the professional writer enters into a history of representation which invokes certain responsibilities as woman's and some as man's. Dickens tends to accept these responsibilities while exempting the writer. The argument proceeds with a certain circularity: woman takes responsibility for representation: woman, in being not the writer, takes responsibility for the writer. (Perhaps nineteenth-century women do not gain as much 'entry' into, or 'income' from, literary professionalism as we might have thought.) Dickens, we have to admit after all, brightens the lands of darkness, is 'so cheery, so fresh, so sensible, so earnest, so . . . ', and is certainly a sunny presence in the Macedonian phalanx of chosen men.

Representing Woman–A Sliding Scale of Mythologies

With woman, the professional case becomes complicated. There are no Woodcourtian equivalents. There is no celebrated woman as a professional ideal. This is because the relationship between work and representation has changed. Dickens' fictional representation has a new set of functions when it transfers from man to woman.

We have seen how an element in nineteenth-century sexual ideology constructs woman in ideal contradiction to the materiality of working life, ('feet do not walk . . . hands do not work'[22]), and how this contradiction has functioned to keep woman, not from work (the law of labour is 'sovereign'[23]) but from power, and from work carrying power. It would follow that when Dickens subscribes to this ideology (or, more precisely, is of it) there would be an absence in representation of a particular relationship between woman and professional work.

To look for an illustration which might fill this absence, it is necessary, for the moment, to look outside Dickens' fiction, to a culture which is at least capable of producing, however occasionally and arbitrarily (or accidentally), a woman professional whom it is ready to acclaim.

FLORENCE NIGHTINGALE

The obvious illustration to take from early Victorian culture is Florence Nightingale. She is what Victorian culture, and history from then forwards, has selected as one of the very few significantly powerful, working nineteenth-century women, particularly outside the literary production process: writer, representation. She is also an obvious choice in relation to some of the more direct concerns of my account, placing as they do an emphasis on the particularity of the relationship between Medicine and the other professions (and representation) in the nineteenth century, the difficulties for women in that set of relationships, and so on . . . It is convenient to select her too for the immediate purposes of what I have to say here about Dickens. They were contemporaries, experiencing similar responses (though taking different directions in action) to the radicalizing movements constituting the professions in the 1840s and 1850s. Nightingale ¡and Dickens also shared, in their lifetimes, public identities through popularity, which have entered into our culture in the form of mythologies. It is these very mythologies which have to be scrutinized to enlighten us about gender-differentiations in representation – or in mythology.

We can now, in the light or dark of accumulating evidence, set some of the mythologies surrounding Florence Nightingale in tension.

In the 1860s, Florence Nightingale became Britain's leading adviser on medical administration. (This is how one history goes.) Since the 1840s, she had put most of her time into matters of medical policy and administration. From the time of the Crimean War until late in the nineteenth century, she committed herself to writing, arguing, influencing government ministers, in order to realize her twin ambitions: the reform of the hospital service and the reform of the British

Army. From 1845 to 1850, her reading of Blue Books about sanitary conditions and hospital reports resulted in her being accepted as the country's leading expert on hospitals. In the ensuing twenty years, she revolutionized the work and status of nurses and soldiers, and did the work of government ministries in proposing reforms to Army barracks, the Indian medical service, the training of nurses, and the reform of medical and hospital services in general.[24] 'As an adviser her position was extraordinary. For the next four years every problem affecting the health and sanitary administration of the British Army was referred to Miss Nightingale.'[25]

In the 1840s, before she was engaged in hospital work, she had rejected both marriage and domesticity as modes of life insufficient to her needs and incompatible with her aims. In response to a proposal of marriage from Richard Monckton Milnes, she writes to a friend:

> I know I could not bear his life, that to be nailed to a continuation, an exaggeration of my present life without hope of another would be intolerable to me – that voluntarily to put it out of my power ever to be able to seize the chance of forming for myself a true and rich life would seem to me like suicide.[26]

Later, she writes: 'I could not satisfy this nature by spending a life with him making society and arranging domestic things.'[27] In her novel *Cassandra* there is a similar range of criticism of the domestic life of the genteel woman: its 'vacuity', 'boredom' and 'false sentiment'.[28]

Between these images produced by and about her, from the 'adviser of extraordinary position' (the 'true and rich life'?) to the critic of the domestic 'nature', there fall the darkening shadows of a plethora of gender types and problems. Autobiography and biography reveal more about the difficulty for any nineteenth-century woman of making that transition from the accepted category of private (woman) to the accepted category of public (man) work. 'She was a young lady in society – was it not peculiar for a young lady to wish for such a post; could a lady take orders, even from a committee of other ladies'. And Medicine poses its own class problems: 'Should a lady, even in those days of strange mingling of ranks, nurse one who was not a lady: was it nice for a lady to be present at medical examinations and, worse still, at operations?'[29]

It is what we can read (as experience) from these questions which, no doubt, prompts Florence Nightingale, in her letters, to justify or agonize, repeatedly, about her work in gender terms (and, on occasions, to attack women).

> The real fathers and mothers of the human race are NOT the fathers and mothers according to the flesh. I don't know why it should be so. It 'did not ought to be so'. But it is. Perhaps it had better not be said at all. What is 'Motherhood in the Flesh'? A pretty girl meets a man and they are married. Is there any thought of the children? The children come without their consent even having been asked because it can't be helped . . . For every one of my 18,000 children, for every one of these poor tiresome Harley Street creatures I have expended more motherly feeling and action in a week than my mother has expended for me in 37 years.[30]

Is this finally the professional ideal – investing in work those feelings and commitments conventionally reserved for family? The shadow falls again: the insecurity of self in work which has no female type attached to it, the questioning of 'motherhood in the flesh' in order to construct for self an image of motherhood ('motherly feeling and action'), the resentful displacement of the mother who has not 'expended' (for 'real' motherhood is about expenditure) in 37 years. Here, the engagement of the received categories of private and public produces the tensions, tensions which are, it might be said again, too close to home: 'Perhaps it had better not be said at all.'

It seems apt to the argument too that increasingly in the 1850s and 1860s, as the professions begin the process of consolidating power, and as Nightingale's political influence begins to wane (these two processes/histories are indeed connected[31]), her gender attitudes change from a rigorous declamation of hostility to women's rights to a tentative identification with the position of the single woman. 'Mine has been such horrible loneliness, but how many women, maids of all work and poor governesses, have been lonelier than I.'[32] Simultaneously, in the 1860s, there is a sense that the inadequacies of individualism (particularly as a woman) in sustaining a position of political influence are becoming self-fulfilling, pushing her into behaviour incompatible with any accepted female type.

> The Tories were now in power, and Miss Nightingale was pushed further outside Government matters. On March 20 she wrote to Clarkey: 'While Sidney Herbert was alive I made most of the appointments. This is no bray . . . *Now* if you can fancy a position where a person can do *nothing* directly, nothing but by frightening, intriguing, 'soaping' or going on all fours, that position is mine.' A letter she wrote to Douglas Galton on June 27, 1866, showed how conscious she was of being outside Government circles . . . 'It is all unmitigated disaster to me. For, as Lord Stanley is to be Foreign Office (the only place where he can be of NO use to us), I shall not have a friend in the world. If I were to say more I should fall to swearing. I am so indignant – ever yours furiously. F.N.'[33]

'Swearing', 'indignant', 'furiously': *not* signifiers of any acceptable type of nineteenth-century woman.

What we have, even with this brief look at some autobiographical and biographical detail of Nightingale, is a complicated set of versions of the woman – which is how it should be: 'leading adviser . . . writing, arguing, influencing government ministers', yet working as a woman and a 'lady' in a work sphere operating against certain gender types, justifying that position, combating that position, capable of swearing. What we have in popular mythology, though, is the retransformation to the feminine ideal, unsullied by material life: the angel of mercy, the 'sweet approving smile', the lady of the lamp, the bedside madonna.[34] The mythologizing of Florence Nightingale, that is, moves her away from professional work to (ideal) representation, ideal woman, in contradiction to the materiality of working life.[35]

It is time to return to Dickens, to see what he makes, if anything, of these transformations and retransformations in relation to popular mythology, to see whether or not there is any sense in his fiction of any of the particular cultural formations of the relationship between woman and work, of which my illustration of Nightingale has been given as an instance. In other words, with the foregrounding, in my account, of the instance of Nightingale, it will be important to see whether Dickens' fictional representations of women carry any of that sense of tension between popular mythology and lived experience, between bedside madonna and complicated subject.

There *are* Dickens novels which present us with women as 'professional persons'. In *Martin Chuzzlewit* and *Little Dorrit*, the idea of professionalism (and the repeated use of the term 'professional') is important, not least in constructions of particular kinds of femininity, of being a woman. Betsey Prig and Sarah Gamp, hospital nurse and 'hired attendant' on the sick poor, respectively, in *Martin Chuzzlewit* are described as 'professional persons', and Amy's sister in *Little Dorrit* is a professional actress. There is, however, a certain stereotypical circularity about these representations. In the mid-nineteenth century, nursing and acting were uneasy in their professional status. Looking now at the nineteenth-century division of labour as also a sexual division of labour, it is not hard to surmise why these two forms of occupation or activity should have been thought dubious as professions. It is clear, with hindsight, that any work done by majority women had a much greater struggle to achieve any status in the hierarchy of labour than work done by majority men. For Dickens, though, the central questions are about individual morality, in ways that it is possible to see now conceal questions of class. It becomes clear that the problem of professional women (as inscribed by Dickens) is one of 'vice', and the solution, through morality. In her drinking, Mrs Gamp is:

> very punctual and particular, requiring a pint of mild porter at lunch, a pint at dinner, half-a-pint as a species of stay or holdfast between dinner and tea, and a pint of the celebrated

staggering ale, or Real Old Brighton Tipper, at supper:
besides the bottle on the chimney piece, and such casual
invitations to refresh herself with wine as the good breeding of
her employers might prompt them to offer.[36]

In the final chapters of the novel, Old Martin Chuzzlewit
intervenes, Prospero-like, to make explicit the Gamp vices
and the necessary moral reforms. 'A little less liquor, and a
little more humanity, and a little less regard for herself, and a
little more regard for her patients, and perhaps a trifle of
additional honesty.'[37] The final admonitions are heard by the
reader and not by Mrs Gamp who, on 'Less liquor!', has fallen
into a swoon.

For Dickens, respectable women ('ladies') simply do not
perform professional work. In other words, sexual ideology is
such in Dickens that the then prevailing norms of women's
paid work (low status) are conflated with that which is morally
tainted. In other words again, while there is some ambivalence in Dickens' representations of male professionals (there
can conceivably be virtuous ones), his representations of
female professionals (who are by definition of the 'wrong'
class: not ladies) are unambivalently hostile. Indeed, in *Little
Dorrit* in particular, 'professional' becomes the touchstone
for all that which women should not be, and for all that which
our heroine, Amy, is not.

Therefore, where Nightingale takes a construction of
femininity which renders 'ladies' incapable of professional
work to be a problem (while working at Scutari Hospital in
the Crimea, Nightingale refused to admit 'ladies' into her
nursing party. 'Excellent self devoted women fit more for
heaven than a hospital, they flit about like angels without
hands among the patients and soothe their souls while they
leave their bodies dirty and neglected.'[38]), Dickens upholds
that construction as his feminine ideal.

The feminine ideal, in Dickens' fiction, is firmly located
outside professional work in various kinds of domesticity.
Mary, in *Martin Chuzzlewit*, is the idealized counter to the
Gamps and Prigs, devoted to service in ways which could
never characterize 'professional' women in Dickens' fiction.

Agnes, in *David Copperfield*, is the acme of a version of womanhood where not only is the class-bound 'lady' the ideal, but any suggestion of work as material life (let alone requiring payment) is evacuated from the writing.

She is David Copperfield's 'good angel . . . pointing upward' to a better place for David's faulty conscience, and is 'good', 'beautiful', 'earnest', 'disinterested', 'dutiful', and more.[39] She, like Mary in *Martin Chuzzlewit*, looks after the interests of two men. She is the guardian of her father's physical health and of her lover's moral and spiritual health. She is also the still point in the turning world of David's (not so) moral and spiritual adventures. The feminine ideal here is invested in the little housekeeper, extending as always into moral and spiritual responsibilities for men:

> Wherever Agnes was, some agreeable token of her noiseless presence seemed inseparable from the place. When I came back, I found my aunt's birds hanging, just as they had hung so long in the parlour window of the cottage; and my easy-chair imitating my aunt's much easier chair in its position at the open window; and even the round green fan, which my aunt had brought away with her, screwed on to the window-sill. I knew who had done all this, by its seeming to have quietly done itself; and I should have known in a moment who had arranged my neglected books in the old order of my school days, even if I had supposed Agnes to be miles away, instead of seeing her busy with them, and smiling at the disorder into which they had fallen.[40]

The feminine ideal here is not so much the female as servicer, as the female *as* those services, as the ideal of service. The narrative, that is, celebrates the signifiers of Agnes rather than Agnes herself. These signifiers - the birds, the easy-chair, even the round green fan – connote the continuities and stabilities of David's domestic existence (Trotwood and post-Trotwood) from the 'old order' to the new.

And the most 'agreeable token' of Agnes is 'her *noiseless* presence' (my emphasis), and by 'its seeming' – the work, that is – 'to have quietly done itself'. Ultimately Agnes appears 'smiling' at the disorder of the 'neglected books', the sweet approving smile which sanctions the work she has done for the man as not really work (it did itself), but service as approval: work as moral signifier, service as its own reward.

The feminine ideal quickly embraces (and at this point class is subsumed in gender) women as service: servicing the male subject.

In *Little Dorrit*, Dickens directly employs the terminology of art to idealize domestic service or Little Dorrit as service. (Working women autobiographers, where domestic servants themselves, find this idealizing process inescapable when they turn to writing: see chapter 7, 'An Itch for Scribbling'). This is the professional writer in his professional art idealizing the unprofessional woman. Is Little Dorrit, he asks, 'Inspired?'. He answers: 'Yes. Shall we speak of a poet or a priest, and not of the heart impelled by love and self-devotion to the lowliest work in the lowliest way of life!'[41] This, too, is in a novel replete with references, disapproving in connotation, to 'professionals'. The accolade repeatedly handed to Little Dorrit is that she is 'not professional'.

Chapter 20 of *Little Dorrit* elaborates some of these 'not man', 'not professional', ideal servant (of man, but not manservant) connections. Chapter 20, 'Moving in Society', plots Little Dorrit (Amy) doing that. 'Society', in its first formulation, is the theatre where Amy's sister Fanny works as a professional actress. In its second formulation, it is the family home of the high society lady, Mrs Merdle. Society is also, in this chapter, the outside world, the public sphere (from professional work to high society) for Amy, which she inhabits uneasily.

Fanny's surprise at finding Amy in the public sphere, her work sphere, the theatre, charts the authorial disapproval of the sister, Fanny.

> 'The notion of you among professionals, Amy, is really the last thing I could have conceived!' said her sister. 'Why, how did you ever get here!'
> 'I don't know. The lady who told you I was here, was so

good as to bring me in.'

'Like you quiet little things! You can make your way anywhere I believe. *I* couldn't have managed it, Amy, though I know so much more of the world.'

It was the family custom to lay it down as family law, that she was a plain domestic creature, without the great and sage experience of the rest. This family fiction was the family assertion of itself against her services.[42]

Amy is indeed made 'quite giddy' by being 'among professionals', but the significant attitudes here are those of her sister. Fanny, though she is 'a professional' and prides herself on knowing the public sphere ('I know so much more of the world'), is too much 'the female' to utilize the common sense of 'quiet little things'. The professional world, as it signifies destruction of 'heart' in man, here signifies affectation of feeling in woman. In the high society of Mrs Merdle, 'professional' reappears again to approve Amy in contrast to Mrs Merdle's affectation. 'Also professional,' said Mrs Merdle, dropping her glass. 'Has not a professional air. Very pleasant; but not professional.'[43] and again 'I again address the non-professional Miss Dorrit'[44].

But it is also significant that, with return to narrative comment on the dialogue between Fanny and Amy, the attention shifts from 'among professionals' (the professional context) to the family, to the critical, relative placings of Fanny and Amy in their own family. The construction of Fanny as 'professional' thus becomes for Dickens the critical signifier of her shaky commitment to family. The argument is not quite as simple as that may sound though, for this particular family is problematic: it exploits Amy through 'custom' and 'law' (which inscribe her as 'plain domestic creature') and in creating a 'fiction' of itself which operates against her services. Her own family devalues the 'love and self-devotion' which commits her to them and to 'the lowliest work'.

The narrative is thus explicit, in charging these caricatures (Fanny, Mrs Merdle) with the force derived from the sign 'professional', and with the force of the knowledge that Little

Dorrit is 'inspired', valued above the 'plain domestic creature' lacking in worldly 'experience'. Ultimately, however, Dickens is compromised in the representation of Little Dorrit by his own kind of 'family fiction', which requires domestic service to be 'inspired'. For instance, this same chapter firmly circumscribes and encapsulates Amy in the plain domestic context. 'Moving in society' takes her out of the Marshalsea home, which, although a prison, is not supposed to be an imprisonment of Amy, who is 'inspired'.

> Little Dorrit was late on the Monday morning, for her father slept late, and afterwards there was his breakfast to prepare and his room to arrange. She had no engagement to go out to work, however, and therefore stayed with him until, with Maggy's help, she had put everything right about him, and had seen him off upon his morning walk (of twenty yards or so) to the coffee-house to read the paper.[45]

As with Agnes and David, so with Amy and Dad: a noiseless presence putting 'everything right about him', so that she is late without even having gone 'out to work' (which is only, anyway, more domestic service, as a seamstress and 'companion'). And the chapter ends with the usual hastening back, after moving in Society, of Poor Little Dorrit, to her prison home, and with Fanny's judgement that she is a 'tranquil, domestic, home-loving, good girl'.[46] So that, ultimately, this judgement of Fanny's is not displaced in the novel; neither indeed is her use of the word 'little' for Dorrit (and why is this word 'patronizing' from Fanny and not from Dickens as narrator, even if an ironic one'[47]) The placement which Dickens has attempted to disturb with irony and inspiration remains intact, or how does Amy remain anything other than the 'tranquil, domestic, home-loving, good girl'?

When Dickens comes to represent Amy's feelings for Arthur Clenham, he is stuck with this same problem of how, in this case, to activate or agitate the feelings of a tranquil, domestic, home-loving, good girl. The Story of the Princess – as follows – is a dream for Freudian analysts. This is the fairy story that Amy tells her strange, childish friend, Maggy.

'The Princess was such a wonderful Princess that she had the power of knowing secrets, and she said to the tiny woman, why do you keep it there? This showed her directly that the Princess knew why she lived all alone by herself spinning at her wheel, and she kneeled down at the Princess's feet, and asked her never to betray her. So the Princess said, I never will betray you. Let me see it. So the tiny woman closed the shutter of the cottage window and fastened the door, and trembling from head to foot for fear that any one should suspect her, opened a very secret place and showed the Princess a shadow.'

'Lor!' said Maggy.

'It was the shadow of Some one who had gone by long before: of Some one who had gone on far away quite out of reach, never, never to come back. It was bright to look at; and when the tiny woman showed it to the Princess, she was proud of it with all her heart, as a great, great treasure. When the Princess had considered it a little while, she said to the tiny woman, And you keep watch over this every day? And she cast down her eyes, and whispered, Yes. Then the Princess said, Remind me why. To which the other replied, that no one so good and kind had ever passed that way, and that was why in the beginning. She said, too, that nobody missed it, that nobody was the worse for it, that Some one had gone on to those who were expecting him – '

'Some one was a man then!' interposed Maggy.

Little Dorrit timidly said Yes, she believed so; and resumed.[48]

Tiny Woman (Amy) had a secret, but not any more because the Princess, being 'wonderful', has the 'power' of knowing secrets. Tiny Woman has not even that power. The Princess knows not only of the existence of the secret, but its inner workings, its psychological motivations. Tiny Woman's response, from the inception, is constituted by guilt (she kneels to the Princess) about the act of concealment and of what is concealed. What she feels called upon to justify, significantly enough, is being a single woman – living alone. Tiny Woman, thus knowing that the Princess knows her secret, takes responsibility not only for having (or rather, having had) a secret (which prompts her to live alone) and for the motivations concealed in having a secret, but also for the act of confession, or revelation. She opens the 'secret place', but does so 'trembling from head to foot', and the compact with the Princess still depends on the exclusivity of the secret: no one else shall know.

But the act of revelation only serves to reveal further concealments, further masks, further sublimations: the shadow which is only of Some one: no flesh, no substance, no name. The 'shadow' is an abstract economy of worth. It is 'bright' (despite the shade), it is 'treasure'. The most difficult acknowledgement for Tiny Woman to make is of her recognition of that worth to her ('And you keep watch over this every day?' And she cast down her eyes, and whispered, 'Yes.'). The narrative concealment (which is at the same time that glaringly obvious revelation that 'the hint' (the mask) can so clearly provide) accumulates or disappears in a series of cancellatons: no one, nobody, nobody, Some one gone on, until only the frisson remains – the 'him', the 'man then'. It's all been about the man.

Revelations, concealments, secrets, exposures: the scenario tempts diverse analyses. There are the taboos of the fairy story; the duality, dialectic of female desire (Tiny Woman, Princess); alter egos in fictional representation; the internal relations of the genre(s), of fiction within fiction, and more. And what seems most important to draw out is the male, authorial, perception of the female perception of desire. The masks, sublimations, cancellations and distortions (revelation which is not revelation) are the authorial masks, sublimations, cancellations and distortions, accumulating into the reduction of female sexuality to a fleshless abstraction which is, simultaneously, a terrible conformity to normative sexual mores: don't live alone, wait for the man, subserve the shadow until you get the flesh.

Perhaps it is needless to add that the Story of the Princess also turns us, again, to the class formation of woman in representation. Lowly woman confesses to aristocratic woman (royalty indeed): ideal constructs, dictates ideal. Woman mediates woman in order to take responsibility for man. That's all right then. The childish Maggy, *ingénue* (idiot woman indeed), displaces the Princess to announce what real women are forbidden to announce: desire for the man. Arthur Clenham is in there then. Amy, tranquil, domestic, home-loving, good girl, wants him, him, him: the man.

Ultimately, these mechanisms sketch the typical narrative resolutions, in the feminine ideal, of much of Dickens' fiction. While woman is forbidden to announce desire for man, Dickens' construction of femininity subsumes all other aspects of being a woman in the realization of that unexpressed desire. This is the cultural and narrative destiny of woman: in cultural terms, to find dependence on man, and in narrative terms, to service the representation of man. This, across his class range from lowly Dorrit to royalty, is what Dickens inscribes as the function of woman. This is 'woman's work'.

In denying the complications, in lived experience, that must challenge such a construction of womanhood, in ignoring Nightingale complexities in favour of popular legends (bedside angels, etc.), Dickens does injustice, despite all his capacity for doing justice in his fiction, to gender relations and to the social relations of work.

Working women (some contemporary with Dickens) did, as I shall argue later, aspire to various kinds of professional work, not least, as writers. There is something of an irony about Dickens' reverence for domestic service as the ideal expression of femininity (being a woman), when female domestic servants were experiencing a similar reverence for literary work. It seems that the very women whom Dickens draws upon in idealizing the pursuit of domestic service are busy doing whatever is in their power to avoid such definitions of subjectivity, doing as much as they can to avoid being tranquil, domestic, home-loving, good girls.

4

The Gentleman's Club, Literature

GASKELL AND THACKERAY

Writing in 1850, Thackeray upholds the 'dignity' of Literature, asserts that the profession is no longer held in 'disrepute' and finds that literary professionalism, the new professionalism, can provide respectable careers for gentlemen writers. By wielding the pen 'no man loses his social rank' (for 'man' read 'gentleman' with a rank to lose).[1] Literature, he proceeds to argue, should not only derive from the shared interests (artistic and material) of writers, but should be a brotherhood, operating in 'manly union' and manifesting a neo-militaristic '*esprit de corps*'.[2] Engaging with the terms of the new professionalism, he concedes that members of the literary profession should 'work and pay' like their neighbours, but believes that they should have the benefits of high rewards and, in particular, should have 'friends'.[3] He thanks God that literary gentlemen do have 'friends', as they should.

Thackeray thus brings together, in his declared interests in literary professionalism and in the position in society from which he speaks, aristocratic and bourgeois interests, in a unity produced by the common gender, male. He eschews fear of literary professionalism (where *Fraser* deplores 'women, children, and ill-trained troops' as encumbrances to Literature[4]) in favour of a consolidation of male interests. He exhorts his fellow gentlemen to a chivalric code of the literary: 'Ah! ye knights of the pen! May honour be your shield and truth tip your lances! Be gentle to all gentle people. Be modest to women. Be tender to children'[5] Unlike *Fraser*, his assumption that the literary club is exclusively male is so firm that there is no room for fear of intrusion.

In invoking Thackeray at this stage of the account of literary professionalism, I particularly wish to avoid the temptation to hand out the prize for unique male chauvinism. I intend rather to take Thackeray as an illustration of some persistent attitudes and ideologies which are, in the nineteenth-century, some of the ways in which the gender, male, mediates class differences. This account of Thackeray will not therefore take his literariness to be either idiosyncratic or, more particularly, archaic, the residue of a previous formation (though elements of this exist) but will rather suggest that he holds an important representative position in relation to the persistence, in the nineteenth century, of a powerful ethos and ideology of the gentleman.[6]

I further intend to argue that this representative position can be read out of Thackeray's polemical statements about literary professionalism, and also out of autobiographical and biographical writings, and perhaps most significantly, his fiction.

> The time had come at last when it was necessary for the gentlemen of England to band together in defence of their common rights and their glorious order, menaced on all sides by foreign revolutions, by intestine radicalism, by the artful calumnies of mill-owners and cotton-lords, and the stupid hostility of the masses whom they gulled and led.[7]

In *Pendennis*, this kind of exhortation to 'the gentlemen of England' is structured into the world of journalists and literary hacks. The language of melodrama and of oratory ('menaced . . . intestine radicalism . . . artful calumnies') voices some of the typical political and class fears of the 1840s and 1850s: fears of revolution, of Chartism. In Thackeray's fiction, and in particular in *Pendennis*, which gives particular attention to the literary world, this kind of language sets up a teasing tension, which is also a class tension between an arguably ironic invocation of political and class cliché ('artful calumnies of mill-owners and cotton-lords . . . stupid hostility of the masses') and an exhorting xenophobia on behalf of the gentleman (that class, that gender). In *Pendennis*, this spirit enters into the individual endeavours of would-be writers, including the central protagonist, and particularly into the rhetoric of the press men. The editor of the *Pall Mall Gazette* is a particularly untiring speaker for those interests which unite gentlemen who:

> love their country, and would keep it what the gentlemen of England – yes, *the gentlemen of England* (we'll have that in large caps., Bungay my boy) have made it – the greatest and freest in the world.[8]

It is not accidental that it is in a novel which gives central attention to writers, to literary endeavours, to a narrative which establishes the professional writer (and *Pendennis*, particularly in its central protagonist, the young man, Pen, is held to be close to autobiography), that those class tensions centring upon the gentleman are so closely focused.

The appeal to the literary gentlemen of England to 'band together in defence of their common rights' is a reminder of that process, traced in *Fraser's Magazine*, of literary professionalism in the nineteenth century.[9] In *Pendennis*, the Major describes to his nephew Arthur, his perception of the changing aspects of 'literature':

> You have got yourself a little reputation by your literary talents, which I am very far from undervaluing, though in my time, begad, poetry and genius and that sort of thing were devilish disreputable. There was poor Byron, for instance, who ruined himself, and contracted the worst habits by living with poets and newspaper-writers, and people of that kind. But the times are changing now – there's a run upon literature – clever fellows get into the best houses in town, begad![10]

Like *Fraser*, the Major is ambivalent in his rating of literature in relation to respectability in its class formations. Literature used to be 'devilish disreputable', but now, in Pen's time, it is more highly valued, and the Major can be appreciative of literary talents in his nephew. Poets and newspaper-writers, once conflated in the 'worst habits' of a particular life-style, are now 'clever fellows' entering the best houses in town.

In this way, through Major Pendennis, Thackeray invokes the process of literary professionalizing which leads *Fraser* to ameliorate the terms (from: 'Literature has become a profession' to 'we may deplore, but we cannot alter it' to 'Literature should be a profession'[11]) in his own construction of certain gendered, class interests. The ambivalence which characterizes Major Pendennis' attitudes has some analogy in aspects of Thackeray's own biography as literary gentleman. It was, for instance, in correspondence with Thackeray that Dickens wrote to express his hope 'of leaving the position of literary men in England, something better and more independent than I found it'.[12] This is as if to say that the differentiated class positions of Dickens and Thackeray (Thackeray shared Dickens' interest in literary professionalism, but found him 'vulgar') come together in the united interests of 'literary men' and in the development of the professionalizing of literature. Thackeray's letters to co-authors and publishers reflect and consolidate this sense of united interest. Even his literary rows (as with John Forster about defamation of character[13]) are characterized by gentlemanly codes of honour: chivalric and heroic defences of reputation, of name, within a paradigm in which name and reputation are understood.

Like *Fraser* too, Thackeray finds ambivalence in the class position of Literature in relation to its history. Most authors, argues *Fraser*, claim to be 'barristers or gentlemen at large'. Warrington, in *Pendennis*, admits that he does not describe himself as a writer because he does not 'wish it to be said that George Warrington writes for bread'. Here is the problem of the cash nexus. The ideology of the gentleman does not permit the acknowledgement of financial transaction. The gentleman does not publish his money motive, because he should not have to do so. Defence of a particular class position thus masquerades as the incorruptibility of financial disinterest. The gentleman assumes high reward (as Thackeray had put it), does not work for it, but works from a sense of 'honour', 'truth' and 'love'.[14] This is the public rhetoric.

The economic reality, though, is that literary men, now bringing the upper and middle classes together in the capitalist process of production, by the mid-nineteenth century need to earn from writing. What sustains the rhetoric, then, is both class (the gentleman as aristocrat and new bourgeois) and gender (the gentleman as male). For whom but the woman: honour, truth and love?

The code of the neo-chivalric is more than a simple embellishment of individualism or respectability. It protects the fraternity of literary gentlemen. It also, because of class mediations, additionally protects the born gentleman who is born to the rhetoric, which is why, for all their united interests, Thackeray still reserves the power to declare Dickens vulgar. Within the fraternity, the families and friends (and the particular colouring of Thackeray's use of the term 'friends' is applicable here) of professional writers are often instrumental in the making of the writer. Publishers support their 'best' writers on occasions of financial stringency. Literary 'friends' combine to offer help to fellow writers threatened by debt. (Dickens worked with friends to plan theatrical performances to raise money to alleviate Leigh Hunt's debts.) Parents risk financial excursions into literary enterprises. (Thackeray's family bought a literary periodical and asked William to be editor, to help his literary career.) So that, while, in *Pendennis*, the literary hack experiences a pattern of work which is as 'dull of routine' and 'tedious of description' as that of any man who must work for money, and the Pegasus, Literature, is seen to 'trot in harness', the ethos of the gentleman is nevertheless there supporting, materially and ideologically, the literary man: trotting in harness with capitalist constraint.

In Thackeray's biography and in analogous elements from the quasi-autobiographical Arthur Pendennis, it is possible to trace some not atypical features of the development of the literary man in mid-Victorian England. It is important to examine some representative elements of these lives, of the courses they take, of their educational and social routes, not to suggest that all professional writers, publishers, editors, share those routes (though we might commonly find that they do), but to glimpse how nineteenth-century capitalism was far from the free market (declassed, degendered, competitive individualism) it might sometimes seem, but was rather operating within a pervasive class and gender inheritance signified in 'the gentleman'.[15]

Thackeray was born into the upper-class society of Anglo-India and inherited many of the assumptions of colonial dominance. He prided himself, above all things, on being a 'gentleman'.[16] As a child, he was surrounded by servants. As a youth, he followed the traditional upper-class route for young males through public school (Charterhouse) and on to university (Cambridge). Despite the death of his father when Thackeray was young, and despite his professed inability to manage his own finances (propensities for lavish spending and accumulating debts), a particular kind of class route is sustained, in large part through his family, conspicuously a devoted mother with a reserve of material as well as emotional resources for her son. Eventually Thackeray is accepted into the fashionable circles of successful, literary London. The educational and social route which his life has taken leads to those 'friends' who can help him with the Pegasus, Literature. He can call upon a network of ideological and material support. This is not, on his part, opportunism, but what exists, simply what is there naturally: literary gentlemen whose assumptions derive from much sharing of personal histories of a particular kind.

In the narrative history of Arthur Pendennis, it is possible to trace some of the detailed meanings which attach to the writer, and to Thackeray as a writer. Pen, also born a gentleman, pursues his route through public school and on to Oxbridge. Helen Pendennis is a conspicuously devoted and resourceful mother. Pen succumbs to and is later rescued from the attractions of lavish spending. When he is introduced to the possibilities of a literary career, there pre-exists for him a network of contacts, associates and relationships which already place him, before he has set pen to paper, in the fraternity. This does not of course mean that he can eschew work or assume success, but that the opportunity to write professionally is in important ways predetermined.

It is not, however, singularly in the proximity or transparency of this fictional life in relation to Thackeray's own that judgements about literary professionalism can be made, for that would be a circular argument. It is rather what Thackeray celebrates in Pen and in *Pendennis* which raises the central questions. The world of gentlemanly value which may be the source of some satire is also the source of celebration and of 'right value': truth, honour and love. *Vanity Fair* and *Pendennis* are pervaded with the rhetoric of masculinity as enshrined in class formations and institutions: army, club, pub, college, smoking-room. These sites and settings, which are frequently in Dickens' fiction the location of vice and foible, are in Thackeray's fiction primarily the location or test of gentlemanly codes of conduct, the source or test of what is right.

In cataloguing the stages of Pen's maturing process, there is constant reiteration of values and activities described as 'manly'. College is attractive to Pen in prospect because it is equated with 'manly pleasures and enjoyments'. The women in his home life (or rather, those left back home), his devoted mother, his adopted sister, Laura, indulge (in Thackeray's construction of femininity) gender difference. For them, Pen, being 'a man', is naturally patronizing. 'It seemed natural, somehow, that he should be self-willed and should have his own way.'[17] And if there is some irony in the 'patronizing', it is very gentle, for Thackeray is as indulgent of Pen as are Laura and Helen.

The authorial perception of self as it emerges in the representation, Pen, elsewhere in the fiction, and in Thackeray's letters, is this very celebration of a particular kind of masculinity. It is a perception which is quintessentially self-flattering and in constant slippage towards an encomium of male supremacy. In his letters, 'manliness' coexists with 'genius' and 'honour' as mutually informing constructions of value. References to women are, conversely, frequently in tandem with diminutives: 'little woman . . . poor little wife'.

In his letters, this use of diminutives as part of a gendered attitude is extended and clarified in the sexual ideologies which inform his attitudes to women, and in particular to

Isabella Shawe Thackeray, his wife. In being declared insane, her biggest failings in Thackeray's account appear to be her inadequacy as a devoted mother: 'Today is her little baby's birthday. She kissed the child when I told her of the circumstance, but does not care for it.'[18] Evidence, for him, of her cure is her reappearance after a savage course of medical treatment as 'happy, obedient and reasonable', a loving wife.

The qualities of devoted mothers and loving wives are also required, as might be expected, of fictional women. In his polemic and his novels, this requirement of various kinds of conforming sexual types is placed within a model of idolatry, a model of sexual type which has its textual moment in mid-Victorian England, in Ruskin's '*Of Queens' Gardens*', with its celebration of 'the angel in the house'.[19] The literary code which Thackeray upholds requires knights of the pen to be 'modest to women' and to serve with love, truth and honour. Literary production is thus a gendered process in which woman (woman is the creature of love, made to be 'Love visible'[20]), the abstraction, is held to be the art object and objective. Amelia in *Vanity Fair* is the 'prototype and exemplar' of this: the Victorian heroine.[21] Some contemporary readers found her less beguiling than Thackeray did, but for him, despite any ironies which fill out her representation, she is 'the kind, fresh, smiling, artless, tender little domestic goddess, whom men are inclined to worship'.[22] Laura in *Pendennis* is a more mature extension or version of the same ideal, and without irony. In being both adopted sister and prospective wife to Pen, the fantasy is flagrantly (doubly) one of femininity situated in home and family. It is also a touch xenophobic:

> Miss Laura Bell, at the age of sixteen, was a sweet young lady. Many thousands of such are to be found, let us hope, in this country, where there is no lack of goodness, and modesty, and purity, and beauty.[23]

Religious language (goodness, purity) enters to moralize the aesthetic, woman. Woman, thus ejected from society, is 'an angel – a supernatural being, all wisdom, love, and beauty', and the love of a mother is a 'sacred mystery'.[24]

In *Pendennis*, the reiterated play on gender attitudes seals, despite ironies (even in the process of 'ironising') the boxed categories of stereotype.

> Does any one dare to suppose that the writer would incite the women to revolt? Never, by the whiskers of the Prophet, again he says. He wears a beard, and he likes his women to be slaves. What man doesn't? What man would be henpecked, I say? We will cut off all the heads in Christendom or Turkeydom rather than that.[25]

The writer 'wears a beard' and does not like to be 'henpecked'. The man addresses the men. Women are men's slaves. We have heard it too often. We have heard the joke too often. The gender-specific intrusion, the assertion of the masculine, does not help.

It is where the novel *Pendennis* takes these gender types into the literary world itself that the old problem of the class and gender basis of representation emerges. Why are the significant women back home? Where are the women writers? And again it is possible to see how the representation of woman (angel, supernatural, sacred, good, pure, modest, beautiful) has removed woman from all contact with material life, from professional work, from 'the rude strifes of reality'.[26] *Pendennis* constructs a literary world which is resonant with 'manly' conversation, and where the significant literary relationships are between men. Pen's close friend, George Warrington, is a 'woman-hater' and 'professed misogynist'. His rhetoric is appropriately 'manly': 'I like to talk with the strongest man in England, or the man who can drink the most beer in England.'

Which brings the argument back to how *Pendennis*, not only in its gender attitudes, celebrates the gentlemanly as the literary.

> On one occasion Pen, riding through the Low Town, fancied

he heard the Factory boys jeer him; and finally, going through the Doctor's gate into the churchyard, where some of Wapshot's boys were lounging, the biggest of them, a young gentleman about twenty years of age, son of a neighbouring small Squire, who lived in the doubtful capacity of parlour-boarder with Mr Wapshot, flung himself into a theatrical attitude near a newly-made grave, and began repeating Hamlet's verses over Ophelia, with a hideous leer at Pen.

The young fellow was so enraged that he rushed at Hobnell Major with a shriek very much resembling an oath, cut him furiously across the face with the riding-whip which he carried, flung it away, calling upon the cowardly villain to defend himself, and in another minute knocked the bewildered young ruffian into the grave which was just waiting for a different lodger.

And, later, by way of explanation to the clergyman, Doctor Portman, Pen's motivations:

The young fellow was so agitated he could scarcely speak. His voice broke into a sob as he answered. 'The – coward insulted me, sir,' he said: and the Doctor passed over the oath, and respected the emotion of the honest suffering young heart.[27]

The Factory boys 'jeer' the literary gentlemen, but it is the 'young gentleman' who is the serious opponent, the serious contestant. The struggle over the grave is, aptly enough, the duel over Literature, over Hamlet's dead body, over Ophelia. The struggle for the gentleman's honour is the struggle to defend the literary. Riding-whips, cowardly villains, insults and oaths inscribe the gentlemanly code of conduct in the process of defence; the literary gentleman, the honest suffering young heart of Thackeray himself.

Thomas Carlyle came to accuse Thackeray of cynicism, despite his 'literary ability'. Thackeray's only conviction, argued Carlyle, was that 'a man ought to be a gentleman.'[28] This is the key, for, far from being a solitary aspect in a world absent of value (which is what Carlyle had thought of Thackeray's cynicism), it *is*, it constructs that world of value. Perhaps Charlotte Brontë both saw this and missed this when she had difficulty with Thackeray's 'worldliness', his lack of 'idealism'.[29] It is the confidence of Thackeray's position in class and gender which may trick readers into believing that his fiction is somehow free of a value system. The importance of this confidence is not that it is unique in characterizing Thackeray, not that Thackeray is relegated, thereby, to an idiosyncratic commitment to an obsolete chivalry, but rather that it is the confidence of Victorian patriarchy and in large part the confidence of the literary profession in that history. It is a confidence which makes that patriarchy and that professionalism appear natural, the only sensible position to hold – indeed the only position which is honourable and without vulgarity.

GASKELL

If I were to take the 'free market' of nineteenth-century competitive individualism, and explore its exchange relations within the book trade, I might be able to show that women writers made a considerable entry into literary production and were, on occasions, the beneficiaries of large profits from the sale of books.[30] An over-emphasis on this would, however, beg some of the central questions about ideology, about access, entry and obstacles to surmount, and ultimately about materialism; about the conditions of existence for women (and men of the 'wrong' class) in the gentleman's club, Literature.

In other words, there are strongly differentiated gender and class determinants of literary opportunity and literary access. How women were received by publishers, how women perceived themselves as literary professionals, and, cumulatively, the difficulties of becoming and sustaining being a writer: these are questions which are not simply answered quantitively according to labour power or profits.

To ask questions about the conditions of existence for women in the gentleman's club, Literature, is also to ask important questions about the profession, Literature, and literary ideology. For, if professionalization involves the crystallizing of certain forms of power in male hands, and yet, women have made some kind of entry into processes of professionalization, then it is important to look at the manner of that entry, at the terms on which women made the entry, and at how those terms operate. This is to reiterate that women who become literary professionals are likely (I would argue 'likely' rather than 'bound' to avoid complete determinism) to attempt to function as men, or, at least, are likely to enter into dominant forms of representation with certain gender attitudes (which may well involve, within the gentleman's club, an assumed collaboration with a notion of woman as art object).

Without further theoretical emphasis on determinations and restrictions, it is necessary now to look at what some of the nineteenth-century women writers who were literary professionals made of the literary production process: to look, that is, around the margins of that gentleman's club which was not entirely exclusive to men.

The women writers of the 1840s and 1850s who are now most famous – Charlotte Brontë, Emily Brontë, Elizabeth Gaskell and George Eliot – all employed pseudonyms at some time in their writing lives.[31] While the adoption of pen-names was not confined at this time to women writers, motivations were different for women than for men. When Dickens called himself Boz and Thackeray called himself Titmarsh, they were subscribing to a convention of literary entertainment in which penmanship was equated with gamesmanship: the gentlemen players were the gentlemen posing as players. The adoption of pseudonyms by women writers was part of a different development, associated with anonymity and gender. In her 'Biographical Notice of Ellis and Acton Bell', Charlotte Brontë explains that the Brontë sisters' adoption of androgynous names derived specifically from a fear that gender might act as a source of discrimination:

> We did not like to declare ourselves women, because – without at that time suspecting that our mode of writing and thinking was not what is called 'feminine' – we had a vague impression that authoresses are liable to be looked on with prejudice; we had noticed how critics sometimes use for their chastisement the weapon of personality, and for their reward, a flattery, which is not true praise.[32]

Writing in the 1840s, Charlotte Brontë and her sisters associate, albeit vaguely, response to authoresses with 'prejudice'. The argument proceeds to focus on the gender attitudes of 'critics', on personality and flattery. The concern, then, is with attitudes within the literary profession, the prejudices of critics who mediate, through the gentleman's club, responses of readers to writers. These same critics are not gender-free in their literary judgements, but have precise ideas (prejudices) about what constitutes unfeminine writing and are not commonly capable of 'true praise'. Androgyny is thus a temporary defence, in gaining access to particular kinds of literary production (mediated by the gentleman's club), against gender-specific prejudices.[33]

Some of these gender prejudices are articulated clearly in correspondence between Charlotte Brontë and Robert Southey (and, as with Thackeray, I use Southey not as a particularly acute example of male piggery, but rather supposing that it is not reasonable to think of him as other than representative of certain perspectives prevalent, within literary circles, in mid-nineteenth-century England). It has been said that Southey was the only person in the fifty years after Samuel Johnson's death to live 'entirely on his writings'.[34] In that sense, he is the obvious literary professional for Charlotte Brontë to approach for an opinion about some of her writing and that of her sisters. Southey is meticulous and careful in his response to the request for a literary opinion, but his response is clearly to the gender of the writers. 'Literature cannot be the business of a woman's life, and it ought not to be.'[35] If a woman, he argues, is engaged in her 'proper duties', she will have no leisure for writing. If she does have time for writing, the effect of day-dreaming (using the imagination) will produce such a 'distempered state of mind', that she will be incapable of performing her 'proper duties'. 'Proper duties' thus complete the circle exclusive of writing.

In her reply to Southey, Charlotte Brontë attempts to clarify some assumptions. Far from being the type which Southey has assumed (a 'lady' whose life is defined by the proper duties of home in tandem with leisure: the angel of the house), she has to earn a living from work. She is a governess, and therefore unlikely to experience the luxury or the ill effects of day-dreaming. Having clarified this position, she adds, without irony: 'In the evenings, I confess, I do think, but I never trouble any one else with my thoughts.'[36] And, again, without irony, she subscribes to Southey's home and duty model of womanhood, inadvertently lining up the men, father and Southey, in some typical attitudes of Victorian patriarchy.

> I have endeavoured not only attentively to observe all the duties a woman ought to fulfil, but to feel deeply interested in them. I don't always succeed, for sometimes when I'm teaching or sewing I would rather be reading or writing; but I try to deny myself; and my father's approbation amply rewarded me for the privation.[37]

Confession, 'I do think', denial (of reading and writing), in order to be dutifully 'feminine' requiring sewing not only to be done, but to be deeply interesting. Thinking is all right, perhaps, but not if it distracts from proper duties, and not as a social act ('I never trouble any one else with my thoughts') and therefore not as writing. Perhaps Southey was one of the readers 'revolted', later, by the imaginative power ('distempered state of mind'?) of *Wuthering Heights*, which was judged unfeminine.[38] Later in the reply to Southey, Charlotte Brontë writes: 'Once more allow me to thank you with sincere gratitude. I trust I shall never more feel ambitious to see my name in print; if the wish should rise I'll look at Southey's letter, and suppress it.'[39]

Elizabeth Gaskell, in whose *Life of Charlotte Brontë* this correspondence is collected, confirms this intention to renounce writing:

> This 'stringent' letter made her put aside, for a time, all idea of literary enterprise. She bent her whole energy towards the fulfilment of the duties in hand; but her occupation was not sufficient food for her great forces of intellect, and they cried out perpetually, 'Give, give.'[40]

It takes Gaskell to recognize and explicate the forces of intellect (the woman writer attaches value to the woman writer: the woman in the woman) and to give these more significance than 'proper duties'. Gaskell, of course, could speak from experience. She writes to an aspiring woman writer: 'One thing is pretty clear, *Women* must give up living an artist's life, if home duties are to be paramount.'[41] Ostensibly, this echoes Southey (and, indeed, it might be expected that a woman who had established a reputation as a writer might adopt the attitudes of a literary, professional, male), but the emphases are different. 'Women', with heavy emphasis: women, rather than men, must give up literary endeavour if home duties are to be paramount. Men will not, after all, do it. And it is only 'if' home duties are to be paramount. Southey's imperatives – 'Literature *cannot* and *ought* not to be the business of a woman's life' – are here replaced with domestic realities as culturally constituted, not as moral imperatives, not the angel forced to inhabit the house. Gaskell, too, being a woman writer herself, cannot utter such a sentiment without making it ironic. It is 'pretty clear', indeed, that in sustaining her own position as a writer, she has frequently had to do battle with the omnipresence of home duties.

It is Gaskell, too, who defends Charlotte Brontë against the charge of being unfeminine in her writing. (Critics had found *Jane Eyre* 'coarse', arguing that if the writer were a woman, she must be one who had 'forfeited the society of her own sex'.[42]) Gaskell, in recounting a remark heard in conversation, inscribes the gender relations which construct and interpret the supposedly unfeminine. 'In certain instances, authoresses had much outstepped the line which men felt to be proper in works of this kind.'[43] Men decide what is proper. Men decide what is properly feminine, fit subjects for fiction by women.

Gaskell, for all her defences, is not invulnerable to gender prejudices. When she discovers the 'true identity' of George Eliot, she declares that it jars against her assumption that *Janet's Repentance* ('the beautiful book') is by a man. 'I should have been more 'comfortable' for some indefinable reason, if a *man* had written them instead of a *woman*.'[44] (This is a reference to *Scenes of Clerical Life* in which *Janet's Repentance* is included.) Her prejudice, she admits, derives from her knowledge of the socially unsanctioned relationship between George Eliot and G. H. Lewes. In a letter to George Eliot she comments, 'I wish you *were* Mrs Lewes'. Judgements about what constitutes the unfeminine frequently slip, like this, from the professional to the personal, and the codes of personal behaviour expected of women are particuarly strict. It is characteristic of Gaskell that she cannot find it in her sexual morality to sustain such prejudice. 'I *have* tried to be moral, and dislike her and dislike her books – but it won't do.'[45]

Questions of gender and writing, of fit subjects for fiction, of pen-names, are not, it appears, only questions about access to literary production. They are questions about the survival of women writers and about the survival of less prejudiced gender attitudes in literary and social circles.

The defence of androgynous or masculine pen-names had limited usefulness in that rumours about the true identity of authors usually drove novelists to claim their own works. Charlotte Brontë made a special journey to London to assure publishers of the real identity and gender of her sisters and herself. Gossip and speculation had rendered the use of pen-names as a defence against gender prejudice ultimately ineffective. For married women writers, who were probably better defended by their marital status against moral judgements about the unfeminine, the employment of pen-names appears to have been less necessary than for single women. It could be that a married woman would have 'professional', respectable status from her husband, from the married name itself (and a married woman might have had a little more leeway for *knowing* something, for not being entirely inexperienced: a sexual connotation too). Gaskell proposed to her publisher Chapman that she adopt the name 'Stephen Benwick', as author of *Mary Barton*, but 'Mrs Gaskell' appeared on the title-page.

The significance of pen-names for women, then, seems to

be as a temporary defence of a writer attempting to make an entry from a vulnerable position in gender and class. Perhaps the persistence of the masculine form, George Eliot, is a measure of the extent to which Eliot overtook moral prejudice to enter fully into the professional, literary world.

Gender prejudice against women writers does not, of course, stop at entry into publication. The Brontë novels are found 'unfeminine'. Gaskell in particular was repeatedly engaged, in defence of her own fiction, in arguments about proper subjects (duly feminine) for women writers. Responses to her novel *Ruth*, which traces the history of a woman seduced and abandoned by an upper-class lover and her attempt to survive in respectable society as the mother of an illegitimate child, were at issue with the subject of 'the fallen woman'. A contemporary reviewer declared the novel and its subject as 'unfit'.[46] Again, a London librarian declared the novel 'unfit for family reading'. Gaskell revealed that the novel was not even allowed in her own home: 'It is a prohibited book in *this*, as in many other households; not a book for young people.'[47] And friends expressed 'deep regret' that the subject had been chosen. Further reactions are recorded in letters: 'Now should *you* have burnt the 1st vol. of *Ruth* as so *very* bad? even if you had been a very anxious father of a family? Yet *two* men have; and a third has forbidden his wife to read it.'[48] The supposed crime of *Ruth* was that it is a challenge to both gender and class prejudices in taking the abused working woman as heroine.

Response from her own Manchester circle to *Mary Barton* contained similar elements, with some book burnings. And again, it is working people who are central, with particular attention to the working woman as heroine. Although the charge of unfit subjects for fiction could be levelled at a writer regardless of gender, it is not accidental that it is Gaskell, a woman writer, who, in dealing with gender formations in class, at this time in history, runs a particular risk.[49] And it is a risk of which Gaskell is aware in the writing. About *Mary Barton*: 'I am almost frightened at my own action in writing it.' After the publication of *Ruth*, in response to critical judgement: 'I knew all this before, but I determined notwithstanding to speak my mind about it . . . I could do every jot of it over again tomorrow.'[50]

There may be a certain irony in seeing the woman writer thus sacrificed on the supposed altar of gentlemanly value: truth, honour, etc. 'I'm sure I *believe*', wrote Gaskell in defence of *Mary Barton*, 'I wrote truth.' It might be appropriate to ask, incidentally, whether Thackeray ever ran the risk of book burnings for truth. This would be to see women as the conscience of the literary profession, as of so much of Victorian culture – that being exactly the measure of women's distance from the central determinants of power within the profession.[51]

Earlier, I traced briefly some of those educational and social routes which 'qualify' Thackeray in making an entry to literary professionalism. Elizabeth Gaskell's life, in comparison, makes for a different kind of entry, from which some arguments about gender can be drawn.

I have shown how Thackeray, through family background, public school, Oxbridge, is introduced into those circles and networks of male power which he then goes on to celebrate in literary professionalism. Gaskell's life follows a different set of educational and social routes, equally gender-specific. She does not experience those particular oppressions of class in gender which characterize the lives of many working women, but she does experience a similar kind of sex segregation and separate sphere. She attends a girls' private school where primary emphasis is on imbuing the girls with those accomplishments thought suitable to femininity, in preparation for marriage into the appropriate class: an education which will define the woman as domestic angel. After learning how to be a wife, she proceeds to marry into the Manchester middle class. Of course, these regional distinctions, Thackeray in London (Bloomsbury) and Gaskell in Manchester, tend to confirm differentiated ways of relating to literary professionalism, so much of which is focused on London. Thackeray's early experiences are thus linear, even predictive, in the direction of fashionable, literary London. Gaskell's early experiences, grooming for what culture has constructed as the peculiarly female position in the family, leads to the wife and the mother, whose 'proper duties' are held to be at odds with the pursuit of literary careers.

While Gaskell is of a class which is combining with the likes of Thackeray to produce a new unity of allegiances in professionalism, generating a wider range of class-related forms of masculinity, that class position is not enough to mediate or subsume gender differences. Gaskell's investment in the provincial city and in a certain kind of radical philanthropy only serves to confirm her difference from Thackeray and his literary ideal, the knights of the pen.

Just as Charlotte Brontë is vulnerable to Southey's views about women and writing, so Gaskell's nervousness about writing, about publication and about criticial reception, is characteristic of an existence on the periphery of the production process. After the critical reaction to *Mary Barton*, she writes to Chapman: 'I am not thinking of writing any thing else; le jeu ne vaut pas la chandelle.'[52] When, two years later in 1850, it is rumoured she is writing again, she tries to still the gossip. She writes to Chapman again: '*No one* in Manchester (except my husband of course) knows of it.'[53] This is just the historical moment at which Thackeray is upholding the 'dignity' of the literary in providing respectable careers for gentlemen. Critical responses to *Ruth* result in similar anxieties: 'I am in a quiver of pain about it' and 'In short the only comparison I can find for myself is to St. Sebastian tied to a tree to be shot at with arrows.'[54]

This nervousness about the subjects of fiction, and particularly about authorial self-perception, also enters into the fiction itself and into fictional prefaces. Gaskell is sure of her moral intentions in writing *Mary Barton* (to speak the truth about 'the agony' of the Manchester factory workers), but is characteristically feminine (culturally constituted) in her disclaimer of politics and theory: 'I know nothing of Political Economy, or the theories of trade.'[55] This is of a novel which deals in imaginative detail with the effects of the 1830 recession, the conditions of the 'terrible years 1839, 1840, and 1841' in trade and economy, the state of revolutionary Manchester in its Chartism (chapter 9) and its internal trade relations (the Manchester meeting of masters and workers in chapter 16), the economic and political determinants of combination and the organizing of men into an 'awful power' (chapter 15), and more of this ilk. This is a strange narrative process for someone who is not supposed to know anything about political economy or trade. The opening of chapter 6 is one example of the way in which these disclaimed areas of knowledge are integral to, indeed sustain, the narrative weave:

> John Barton was not far wrong in his idea that the Messrs Carson would not be overmuch grieved for the consequences of the fire in their mill. They were well insured; the machinery lacked the improvements of later years, and worked but poorly in comparison with that which might now be procured. Above all, trade was very slack; cottons could find no market, and goods lay packed and piled in many a warehouse. The mills were merely worked to keep the machinery, human and metal, in some kind of order and readiness for better times. So this was an excellent time, Messrs Carson thought, for refitting their factory with first-rate improvements, for which insurance money would amply pay. There were in no hurry about the business, however. The weekly drain of wages given for labour, useless in the present state of the market, was stopped. The partners had more leisure than they had known for years.[56]

There can be no doubt that the disclaimer is in part an attempted defence (as I have argued about pen-names) against certain gender and class assumptions. Gaskell writes: 'If my accounts agree or clash with any system, the agreement or disagreement is unintentional', taking the form of the all too commonly sex-specific plea of political ignorance. Subsequent reactions to *Mary Barton* do bear out the idea that Gaskell needed to attempt some kind of defence against accusations of political subversion. The disclaimer is also part of that very uncertainty about fit subjects for fiction by women writers. The act of putting the working woman and man at the centre of fiction is a particularly vulnerable move for a woman writer. Contemporary reviewers, however, were far from recognizing the dilemma of the woman writer. The tendency was to accept the implied judgement of naivety or superficiality ('I know nothing') all too readily, dismissing the novel as 'light and transitory'.[57]

Gaskell's vulnerability in relation to attacks on the class and gender interests of *Mary Barton* is later manifest in the writing of *North and South*. Although she had resisted one direct attempt to persuade her to 're-write' *Mary Barton*, giving the narrative perspective as that of the employer rather than the worker, the manufacturer, Thornton, in the later novel is clearly a concession to that kind of persuasion. Perhaps this signifies too her further entry into literary professionalism by the time of the later novel.

None of which is to doubt that Gaskell does become a literary professional, in terms of her relations to and within the profession and the literary production process. Some of the tensions which she experiences within the profession, however, continue to raise questions about gender, for, once again, it is not good enough – as with Thackeray, as with Southey – to treat Gaskell as idiosyncratic, unrepresentative, whatever the mediating factors of personality. Gaskell clearly had strong reservations about the power relations involved in writing for male editors. She had problems, not least, with Thackeray and Dickens. Dickens was open in his praise of *Mary Barton* and found it an inspiration for *Hard Times*. That kind of response might have compensated Gaskell in some measure for bannings and book burnings. Nevertheless, she was unimpressed by his praise which she described as 'soft sawder'. (Remember Charlotte Brontë worrying about 'a flattery, which is not true praise'). When Dickens was in control of *Household Words*, they continued to experience difficult working relations, and Dickens resorted to an attack which was indeed crudely gender-specific.[58]

Her aversion to writing for Thackeray was even stronger than for Dickens. She wrote to the publisher George Smith that it amounted to 'extreme dislike'.[59] Charlotte Brontë, despite her initial lionizing of Thackeray, centres the gender problem – after the publication of *Henry Esmond*, she writes: 'As usual, he is unjust to women; quite unjust'. Gaskell had written earlier that Thackeray did not reciprocate the esteem in which she and Charlotte Brontë held him.

It is indeed doubtful that Thackeray, who during his literary life juggled, sometimes in serious rivalry, sometimes in friendly competition, with the order of the two names he deemed big – Thackeray and Dickens, Dickens and Thackeray, Thackeray and Dickens – ever regarded 'the women' as serious competitors (Gaskell and Thackeray, Brontë and Thackeray). It is uncertain, in that sense, whether Gaskell or other women writers were fully accepted into the gentleman's club, despite 'soft sawder'.

It could be argued that that acceptance (or not) is an irrelevant question, that the Brontës and Gaskell found publishers and have taken up firm places in canonical history. The important questions, however, extend beyond individuals (as I continue to insist) to the gender and class implications for Literature which can be read from the lives and writings of Gaskell and Thackeray. Literary professionalism, throughout those lives, prevails as an organization of labour with particular gender and class interests. That organization does not fully determine what is written and what is published, but it *predisposes* what is written and what is published. I have argued that this influences not only access to literary production, and the process of sustaining a position as a writer, but to the definitions of fiction and Literature, to the whole question of fit subjects for fiction, differentially gender-linked (according to novel content and sex of writer), to relations within the gentleman's club, and 'backwards' to the kinds of lives (social, educational routes, etc.) which prepare for an entry into literary production, prepare for becoming a writer.

This raises some questions about what may be missing, in gender and class terms, from nineteenth-century fiction, and this is a large part of my motivation in looking, later, at the writings of working women autobiographers. But it also raises important questions, as I have systematically argued, about what, in gender and class terms, is present. With Dickens and Eliot, I have shown how the strong elements of regulation and self-regulation within the professions, and within 'the literary', affect and constrain representations in and of gender and class. Examples from Thackeray's fiction and even from Gaskell's fiction could demonstrate similar effects and limitations, although in relation to them I have emphasized lives rather than texts and the gender differentiations in the self-perceptions of writers.

We can only speculate now about how many women and working-class men in the nineteenth century were excluded from the gentleman's club because of various kinds of nonconformism to 'the literary'. What it *is* possible to conclude is that the nineteenth-century novel and, for particular reasons, the canonical text, is not always the liberated spirit we sometimes think it. The representational influences (their sexual and social ideologies) of the nineteenth-century novel, continue to be complex and pervasive, which is all the more reason why the gender and class terms of those representations should continue to hold our interest and why that interest should be politically informed and critically sceptical.

Part 2
Working Women
Autobiographers

These things by women saved
are all we have of them

or of those dear to them
these ribboned letters, snapshots

faithfully glued for years
onto the scrapbook page

these scraps, turned into patchwork,
doll-gowns, clean white rags

for stanching blood
the bride's tea-yellow handkerchief

the child's height penciled on the cellar door
In this cold barn we dream

a universe of humble things –
and without these, no memory

no faithfulness, no purpose for the future
no honor to the past

From Adrienne Rich, 'Natural Resources', *The Dream of a Common Language*, 1974-1977.

5

Working Women Autobiographers

1840s: the age of the 'clever amateur writer'[1] and 'the classical age of autobiography'.[2]

INTRODUCTION

I began reading and studying the writings of nineteenth-century working women autobiographers for two central reasons. One was my sense that, for all the complexity, diversity, and density of representation of women in fiction, for all the multiplicity of representations of the female, femininity, womanhood, in that nineteenth-century fiction which lives on in the canonized text, there remains something to be said, there remains something missing about women, our experience, our lives. My sense of something missing can thus be seen to derive specifically from a reading of fiction, and more specifically from a reading of the nineteenth-century novel. This is because of my belief that fiction, and in particular the nineteenth-century novel, that genre, that history, is peculiarly influential, then and now, in the construction of gender relations and of sexual ideology.

This sense of something missing also begins to lead to the second reason. It was because of it that I began to read some nineteenth-century working-class autobiography. This seemed a possible source of those representations, those versions of experience in writing, which might form or might be predicated on some notion of opposition or challenge to dominant forms of representation, and there are a number of such autobiographies written in the particular period under scrutiny, the nineteenth-century, and in particular in the 1840s, an important moment in the production of texts.

Finding that these autobiographies are now strongly mediated by twentieth-century social historians, I was thus drawn to the beginnings of a contemporary theory of working-class autobiography, in the context of particular notions of class-conscious history.[3] And with the finding of that class-conscious history, there was also the problem of being presented with some of the recently familiar understandings and readings of women in history, or, more accurately, of women's supposed absence from history. 'The most significant silence is that of women', we learn, and true enough and unsurprisingly, not nearly so many nineteenth-century autobiographies of working-class women as of working-class men have presented themselves for our reading to date.[4]

In making the transition in this way, from reading nineteenth-century novels, to reading working-class autobiography, to discovering the terms of women's supposed silence and beginning the search for working women's autobiographies, I have been particularly concerned to retain a commitment to saying something about textuality and 'the literary', in its vexed terms, and to utilizing various kinds of literary methodology. This attachment derives from a sense that it is through a consciousness of 'the literary' (in all its vexed terms, to which I shall return) that the yield from texts continues to be at its most productive. Indeed, I would go further and suggest that the reading of historical texts, of social history, is restricted without a sense that texts themselves are imaginative constructions with their own biases and partialities, and that it is through a critical awareness of the partialities of the text in our readings that a complex understanding of history emerges.

But the notion of bringing together literary and class-conscious readings of history is still suspect in certain quarters of the academy. It calls not only on the new-fangled – social history, oral history, the study of popular memory - but on inter-disciplinary approaches: a sense that English Literature as subject discipline is not quite adequate to the task, that there might be a need to call on History, even Sociology. And those opposed to inter-disciplinary methods will always tend to find the student rather than the subject inadequate to the task. Inter-disciplinary study is still held to be unspecialized, inexpert, a thinning of the gruel of academic scholarship.[5] A class-conscious history is, moreover, always more vulnerable in what it announces about itself, always more likely to be pressed into declaring its ideological hand than other more consensual forms of history which blind us to, and are blind to, their own ideologies. Sometimes it seems that only those on the Left see, in a paranoic way, the ideological constituents of much academic history, and see those constituents glaringly, as if written in neon.

The class-conscious history which I wish to pursue (moving further into risk) is also primarily a gender-conscious history: both a women's history and a feminist history.

Recalling the first Women's Liberation Conference (Oxford, 1970), Sheila Rowbotham makes the connection between 'the reawakening of feminism' and 'the search for a past'.[6] In that search for a past, in 'the cherishing of memory', we uncover, discover, recover those continuities of experience which consolidate grounds for opposition to subordination, grounds for rebellion. Memory is directly a tool for 'breaking the silence'.

> In Barcelona after Franco died I asked socialist feminist friends who had been active in the anti-fascist underground, 'How did you become socialists under fascism?' They looked at me incredulously. 'The historical memory,' one replied patiently.[7]

Despite the 'incredulous' look of Sheila Rowbotham's socialist feminist friends, it is clear that 'the historical memory' is no simple unity in any culture. Nor is it simple to construct or reconstruct a unity called memory which will function to consolidate a potentially subversive or oppositional experience. Perhaps propaganda is ultimately the dislocation of such a memory from experience, to construct an artificial unity. Undoubtedly, regimes do frequently rely on such a construction. James Cameron, writing about Vietnam before and during the government of Ho Chi Minh, describes his attempts to relocate the Maison de la Presse in Hanoi after the Vietnam War.

Useless for me to protest: 'But I was there; I remember everything about it, except where it was.' They would look at me with considerate incomprehension. 'You really must be mistaken!'[8]

James Cameron perceives this as a new regime endeavouring to write the colonial past 'out of memory'. Less flagrant reconstructions must surely occur in all countries and cultures, like the post-Maoist rewriting of Mao or our reconstructions on television of Victorian England. The investment which certain regimes have in engineering a unitary memory only serves to emphasize how important it is for oppressed groups to write themselves back into the past-present relation. We will find that any popular movement, like the women's movement, which has not yet secured the time and space to shore itself up with institutions and texts, will find itself, by way of that very vulnerability, susceptible to dissolution. The women's movement has not yet, for instance, secured sufficient of the past to write male chauvinism 'out of memory', and it might take a while yet! It is rather the case that a movement which has been one of the powerless, depending on oral rather than written words, on lived culture rather than text, is in constant danger of losing its memory. The women's movement has repeatedly been in danger of slipping into amnesia. 'Even as we scan the past our own beginnings slip away.'[9] Memory . . . dissolves.

> What about those who were left at the washtub, or who acted without belonging to formal organizations, or joined everything and evaded the spot light, who dreamed, thought, met, picketed, marched, tub-thumped, plotted, died without trace or echo?
> They might have a few words with history.[10]

The constitution of memory continues to be an essential task for the women's movement, in fuelling rebellion, in breaking the silence. It is not sentimentality which prompts us to continue asking what our mothers and grandmothers were doing, how they were living, but an essential prerequisite for change, an essential utilization of and function of the past-present relation.[11]

What we are looking for from this relation is a basis in experience for a feminism demanding freedom for women as 'the precondition for a general social liberation'.[12] And in the syntax of that sentence, it is 'in experience' which negotiates the move from past to present, and 'precondition' which negotiates the potentiality of a move from present to future.

Why the choice of autobiography to carry the burden of this 'basis in experience'? Any thoughts here about autobiography will not be attempts to define conclusively the constituents of autobiography as a genre, but will rather suggest a set of possibilities about a special relationship between the genre and the kind of history (class-conscious, gender-conscious) to which my account is committed.

Much of the recent study of working-class autobiography derives its theory from Gramsci after Marx, a belief that social classes are characterized and distinguished from each other by their conceptions of reality. 'Class consciousness can only exist when a social group holds a common conception of reality, and the resolution of class relations depends, in the last resort, on the content of that conception.'[13]

E.P. Thompson is important in premising class-consciousness as central to reading history.[14] F.R. Leavis wrote that 'the consciousness and memory of the people' was formative in the constitution of cultural traditions.[15] In David Vincent's work on working-class autobiography, he gives particular significance to autobiography, to autobiographical *content*, as 'the content of that conception' of reality held commonly by a particular social group, in his instance, the working class. Autobiography, which might at one time have been taken to be super-structural frippery, can now be seen by social historians as something more than effect, something potentially constitutive. More particularly than that, autobiography, in its intense consciousness of its own subjectivity, its own subject, might be seen (if that consciousness is informed by gender and class) as a conspicuously direct posing of a relationship between individual and social group. This relationship will be different from that posited by a theory of high art, which might in one case constitute the individual artist as unproblematically representative of a particular group (the genius of the age, the spirit of the times, the mind of medieval England) or, in another case, insist on the specific as 'the unique' of the artist's individuality (the special vision of Yeats, the unique qualities of D. H. Lawrence). A preferable method, which the kind of autobiography of interest here might give rise to, would question the requirement that any individual could stand for an entire social group, age, epoch, while also questioning the notion of a hermetically sealed or idiosyncratic, eccentric subjectivity which attempts no connection between individual and social group. The individual neither constitutes nor is constituted by the social group, but is in tension with it, and autobiography, the genre, and working-class autobiography in particular, displays and produces meaning from and through this tension.

Working-class autobiography can, in this way, be seen as producing working-class consciousness as well as being produced by that consciousness. Although its productivity is that of individuals, individual writers, working-class autobiography has and is the content of a conception of reality with elements common to the working class as social group.

It is this constitutive aspect of genre, of autobiography in particular, which brings the argument round to a consideration of the literary. David Vincent, as social historian, argues his own commitment to a study of genre. He wishes to study autobiographies as 'units of literature' where individual experience is not aggregated to or coterminous with social experience.[16] This is a commitment to autobiographical content as socially constitutive.

Despite this commitment to the autobiographies as 'units of literature', as genre, as self-contained, there is a sense in which the crucial decisions about what constitutes working-class consciousness have already been made in the selection of objects for study. In other words, a large part of Vincent's understanding of that consciousness has been arrived at previous to the study of the actual content of the autobiographies. He has predefined and prescribed the social group (and the research methodology in large part) which locates the autobiographies. In a study of class-consciousness, it seems quite legitimate to use these prescriptions and predefinitions, but there are problems if these prescriptions and predefinitions are too restrictive, and if they ignore the existence of texts which are difficult to classify.

Some instances . . . Vincent locates the emergence of autobiography as a consciously generic pursuit by working-class men in a political movement, supported by spiritual and oral-narrative traditions, which sees its moment of self-realization in the establishment and activities of the London Correspondence Society. He can thus, in his analysis, work from what is already known about some aspects of working-class experience and working-class institutions. He draws attention to autobiography as a political activity or mode, often in questioning tension with established written history and other widely accepted versions of experience. In terms of cultural theory, this might place working-class autobiography somewhere between 'text' and 'lived culture'.[17] At the heart of this tension are directly political questions about the relationship between experience and knowledge, about which kinds of knowledge most easily legitimate themselves as experience, about the class structure in relation to types of knowledge and about whether working-class autobiography as knowledge would have been in the nineteenth century 'a means of reinforcing or undermining the edifice of political and economic power which the middle class was attempting to construct'.[18] What this kind of approach does is to establish, prior to a study of autobiographical content, an understanding of working-class consciousness as potentially, latently in tension (reinforcing or undermining) with dominant or middle-class versions of knowledge. This kind of strategy is at its most noticeable in Vincent's outline of some aspects of his research method, for instance, the assumption of an understanding of what constitutes 'the working class' in his intention to study only those autobiographies where the autobigrapher is the child of a working man and has 'remained a member of the working class until the composition of his memoirs'.[19] For a variety of reasons, these kinds of classification are unlikely to lead Vincent to women's texts.

Nevertheless, in women's history, it seems important to keep hold of some of these ideas, or analogous ones, about prescription and predefinition of social group and the consciousness of that group. This is what I have tried to do in my study, whilst giving an even greater emphasis than Vincent does to autobiography as a genre, to the literary aspect of the study, and to experience as importantly constituted within text. I have, in other words, eschewed the identification of women *per se*, as a social group determined by the biological category, female. What I have tried to do instead is to utilize some of the ideas from class-conscious history in two ways. One way is the attempt to identify women autobiographers through known, gender-conscious movements: the nineteenth-century women's movement and some of its culminations in militant suffrage. The other way is to use some prescriptions and predefinitions of class, though these cannot be the same as those employed to define working-class men autobiographers, to establish my category of working women. I have, that is, wanted to retain some notions of class in gender, though the taxonomy of class which Vincent, for instance, employs will not do, creating, as he sees it does, a constitution of male experience but only a 'silence' of women. Those categories of class which may be appropriate to men are not, as the women's movement has shown, wholly appropriate to women. Even Vincent has a tendency to refer to 'working-class men' and 'working women'.[20]

My particular emphasis, I repeat, is on working women, an emphasis in which the terms of work are informed by understandings of class and gender which are, in turn, mutually informing. This is not to take either class or gender to be a superstructure on the other's base, but to suggest that neither can explain nor displace the other.

What follows is about working women autobiographers in a study primarily grounded in literary critical methods of close reading, taking only a smallish number of autobiographies in an attempt to do justice to these methods, and to avoid the assumption of a comprehensive survey which aggregates individual women into a gender constituency which speaks for all women, that is, to avoid that inventory of experience, which social history sometimes seems to be. The task is to see how gender consciousness, with class, is constructed within autobiographical content and within autobiography as a genre, to see what can be learned from individual women about gender-linked subjectivity and about the gender consciousness produced by relations between that subjectivity and the social group, working women.

WORKING WOMEN AND INITIAL EXPERIENCE OF CLASS

The common reference point of the autobiographies referred to is that all were written by working women living for some part of their lives between 1800 and 1880. Not all were written in the nineteenth century, and of those which were completed then, not all are available in their nineteenth-century form. Some are only available in that form and have remained uncut on library shelves from then until now. I must stress that the selection is by no means comprehensive and relies to a certain extent on the arbitrariness of that which was available, given limited resources. In any case, such a search does depend on the arbitrary. Edward Hall, for instance, salvaged Ellen Weeton's letters and autobiographical sketches from a Wigan bookshop just before the owner was about to throw them out with the rubbish.

For the sake of facilitating what follows, I shall give here a rapid reference list to the autobiographies which are most significant in my account. Dates of publication (and in some cases, separate dates of completion) are given in the notes to individual chapters.

The Autobiography of Rose Allen
Life of a Licensed Victualler's Daughter (Mary Ann Ashford)
Bread-Winning or The Ledger and the Lute (Mary Barber)
Elizabeth Ham
The Factory Girl, autobiography of Ellen Johnston
Schoolmistress and Nonconformist (Mary Smith)
Memories of a Militant (Annie Kenney)
Memories of Seventy Years (Mrs Layton)
'A Retrospect' in *Miss Weeton: Journal of a Governess 1807-1811*
A Fire in the Kitchen (Florence White)

Many of the autobiographers share with working-class men a preoccupation with class as a commitment to a position differentiated from the middle class, and as having an intense bearing on subjectivity, self-definition. A measure of the significance of class is the extent to which it is used to foreground narrative. This often takes the form of initiating self-perception through relation to paternal occupation.

Ellen Johnston and Mary Smith connect the occupations of their fathers directly with the low social status of their own occupations. Ellen Johnston's father is a stonemason. She is a factory worker, aspiring to be a poet. Mary Smith's father is a shoemaker whose experience of financial hardship, throughout her childhood and young womanhood, she sees as defining and prescribing her own lack of social status. She is a domestic dogsbody, progressing to schoolteacher and very much later to journalism and the women's movement, a progress to which I shall return.

Annie Kenney constructs her own identity in terms of the traditional working class, but in her particular advocacy of the women's movement also identifies women as a particular class. Appropriately, her initial autobiographical interest is with her mother's rather than her father's influence on her experience.

Mary Barber describes her initial class position as middle-class, but she explains in the first chapter of her autobiography that what she wishes to present to her reader is her experienced version of 'poverty of a peculiar kind'. This is the poverty of 'losing caste' which engenders the poverty of 'unsuccessful labour and unsatisfied desires'.[21] It is the 'peculiar' or particular quality of this poverty, its metonymic aspect, which begins to hint at an economic and social position which Mary Barber shares with Annie Kenney, and indeed with Mary Smith and Ellen Johnston. It is not that 'losing caste' is an experience unique to women, nor that it is an unambivalent statement of hardship or low social status. Mary Barber is not alone in writing out a certain romantic evocation of the term, for Mary Ashford gives a similar significance to the phrase. The poverty of losing caste is 'not that which hides in the dark narrow street, the hovel, the

cabin, or the cellar, but the poverty of the middling classes.'[22]
The insecurity and precariousness of 'losing caste' is thus the
memory of respectability or gentility, idealized because lost.
What is also important, though, is the extent to which 'losing
caste' is the inescapable experience of that nineteenth-
century woman of 'the middling classes' who seeks to define,
or is required by circumstance to define and discover, an
independent self. Self-definitions in relation to class thus
already begin to hint at a gender-specific aspect.

Mary Barber (and Elizabeth Ham is another of the
autobiographers who experiences an uneasy self-definition in
relation to class) in this way defines herself as from 'the
middling classes' of the parental home, but the process of
personal history has, like that of Elizabeth Ham, removed her
from the security of that definition, and removed her further
as chronological distance from the parental home increases.
This is to say that the occupational route for women who do
not marry (and also for some of those who do) is from class
defined by paternal occupation, to 'women's work', almost by
definition in the nineteenth century work of low status.
'Losing caste' now becomes the metonym for the process by
which the woman born to affuence or relative affluence copes
with a personal history of social descent. And it is a metonym
which denotes the gender-specific aspect, a levelling to the
common experience of the social group, women, culturally
constructed, around 'women's work'. From different class
routes (and roots), Mary Barber and Elizabeth Ham thereby
arrive at similar conditions of social and economic circumstances to those of Mary Smith and Ellen Johnston.

After these placements in class, most of the autobiographical narratives maintain a conventional chronology,
settling to the birth of the subject, the family context of that
birth, and to accounts of family and childhood. Mary Barber's
story is exceptional and powerful in opening not with her own
birth, but with the death of her mother when Mary is a grown
child. In Mary Ashford's account, the deaths of both parents
follow closely on opening statements about her own birth and
childhood.

Much of the recounting of childhood shares a conception of

reality with working-class men, but even here culture constructs a peculiarly female experience. Preoccupation with family deaths and with the proximity, chronologically and in narrative chronology, of deaths of parents to births of subjects, is characteristic of the autobiographies. For Mary Barber, the death of her mother is not only a crisis in feeling, but a change in the autobiographer's material circumstances. It marks discontinuity and disruption, from a relatively secure domestic environment to isolation and self-dependence. This is because the loss of her mother, though not a loss of the bread-winner, removes protection of the interests of the daughters, the only connection (gender) which has defended Mary Barber against social isolation. For her, the emotional trauma is also a social one. For Mary Ashford, an orphan at thirteen, the break from family dependence is absolute, and she has little alternative but to enter domestic service, obliged to sustain the lie that she is of the right age for employment.

Much of the experience of schooling is also similar to that of working-class men. Most judgements of formal schooling are condemnatory, although this is nearly always set against a strong approval of the idea of knowledge, and in particular, the love of books. Indeed, the pursuit of learning meshes with and derives from a class and family experience which is frequently at odds with the realities of formal schooling provision. The pursuit of books is often a passion. Mary Smith reads Addison, Steele, Carlyle, Emerson and, clandestinely, *Dr Faustus* and others, spending a last half-crown on one occasion on a book of lectures. Elizabeth Ham repeatedly bemoans her lack of access to reading matter, in particular books. Mrs Layton craves for 'a good book'. Ellen Johnston is enraptured by Walter Scott. Rose Allen loves reading.

This passion for knowledge is part of a class perception of spiritual and intellectual self-advancement which departs from and may indeed be divorced from material self-advancement. Interest in reading is part of a lifelong commitment, initiated in childhood but not confined to childhood, pursued frequently as clandestine, potentially subversive, functioning more as class otherness than social aspiration.

Beyond rooting a shared experience of the desire to learn in a particular kind of autodidactic ethos among working people, in community and family, it is necessary to engage with a certain amount of arbitrariness in individual women's experiences of the pursuit of learning. Part of this diversity derives from the position of the family in Victorian society, and the range of subjectivities to which the family can give expression. The individual family, the parental home, the married couple's home, the employer's, can contain within it a range of possible responses to the education of children and of women, although that may not be the variety it sounds if we remember that, in very real ways, those three categories of family could be relabelled the father's home, the husband's home, the male employer's home. Benevolent parents can, for instance, offer individual challenges to gender and class restriction in their attitudes to learning. Here again we see that, in childhood, the experiences of working women and of working men might have been similar.

Rose Allen describes her father as 'indulgent' and particularly concerned that his children, daughters as much as sons, should be well educated. Rose's grief at his death ('I cannot speak of the closing scene') is powerfully rooted not only in individual loss, but in being deprived of an exemplar and mentor, 'one whom I loved as the model of all that was excellent'.[23] She knows that the particular attention given to her intellectual development has disappeared.

Mary Smith also believes that she owes the strength of her interest in learning to her father. She recalls being able to read and participate in learned conversation before starting school at the age of four. Her father is alone in her acquaintance, including teachers, in believing that scholarship, for girls, is more important than needlework. School, with its emphases on ladylike manners and sewing, presents both a reified notion of womanhood and a prefiguring of womanhood, which in their own experience of girlhood and womanhood, most of the women autobiographers neither recognize nor value.

Benign paternal authority (and the male term has its own patriarchal history) in the mediating of knowledge and in the acquiring of curiosity for learning is not, however, by any means universal to the autobiographers. A parity, by fathers, in the treatment of daughters and sons is unusual, as is a lasting interest in children's education.

Of the autobiographers I write about here, it is the daughters of literary or would-be literary men who are most conspicuously ignored by their fathers, which might indicate that competition within the family, amongst the family members, can be as intense as in other sites of capitalism. Ellen Johnston shares her father's literary ambitions, but he is 'proud and independent' in attempting, unsuccessfully, to make the transition from stonemason to man of letters. Mary Barber's father, also aspiring to the profession Literature, is a shadowy figure in her autobiography. His absences and presences in the narrative are not fully explained, to the extent that there are moments when it is not clear whether he is alive or dead. What is clear is that, after their mother's death, he does not figure in caring for the two daughters. From then, he appears at moments of narrative crisis (which are often also moments of domestic crisis) frequently to compound the crisis, on one occasion requiring Mary to meet his debts. In addition to her lack of commitment to representing him fully, there is a sense of evasion, concealment, in the representation, in ellipsis. His was 'a sort of visionary existence; he was wanting in that judgement which relates to the need and the duties of everyday life.'[24]

Ellen Johnston and Mary Barber, like Rose Allen and Mary Smith, emulate their fathers, and could in that sense be said to have inherited a love of knowledge, or acquired a love of knowledge in the context of family, but the difference is that they pursue learning without the benefits of family support – and their insecurity, greater than that of Rose Allen or Mary Smith, is constructed into the way they write.

When it comes to the experience of formal schooling, there is little substantial diversity in the perceptions of the autobiographers. While almost all hold out illusions of school, particularly in relation to self-improvement in the arts and in religion (frequently, nonconformism), almost all discover that the actuality of school is at odds with those illusions. In other words, while reverence for learning may, before the actuality of school, conflate with a certain respect for and high expectation of formal education, the practices of school invariably disturb any idealizing of it as a source of self-discovery and moral development, disturbing the conflation of learning with formal education. In what Mary Smith writes, she generalizes a fairly common experience of school as limitation and constraint, which has its gender-specific aspect.

> Correct and lady-like manners were considered to be almost the be all and end all of a girl's education . . . For long years English-women's souls were almost as sorely crippled and cramped by the devices of the school room, as the Chinese women's feet by their shoes.[25]

More anecdotally, Elizabeth Ham writes of the same kind of lack.

> John and Tom went to a day school in the same street. In the Winter they went again in the evening. As there were a few girls who attended this class, I begged to be allowed to go with them. I was exceedingly anxious to learn to write, but I do not recollect learning anything here, and soon ceased to go. After that I went to a day school kept by a little old widow lady, who was always called Ma'am Tucker. Here I learnt nothing but reading, spelling and sewing. When I first went to school Ma'am Tucker lived near the Quay. A memorable spring-tide, one day, completely flooded that part of the town, to the great delight of all Ma'am's pupils.[26]

The sense of being 'exceedingly anxious to learn' is clearly in tension with disappointment at the experience of school. It is worth speculating, from knowledge of the nineteenth-century curriculum, that 'reading' is probably reciting out loud, and 'spelling' is learning lists by rote.

When working women (and here again there is some similarity to working-class men) idealize schooling, they do so, it seems, under the illusion that there is some connection between that moral and intellectual development associated with self-education and self-improvement, and the experience of formal education. In actuality, though, school and learning operate not in harness, but in ironic polarity. Formal education tends to confirm and consolidate existing class and gender positions even at a time when some element of class mobility fosters the illusion that a change of class position is a possibility. While working-class men have to deal with some hegemonic strategies on the part of the middle classes (an example might be the Society for The Diffusion of Useful Knowledge) to incorporate the drive for self-improvement in social conformity, working women experience a double restriction. For them, it is not only that there are class problems involved in engaging with formal education, but also that sexual ideology requires formal education to mediate 'woman's sphere'. In other words, even the residual notion of mobility through formal education is removed by prevailing definitions of sexually appropriate labour.

In this context, it is not only the experience of school, but predictably enough, that of later employment which reinforces the culturally constructed contradiction, for women, between their own definitions of learning and those of dominant groups. That most of the women autobiographers retain an attachment to books and to knowledge as crucial aspects of autobiographical self-perception is a testament to the power of the illusion of the possibility of change through learning, but it is also a testament to acts of daring in the teeth of the pressures of conformism.

Although this section is primarily concerned with initial experiences of class and learning, it is worth looking forward to the attitudes of employers to self-improvement.

Mary Ashford, who recounts an inventory of 'situations' held in her attempt to find congenial labour in domestic service, specifically articulates 'knowledge' as a problem between servant and employer. At her second post, in Hoxton, she sees the extent of her workload as a conscious strategy of her employer's to keep her from applying for more prestigious work, to keep her in ignorance. She believes that her employer so structures the employee's work and her 'leisure' hours as to prevent her from finding time to read. She quits the post after a winter in which she is expected to commit that 'leisure' to pumping out a flooded cellar.

Rose Allen, who also produces an inventory of positions in domestic service, also describes how love of books and the pursuit of knowledge can offend employers. She recounts an interview with a potential employer:

> 'You can write, I suppose?'
> 'Yes, Ma'am.'
> 'I should want you to write always to trades-people, and invitation notes for my whist parties. Do you like reading?'
> 'Yes, Ma'am! very much.'
> 'I don't know, then, whether you'll suit me. The last maid liked reading, and she kept my poor Polly waiting for his supper twice in one month; and sometimes she forgot to wash the cat on Mondays, Wednesdays, and Fridays, and would do it on Tuesdays or Thursdays, which I never can permit, and I'm sure it all came from her love of books.'
> 'Indeed, Ma'am, I would never read unless you gave me leave, and I really would endeavour to keep to the hours and days you wish.'[27]

The licence of caricature – parrots demanding prompt meals, cats in need of a wash – serves to emphasize the triviality of the domestic task which is being privileged as indispensable, a displacement of the need for reading.

Mrs Layton's account reminds her readers that reading, for domestic servants, is potentially subversive, clandestine. It also reminds them again of what working women share with working-class men.

> After the death of my mistress her mother and sister came to take charge of the home and children. This made a great difference to me. My mistress used to teach her children instead of sending them to school. I had often to mind the youngest child while the mother in the same room taught the two elder children to read. In this way I learnt how to spell and pronounce a good many words. After the baby came, the children went to school, and as I had the principle care of the child, I had very little time to myself. If by chance I was seen

reading, I was told that I ought to be able to find something
better to do, and generally speaking a job was found for me.
The result of this treatment caused me to read when I ought to
have been doing my work. I managed to do so when I went
upstairs to make the beds, etc . . . I had heard my brother had
been discharged from his employment for reading whilst he
should have been at work, and that my mother was upset
about it. It required a good effort, but I managed by not
beginning a fresh tale. I have often thought how different my
life at that time might have been if I had had a good book lent
me to read and that I could have read it openly.[28]

In a job of slightly higher status as an assistant teacher,
Mary Smith describes how she must not 'reveal' knowledge if
she wishes to remain on good terms with her employers. On
the one occasion when she finds herself lucky enough to be
thought valuable, as governess and friend, she proceeds as if
conversation with her employer is a very delicate thing, only
revealing the extent of her learning in carefully graduated
stages.

It is rare, particularly in the autobiographies of earlier date,
for self-improvement through reading to be seen, outside its
immediate personal satisfactions, as anything other than
dangerous. Whatever their early illusions about school,
women autobiographers, like working men, discover in
employment that education has different meanings according
to class differences. Whatever the previous illusion of formal
education provision as benign, in its lack of self-interest, to
those who want to learn, regardless of gender and class, the
discovery in employment is that education means threat, that
love of reading is more likely to lead to being discharged than
to promotion, that the pursuit of learning is more likely to
lead to problems with employers than ameliorations, and that
if education is supposed to benefit some people in improving
their status at work, it is not *these* people.

Material advancement through education is, for women,
particularly illusory. The sexual division of labour is such that
self-advancement through labour is not a possibility. In this
sense, the pursuit of learning operates differently for working
women and for working men.

It is not only that sexual ideology prefers women to be ignorant rather than educated but the jobs and skills which might allow for self-advancement through labour are not available to women. This is what makes the women's commitment to self-improvement through learning, whatever their illusions, frequently courageous.

Apart from this later section about learning in relation to employment, most of my account of working women's autobiographies so far has been about childhood experiences. This might well be how a conventional social history would approach women's lives. If this account were primarily about working-class men, I would probably proceed, after writing about education and the pursuit of learning, to writing about skills and occupations in waged labour. While the implications of waged labour are, of course, as important in working women's lives as in men's, I have rather chosen to proceed in the account with those other powerful material and ideological constraints and formations in women's lives, the ones which operate in the name of sexuality and domesticity. In doing so, I shall also proceed to attach a greater significance to textuality than I have so far, to the detail of the writings themselves as that construction of subjectivities from which I am able to produce readings of the women autobiographers.

They write poems about
the softness of our skin
the curve and softness
in our eye
the declivity of our waist
as we recline

we are their peace, their consolation

they do not write of the rage
quivering

we snuggle perfection in
the ball of our foot
our hair weaves
glowing by lamplight
as we wait for the step
on the step

they have not written of
the power in

we approach divinity in
our life-source
we are earth-mother
yearned for
absent muse
shed a silent tear for
missed and loved

we are their comfort, their inspiration

sometimes we are regretted
when we behave
like a jealous woman
and loved for
our jealousy which
shows our devotion

they have not written of

and when we have begun to
speak of it, limping
coarsely, our eyes
red with sleepless pyramids

they have written of us as
whores, devouring Liliths

and never as

Michelene Wandor, 'Some male poets',
Up Beat, 1982.

6

'Women's Issues'

I have been placing the emphasis, in writing about working women autobiographers, on an experience which, though it has its individualistic and gender-specific aspects, is in important ways shared with the experience of working-class men. From now on I intend (indeed, I can do nothing else) to give more emphasis to gender differentiation. This is to say that, in my reading of the autobiographies, I am concentrating more specifically than before on the subjects and subjectivities of adulthood and that that concentration properly pulls towards a greater consideration of that which is gender-specific. This is partly to say that the accounts we have of working-class womanhood have tended to place the emphasis, whether by author, editor or collector, on childhood, girlhood, schooling, rather than adulthood. Women, it seems, have been most interesting as children (and there are other histories and symbolization processes which see women as children), sharing with men or boys those common features of oppression residing in childhood. Recently, there has been more interest than before in working women as wives and as mothers (*Working-Class Wives* and *Maternity, Letters from Working Women* being two examples[1]), but, as with accounts of women which turn out to be accounts of childhood, many of these accounts, or rather the criteria of historical and editorial selection which have operated in relation to them, leave that same sense of a very limited subjectivity, bound and categorized by limited, often stereotypical or prone to the stereotypic, paradigms: childhood, the wife, the mother. A move towards a greater concentration on the gender-specific is therefore a move towards a greater concentration on subjectivity.[2]

This greater emphasis on gender differentiation, on female experiences, than has so far been the case in this account, is also a move towards a consideration of some of those experiences which are aggregated in the cliché, 'women's issues', and ultimately it will challenge that taxonomy. It is a revealing paradox that those experiences catalogued or typified as 'women's issues' are frequently the very matters which have been least articulated by women. 'Women's issues', it seems, are part of a male discourse which signals with that cliché, that containment, those subjects which the man judges too difficult for discussion in mixed-sex company. The male discourse thus signals that which it prefers to render or retain as inaudible, invisible. And since it is the male voice which has so frequently articulated, formulated in the name of the public, that discourse which misconstrues the private, the label 'women's issues' (its signals, its implied absence, difficulties) has not had the challenge it should from women, from women's experiences.

Initially, I therefore intend to write about that experience of 'woman's sphere' (man's construction of the site of 'woman's issues') which women have articulated so little, about which we know, in that sense, so little. This is to commit myself, too, to a belief in a materialism which is open to different constructions in discourse. 'Women's issues' do, in this sense, signify a material reality.[3]

The aspects to which I wish to give significance in my own partial account are, as I argue in my previous chapter, to do with the social group, working women, in tension with individual, autobiographical subjects, taking, initially, sexuality and feminist politics as signal female experiences, women's issues. In writing about sexuality, I give emphasis to those ideologies of marriage in the nineteenth century (located more broadly than in the institution of marriage alone), which define, for women, prospective relationships with men, actual relationships with men, and also relationships with work, although I do not give that set of relations centrality at this stage of the account. Emphasis is also given to the collapse of these ideologies at such moments as domestic violence, which has been treated, frequently, as outside public discussion – a woman's issue.

In writing about politics, the primary interest will be in that range of activities in the nineteenth century which is embraced in descriptions from 'women's rights' to 'militant suffrage', having its basis in dissatisfaction with practices and definitions of 'woman's sphere'.

One of the characteristic features of autobiography as a genre is that the relationship between authorial subject (the 'I' central to the narrative and to a particular social group) and narrative movement is peculiarly direct. Frequently, this means that the autobiographer attaches to the construction or dramatization of self a notion of progress in society, which is also the narrative progression. The rise of the working man from rags to riches, stereotypical of a certain kind of autobiography, takes the form of a narrative development which is also that social progress named success, in conventional, normative terms. Autobiography has a particular investment in this idea of a unique or exceptional advance – and sometimes in the inversion of failure, the decline from fortune, which nevertheless has many of the same assumptions. Self-advancement is also a social and narrative progress.

In class-conscious autobiography, the relationship of the subject to this social and narrative progress does not comply with this obvious fit. A class-conscious autobiographer invests in furthering not only the individual, the autobiographical self, moving through the narrative and through society, but a particular social group such as the working class. This type of autobiography therefore carries the freight of a narrative direction which subsumes the autobiographical 'I', with its conventional association with individualism, with personal interest in the interests of a particular social group. This kind of autobiography is thus a more complicated, even contradictory, version of the genre than the more easy fit of conventional autobiography.

In reading women's experiences in autobiographical form, the formulation of self-advancement and of subjectivity, their relation to the genre, is more complicated again. And for working women, the relationship between social status and narrative structure is peculiarly problematic. For working women, particularly in the first half of the nineteenth century, the models of social advance (and of the advance of the social group, working women) barely exist, in any form, in the social formation. Neither can working women call upon a clearly defined class consciousness which unites the social group, working women. What working women autobiographers have to do therefore, given that absence of a model of material progress, given that absence of routes, is to construct subjectivities by calling on particular representations, particular genres, in which women are at least visible, though frequently in a reified, idealized form.

We could not have expected, anyway, that, having discovered working women writing about ideologies of marriage and about women's politics, the discovery would also be of a discourse suddenly liberated from the containment of 'women's issues' or from a history of representation which understands and creates sexual ideology (in terms not confined to texts) in particular ways.

While working-class men may frequently organize their autobiographies around particular notions of advance in waged labour – through acquiring skill or various modes of organization – working women are more likely to turn to 'the literary', to genres, for terms in which to express and construct the experiences central to their lives. What is significant, indeed, is the apparent inescapability of genres (of fiction, of melodrama, of romance) in the autobiographies, as if 'the literary' itself is the key (possibly the only) means of construction of self. When such a use of 'the literary' is at its most acute or most transparent, it almost invariably means that experience has moved into the most fraught areas of sexuality, of 'women's issues' as that category allocated to women as not public, kept from articulation. It is the tensions between genres and harnessing genres (melodrama, romance, and so on) which express female sexuality and its problems. And occasionally in the writings, there is a slippage from 'the literary', from intertextuality, to a more direct materialism: the glimpsed material world itself in tension with 'the literary'.

An understanding of subjectivity in the autobiographies and of their narrative modes therefore requires a concentration upon the detail of the writing, upon textuality itself as the response to that which is unprecedented and that which is difficult in formulating experience. In order to understand this difficulty, it is necessary to take sexuality in its broadest terms, for it is not only the sex act or the interpersonal relations of the sexes which are at issue, but the whole range of female experience of the world. And it is not only, for the autobiographers, that textuality is a response to difficulty, indeed impossibility, but that areas of sexuality, particularly of domesticity, are in their gender-specific histories, somehow tainted, lacking in legitimacy as significant discourses. 'The literary' here enters as the moral mediator, in a sense as the compensation for those areas of experience which are tainted.

In harnessing literary genres as central in the construction of subjectivity, the autobiographers thus tend to operate within dominant sexual ideologies which are nonetheless revealing in their slippages, their fraught relations. They even utilize different versions of the feminine ideal to make good the 'lack' (the taint) in a given area. For instance, when Mary Smith rejects the idea of marriage (presumably not a very feminine thing to do), she is called upon to replace it with a competing ideal (a 'higher vision'). 'I had higher visions than matrimony: literature, poetry, and religion gleamed fair before me.'[4] (Most of the autobiographers quoted here pursue ideals competing with matrimony, all but two being unmarried, separated, or widowed.) Similarly, in compensating for a bad marriage, Ellen Weeton idealizes motherhood, with herself as mother, through 'the literary':

It seems probable from present circumstances that my child will know no more of her mother than what she may learn from these pages. Nay, even these may be withheld from her by the same influence that has poisoned the comforts of my later years, should it come to the knowledge of my husband that such a writing has been produced. I therefore earnestly desire anyone who may see this History, not to betray me to him; for it is surely proper that my daughter should be acquainted with the truth, and all the truth, as regards a mother who loves her dearly, and of whom, could she but know her, she would find she would never need be ashamed.[5]

Again, as with Mary Smith, 'the literary' enters as the defence against moral fallibility. It is through writing this 'History' that Ellen Weeton can make moral good. 'It is surely proper', it is 'the truth', it is the protection against 'shame'. The reader is requested to enter into this moral code of literary chivalry.

'The literary' thus carries the moral force which the life, from the perspective of the autobiographers, appears to lack, because it is working women's experience.

When Rose Allen writes about a congenial marriage and courtship, the move is directly across the genre, from autobiography to fiction. The scenario is as follows. Throughout the early part of the narrative, an arbitrary intervention occurs in the form of a friendly and handsome young man, rescuing Rose at moments of acute domestic and emotional trauma. The character has no substance except for the mystery of the romance hero: he has no history in the narrative process, no motivation from that process (except for the woman's fantasy), no momentum within it (except to realize that fantasy). In terms of the autobiography's realism, he comes from nowhere, but drops, like one of Carlyle's heroes, from the sky. In the move to fiction, though, he is all important: Rose's devotee, functioning to rescue 'the plot', her life. Later in the narrative, a second, analogical, intervention occurs. This time the form is a benign and considerate 'older man'. His function is also rescue, his entry timed to alleviate intolerable material circumstances for Rose and her mother. Narrative contrivance increases, complicates, as the said older man reveals to Rose and mother that he is no other than the disguised guardian uncle of the handsome, devoted follower of Rose who is about to become her spouse (the younger man, that is). There even follows the classical year's trial, in which the intentions and affections of the younger man are put to the test. This is marriage as feminine ideal, maintained as ideal, but so transparently that it cannot transfer back from fiction to autobiography. Happy families.[6]

This whole sense of marriage as the feminine ideal of fiction, bound up so closely with constructions of self, carries over into conceptions of sexuality and of sexual encounter. Elizabeth Ham writes:

I saw nothing more of him for many days. The next time we met, I was going for a walk with Beata Langley and some of the Joneses. There was a knot of Officers standing near the door when we came out. They immediately joined us, all but he. As he was drawing back, Beata said, 'Won't you join us Mr Jackson?' He said not a word, but walked on by my side. By the time we had reached that very spot where first our acquaintance had commenced, we were left alone. We walked on still in silence. To break the spell, I remarked, 'that Beech is a very fine tree.' 'There is but one tree that interests me, and that Miss H--- has suffered to die from neglect,' he replied. 'Who told you it was dead,' said I. 'Yourself.' 'How was it that a whole day passed after your return without your coming to Ardnaree?' 'I was very ill in bed all that day. I had a Detachment of men under my charge, and was obliged to ride slowly in all the heavy rain. I could scarcely move the next morning.' 'Then I am sorry I answered you so cavalierly about the tree. It is still alive, tho' it had been in great peril.' . . . But I do not know how it was, our intercourse was never again so *cordial* as it had been, tho' we had again our interviews in the Garden, and our *tête-à-tête* walks.

He was very captious too at times. One evening, as we were walking to and fro in the front of the House, my eyes happened to fall on the L.U. on the tree, which threw me into a reverie. I had not been attending to what he was saying, and answered 'yes' at random, to his 'Don't you think so?' 'I feared as much. - I now find you are all alike,' said he, seemingly much hurt. 'What *is* the matter?' exclaimed I, 'I confess I was not attending to what you were saying; will you repeat it?' 'Since my conversation possesses such small interest for you, I will no longer intrude on your time', said he, with an offended air, and leading the way to the door, took leave with a bow only.

The next morning he came as usual, and I asked him what he had been saying when my inattention offended him. 'Nothing of any consequence,' was all he would say.

One evening Mary and I went to drink Tea at the Widow Brady's to meet Margaret and Aleck Garrett. They were a fine specimen of the Irish *genus*. Brother and Sister to Mrs Faucett, to whom they were on a visit. We knew them well, for they spent a great deal of time at Ballina. Mrs Brady's windows commanded the Parade ground too, and as the Band was playing we had them open. Mr J. as usual, came to me to name the Music, and got invited with one or two of the others to come in and take tea. The days were now shortening, and when the candles were brought in we commenced a game of forfeits.

Mr J. had to redeem one of the first. He was to take a Candle from the Candlestick and place it in the hand of the Lady he loved best, and then *kiss the Candlestick*. He took the Candle with the socket and placed it in my hand, and then looked in my face with a comical expression that seemed to say 'May I dare?' and showed plainly that he understood the trick. I lifted the arm that held the Candle as a shield to my face. He took it in both his hands and pressed it with his lips. The grace and delicacy of the action was much admired.[7]

This is the romance genre, the construction of possible meanings from love tokens, love games, gallantry – the 'grace and delicacy of the action', though there are some significant inversions of the sex types of romance, following from the first person, woman narrator, observing the man. It is the man who is touchy, 'captious'; it is the woman who takes responsibility for hurting the man ('What *is* the matter?') and for causing offence. Elizabeth Ham's representation of the relationship with Mr J. thus repeatedly displaces, through the rituals of gentility (taking tea, naming music) which are also the rituals of romance, the writing out of her reservations, problems with the man, the discovery of the terms of her own sexuality. And yet, the intense, troubled concern throughout her autobiography with the romance genre does afford us a glimpse of the shortfall, as does the occasional lapse from that genre into something more firmly grounded in materialism:

> Nancy Shield kept whispering in my ear praises of the very *gentlemanly* young man to whom every one supposed that I was engaged. I could not but feel in the midst of these public manifestations on his part, how very slight was the tie by which I held him.[8]

(And here, again, in the life of Elizabeth Ham, it is the whole question of how to progress, how to live, which works in competition with ideals, sustained by different kinds of genre.) In contrast to Mary Smith, she retains a conception of marriage as a mode of self-advancement, but only relatively to her perception of the impossibility of financial self-support. Matrimony is the hoped-for escape from 'the utter loneliness of being a governess' and from 'heart-sickness of hope continually disappointed, and the despair . . . of ever attaining anything like a means of self-support.'[9] This returns us to the perception of competing ideals, in this case, marriage and satisfying labour as mutually exclusive competing ideals, competing possibilities, for women. (Working man's history under capitalism sets up a different and compatible, relationship between marriage and labour called the bread-winner.)

In her imagined solution to the problem of her future, of how to advance, Elizabeth Ham juxtaposes the pursuit of a husband with the pursuit of knowledge, as mutually constructing ideals:

> The gift of sympathy, the interchange of heart thoughts, had been what I had pined for all my life ...
> If I could have procured books at this time, I might have improved myself, but I had no money to buy them, nor any one to recommend me what to buy if I had.[10]

But 'no money' and no one 'to recommend' only serves to emphasize what has already been glimpsed as an illusory promise.

In the autobiographies the dramatizing, constructing of

sexuality as romance frequently slips into or culminates in a
preoccupation with suicide or the death wish, a logical
extension to the fate of the literary heroine who cannot find
solutions to the problems of sexuality.

> By this time my mother had removed from Anderston to a
> shop in Tradeston, and my stepfather and myself worked in
> West Street Factory. When one morning early, in the month
> of June, I absconded from their house as the fox flies from the
> hunters' hounds, to the Paisley Canal, into which I was about
> submerging myself to end my sufferings and sorrow, when I
> thought I heard like the voice of him I had fixed my girlish love
> upon. I started and paused for a few moments, and the love of
> young life again prevailed over that of self-destruction, and I
> fled from the scene as the half-past five morning factory bells
> were ringing, towards the house of a poor woman in Rose
> Street, Hutchesontown, where, after giving her my beautiful
> earrings to pawn, I was made welcome, and on Monday
> morning following got work in Brown and McNee's factory,
> Commercial Road.[11]

In Ellen Johnston's autobiography, this kind of movement
works against a recurrent hyperbole of success. The reconstruction of the experience is the invocation of romance
fiction with strong elements of the gothic. The voice which
prevents the attempt at death is significantly not the divine
intervention, but the voice of the 'divine' lover, the romance
hero, 'the voice of him I had fixed my girlish love upon'. (Not
for nothing had Ellen Johnston read Walter Scott with
passion.) The memory of 'the love of young life', invoked at
the moment of crisis, prevails over the wish to attempt
suicide, the urge to self-destruction. The autobiographical
subject is the heroine of the piece. The bank of the Paisley
Canal is the 'scene' from which she had 'fled' as the bells (the
bells, the bells) were ringing. Images from romance are in
sharp (if a touch bathetic) contrast to the solid realities of
canal and factory. The fox (autobiographical subject as
victim) flying 'from the hunters' hounds', in suffering and
sorrow, arrives at her Lethe, the Paisley Canal. The pawning
of 'beautiful earrings' (the literary heroine in her class and
gender terms, rich and feminine, as against the destitute

daughter of destitute working people) precedes Monday morning in the factory on Commercial Road (the acme of 'the real').

Ellen Johnston later calls upon religious discourses, the crusading, the zealous, the martyred, to substantiate the romance intervention with the divine intervention. 'I did not then want to die, although I had wished to do so a thousand times before, to relieve me from unmerited slander and oppression' and 'had it not been for the bright Star of Hope which lingered near me and encouraged me onward, beyond doubt I would have been a suicide.' Ellen Johnston is not alone in experiencing the urge to self-destruction (itself a more dramatic term than suicide). For many of the autobiographers, the unresolved problems of self-advancement, of narrative progress, slide towards a dramatic contemplation of death, frequently in tension with fraught terms of sexuality. In Elizabeth Ham's autobiography, these take the form of moments, 'depressing, physical and moral', and she also recounts a contemplated suicide. In Ellen Weeton's 'A Retrospect' the 'longing for death' constitutes the central mode of the narrative.

Often and often, for years I may say, I went to bed with the idea that I should not rise again with life. I thought so much on death, I at length became inured to it; its horror disappeared, and I most earnestly wished to die – and if I had, I might have lain and grown putrid many days before anyone would have known. The idea of dying by myself would at times appear very terrible; at others, I was indifferent about it. I almost wished it; and then, thought I, my cruel unfeeling Aunt will reflect, and repent in time her treatment of me. Mrs Braithwaite would often invite me to spend my evenings there, which I did when well enough. One evening, a few months after my mother's death, whilst I was with Mrs B. I felt an unusual kind of whirling in my head, as if I shoud lose my senses. A palpitation came on. Mrs B. seemed much alarmed, and entreated I would stay there than I was better. I staid some time. At length becoming better, I came home, Mrs B. insisting that one of the servants should come with me and stay with me all night. However, when I got home I found myself so much recovered, I dismissed her; and it being then just nine o'clock, I went immediately to bed. When I got into bed, I sat awhile as I often did before I lay down, when all at once a coldness overspread my face, and I sank senseless on the bed. When I came to myself, I was unable to rise. The Church clock was just beginning to strike eleven, so that I must have lain in that state near two hours! I thought I was dying. And must I then, Oh Father, not have even *one* human being near to render the last assistance! not so much as the hand of *a stranger* to close my eyes! Thy Will be done! And yet, to die by oneself is terrible indeed! A palpitation again seized me, my terror lent me strength, and I rushed out of bed, but through weakness I fell on the floor. If I could but get to the opposite house, thought I, I should I think be better. I tried to rise and with some difficulty got down stairs, putting my feet before me, and sitting on each stair as I descended. By the help of chairs and the wall, I got to the front door, and sunk upon a chair, where I rested awhile; but hearing Mr Walmsley's door locked – 'They will be gone to bed,' I thought, 'and oh, what shall I do?' I opened the door and ran across the street and knocked at the door, when I recollected I had nothing on besides my night dress and a pair of shoes. I crawled back into my own house again as fast as I could. He opened the door, and seeing no one, went in and locked the door again. 'Oh dear! Oh dear! I never can live than morning,' thought I, 'and now they will indeed be gone to bed!' I reached a red cloak which hung behind the front door, and ventured out again, but trembled so, that when I got to Mr W.'s door, in attempting to knock, I fell against it. He heard the noise, and I could hear him say – 'They are there again.' 'Never heed 'em,' said his wife, 'it is only somebody for mischief,' and they were proceeding up stairs to bed. The sound of human voices revived me, and I had strength to knock with my hands. I was heard. Mr W. came again, but seeing no one (the night was so dark, and I sat on the steps) he was going to shut the door again. 'Oh, Mr Walmsley,' I said. 'My God, Miss Weeton, what is the matter?' 'I am very ill', I answered. 'Would you have the goodness to send up to my aunt Barton's?'[12]

The term recurs – 'I thought so much on death . . . I most earnestly wished to die . . . The idea of dying . . . my mother's death . . . I thought I was dying . . . to die by oneself is terrible indeed . . . I never can live than morning' - in a dramatic inversion (through the hyperbolic and fictional), which is also a perversion, of the whole notion of self-advancement, of subjectivity, of narrative progress. The past-present relation here hardly attempts autobiographical reconstruction, hardly attempts memory. Past slides into present -'I thought I was dying. And must I then, Oh Father, not have even *one* human being to render the last assistance!' The latter is not a question (not expecting a 'response' from the Father) but a despairing imperative – not *one* human being to render the last assistance. And with the collapse of the past-present relation, the move into fiction is complete: raising Mr Walmsley, failing at the first attempt, and again at the second, and succeeding, as we know it must in such a construction of plot, at the third.

The invocations from melodrama, horror and the terrible are no mere embellishments, but the fabric of subjectivity itself, as is the narrative movement, failing to advance, falling. 'I went to bed with the idea that I should not rise again with life . . . I sank senseless . . . I was unable to rise . . . I rushed out of bed . . . I fell on the floor . . . I tried to rise . . . and sunk upon a chair.' This whole battery of imagery, accumulating around that process – effort interrupted by failure – is sustained by terms of sickness: 'an unusual kind of whirling in my head . . . lose my senses . . . palpitation . . . a coldness overspread my face . . . I sank senseless'. These are the constructions of self, of subjectivity, in pathology and despair, available to Victorian women. It is only the incidental reference, the understated comment, which puts these dramatic constructions of self in question, which moves against this kind of grain. 'No sooner did Miss W. begin to talk with me than I felt quite well . . . It was only the want of society out of school hours that depressed my spirits in such a manner.' Suddenly, taking us by surprise, the problem is articulated as simply sociological: loneliness, 'want of society'. Sickness is a symptom, not a causal factor. The dominant representations, which the account cannot avoid, are of woman as sick, womanhood as sickness, woman as the emotive, emoting victim of her own fiction.

And the representations of woman in sickness, wishing for

death, are also those of sexuality, as in so much Victorian
fiction. Wilkie Collins' *The Woman in White* is a striking
example. In this account of Ellen Weeton's, the details of
night-dress and red cloak assume the key importance, even
where life is at stake, in negotiating the necessary social
relation, raising Mr Walmsley, the hero, to rescue the
heroine. It is inescapably the man, not the other available
characters (wife, daughter, aunt), who alone can initiate a
solution in narrative to the problem, woman.

I return, for a moment, to Ellen Johnston, because it is in
her autobiography in particular that romance fiction deter-
mines subjectivity. This does not mean, though, that sexuality and love, for all their literariness, are idealized, utopian.
Sexuality as problem is not explicated, but there is a veiled
and recurring reference to a construction of self in which the
'living martyr' must defend herself against the accusation of
being 'a fallen woman'. The romantic idyll is here in tension
with 'a dark shadow . . . a shadow which has haunted me like a
vampire, but at least for the present must remain the mystery
of my life'. Her autobiography and her poetry inscribe a
powerful sexual desire alongside a romanticized sexual
oppression. In the following, the 'factory poet', woman poet,
working woman, inverts the poetic convention with an
encomium to the gentleman:

> Lines to a Young Gentleman of Surpassing Beauty
>
> And what art thou? – An honour'd son of wealth,
>   Gay fortune's diadem sits on thy brow;
> Bless'd with a generous heart, with youth and health
>   And beauty's self before thy shadow bow;
> Yet thou may'st never know whose humble lays
> In sadness sung thy dazzling beauty's praise.[13]

And the slight gaucherie of this is in that gender inversion
and in that resort to 'the literary', to a sense of how the poets
do this sort of thing. For what precedents has a working
woman got for writing about an experience of sexual desire,
from a woman to a man, in particular one of another class?

Women's sexuality thus steps into discourse as the melodramatic, the sinister, the spiritual, the romantic; with different genres in competition, via the moralizing code of 'the literary', for subjectivity. 'Women's issues' and the fraught area of sexuality in all its taboos are presented for contest by our reading of the autobiographers, presenting those contradictions, those contrary movements, which produce meaning from the relations between representation and experience. Descriptions of marital difficulty are understated, shadowy, but where they do exist, as in the accounts of Ellen Weeton and Mary Ashford, they are characterized by a call on the moral force of particular genres, such as that sexual ideology inscribed in melodrama.

When Ellen Weeton breaks the taboo of writing about domestic violence, she does so with that kind of force, though this is in a letter to a friend, not in the more measured autobiographical fragment, 'A Retrospect'. The more intimate genre of letter appears to sanction a more direct entry into the 'women's issue', domestic violence.

> Cruelty from a *monster of a husband*; extreme want and houseless at one time; imprisonments and bruises at another; my life daily in danger, attended with constant terror for many months, supposing each hour might be my last, and not knowing in what shape death might come – expecting at one moment to be poisoned, and therefore afraid to eat or drink anything that my husband could possibly have meddled with; obliged to be constantly on my guard against the deadly blows he would sometimes give me at the back of my ear, unprovokedly, and when I was least expecting it.[14]

I shall argue later about how editors intervene to mediate the monster, husband: as if Ellen Weeton's 'word' in this particular territory requires witnesses, attorneys. Similarly, in the courts a rape victim is frequently required to produce corroborative evidence, while the victim of a mugging is not. In 'A Retrospect', allusion to the monster enters again: he who has 'poisoned...the comforts of my later years'.

Mary Ashford's account of a marriage promise employs

similarly melodramatic terms (with resonances of the thriller)
to carry moral force in a defence of self.

> He soon proposed marriage, but at the same (time) he should
> wish me to remain in my place for some time afterwards. To
> this I did not object, as he said it was on account of his brother
> and parents; and as he went to London with the market-cart
> every week, he one time put up the banns, at Shoreditch
> church, and after that gave some hints that we were as good as
> married. But I had once heard, when waiting at tea, one of the
> curates of Lambeth say to a lady he was conversing with, that
> 'putting up the bands' was often made the instrument of
> seduction. This I had not forgot. I used, if I liked, to go out
> every other Sunday, and my suitor asked me to go with him to
> pay the ground-rent, a few miles off, which he said would be a
> very pleasant walk. So it was; but part of it lay through a wood,
> by a lonely footpath. I requested him, as evening was coming
> on, and it was so dismal, to come back the roadway; but he
> declined, saying it was a great way round.
>
> We were kindly treated at the house we went to, and after
> tea set off on our return. I think it was in about the middle of
> the wood, when he began talking about a man who had been
> lately executed for an outrage on a female, and asked if I did
> not think it very hard, and whether I could have the heart to
> swear a man's life away. I became dreadfully alarmed, and,
> letting go of his arm, which I held, I stepped boldly in front of
> him, and said, 'Ask me no questions, for I will not answer
> them;' and I hurried forward, saying it was time I was at home.
> He seemed rather confused, and was silent for some time; and
> then muttered something about meaning to marry me; and I
> was thinking that I would never go walking again without
> knowing what sort of road I had to go.[15]

Virtue is saved via caution and common sense ('But I had ·
once heard . . . This I had not forgot . . . I requested him . . . to
come back the roadway') from the monster, man, and his plot
– putting up the banns as an instrument of seduction. The
concluding moral ('I would never go walking again without
knowing what sort of road I had to go') rounds off a narrative
foregrounded in Christian morality, which is also the chief
informant of common sense ('I heard one of the curates . . .

This I had not forgot'). The heroine proceeds to take up the bold, moral stance. 'I stepped boldly in front of him . . . I hurried forward', onward, forward in virtue against the villain, characterized as such in his tactics and deceptions. 'He said . . . he gave some hints . . . he said . . . he declined' and in his response to the lady's refusal he was confused, silent, muttering.

Later in the account, the man shows 'his cloven foot with a vengeance' by threatening to expose her (her what? her virtue? but the precariousness of woman's reputation is enough to make the episode frightening) to her employers, and in displaying 'an envious and covetous temper' in a fit of 'violent passion' (Heathcliff without salvation).

These are the lives, irreducible, of working women. Self-advancement, subjectivity, does not have its simple reification or typification in a genre, in genres.[16] The heroine, the victim, the martyr are the only means of representing an experience unprecedented in discourse (the working woman by the working woman), but they are also the signifiers of lack, of what is missing. The echoes and hints of material circumstances, finding their resonances in the discourse, will always remind one that the heroine, the victim, the martyr, is never the full subject. That resides somewhere in the realms of a knowledge that there is no simple advance, no simple route or progress, but a continuous, precarious adaptability, signified from the brink of despair.

> I knew, indeed, the worse was past; and in a few years the family ship righted itself, every bill being eventually paid, and every account settled. But for myself, as is often the case with women, even the most capable and energetic, the one small event of my brother's marrying had stranded me without occupation.[17]

WOMEN'S RIGHTS

It is a relief to find that, because of recent feminist research in history, there is no longer the pressure there was to insist that the women's movement is more than synchronic, historically more than a phenomenon of the post-1950s.[18] It has become clear that the nineteenth century had, even before the obvious suffrage action, a women's movement which shared characteristics of our own contemporary one.[19]

The challenge to containments such as 'women's issues' and 'woman's sphere', which might be seen as part of that movement's motivation and practice, enters into the auto-biographies of working women in a variety of ways. It is in this territory of gender-conscious politics that the articulations only implied in the writing, about such taboos as female sexuality, domestic violence, marriage, begin to enter more explicitly into discourse. In other words, it is dissatisfaction with those very containments signalled in 'women's issues' and 'woman's sphere' which produces the discourse of the women's movement.

In this sense, it is possible to begin to see that the activity and language of 'women's rights', for instance, is a response to taboos such as those on sexuality, and therefore a response to the taboos of discourse itself, 'women's issues', 'woman's sphere'.

Many working women autobiographers engage, in some way, with gender-conscious action. This is as if to say, as if to feel that such tensions as those involved in experiencing, in writing about sexuality, courtship, marriage and its ideolo-gies, and of course, paid labour, require an additional kind of response to that experience and that writing.

One of the first signals of dissatisfaction with the contain-ments is a turning away from the orthodox Church to different kinds of nonconformist religion. That conventional religious rhetoric most accessible to women, having an exact fit with dominant constructions of Victorian womanhood as martyred, passive, appears to be rejected at such moments in favour of a religious experience which is closer than that to different kinds of radicalism. Although this shift to noncon-formism is not always articulated as an issue of gender (and indeed has its limits as an issue of gender), it is frequently precipitated or occasioned by that experience of oppression which may also instigate more obvious forms of political action.

Mary Smith does not 'turn' to nonconformism (she is rather born to it), but in her autobiography she does equate that inheritance with her anti-authoritarian tendencies and her struggle for rights. In illustration, she recounts episodes from childhood, such as the occasion on which her refusal to curtsy to the local vicar (vicars are 'fox-hunting, wine-bibbers') is approved by her nonconformist father (father, sober and self-educated, 'Puritan in life and Calvinistic in creed'). Elizabeth Ham becomes a Dissenter in response to a 'monotonous, not to say, miserable life'.

Conversely, a reliance on the orthodox Church is nearly always symptomatic of a failure or absence of opportunity elsewhere. Mary Barber searches for waged work, fails to find it, and decides to work for God. The orthodox Church here functions as metonymic construction of women's isolation from the social and economic sources of action, in that sense symbolic of political impotence.

Sometimes, the easiness of the fit between Victorian sexual ideology (woman to suffer and be still) and the Church's prescriptions of womanhood means that religious discourse enters into the very perception of 'rights'.

> I was discharged by the foreman without any reason assigned or notice given, in accordance with the rules of the work. Smarting under this treatment, I summoned the foreman into Court for payment of a week's wages for not receiving notice, and I gained the case. But if I was envied by my sister sex in the Verdant Works for my talent before this affair happened, they hated me with a perfect hatred after I had struggled for and gained my rights.[20]

Ellen Johnston's account of her fight for rights at the factory combines the rhetoric of militancy ('I was discharged by the foreman without any reason . . . I summoned the foreman . . . I . . . struggled for and gained my rights') with a rhetoric which is sexually reactionary ('I was envied by my sister sex . . . they hated me with a perfect hatred'), sustained in the religious discourse of the martyr ('smarting . . . envied . . . hated'). I shall return to questions of how working women's relationships to waged work and labour relations function in relation to the construction of subjectivity.[21]

On other occasions, the struggle for various kinds of rights for families informs a developing gender consciousness, even in the midst of preoccupation with 'women's issues'. Ostensibly, this kind of struggle might seem conventional, part of woman's role, but it is a territory in which women are brought into contact with those kinds of experience which inform a gender and class politics. In the following, Mary Ashford, who also fights for her husband's pension rights, is interviewed by a committee of gentlemen, as part of her application for special accommodation for her lying-in.

I dreamed that night, that I was going through Chelsea market, and was much annoyed and frightened by a porcupine, which lay at my feet, and its quills kept going off like squibs; and all attempts to get away from it were vain; at last, I thought it burst suddenly open, and the face of a very cross, ugly, old man came forth. I just then awoke, and a dreadful fright I was in. By twelve o'clock the next day I was to be at Brownlow Street, and it being a very hot day, I was much tired with walking there, as omnibuses had not come up then. There were several other women there, each of whom was called into the committee room separately. When it came to my turn, I went in, and at the head of the table, round which sat four or five gentlemen, there was (or, at least, I thought so) the very cross, ugly face I saw in my dream the night before. I was called forward, but all presence of mind and self-possession had forsaken me; I trembled, and was much confused. The gentleman (who, I think, they called Sir William Knatchbull, or something like it) said in a stern manner,

'Why is this letter not signed by the Hon. Mrs Percival, but by a Mr M.? - Pray, who and what is he?'

I stammered out that he was the head doctor of the Duke of York's School, and His Royal Highness's medical attendant.

'We don't care for the Duke of York, here, nor anybody else,' said he; 'the rules must be complied with. Where is Mrs Percival?'

I replied, 'Gone to Northumberland.'

The other gentlemen looked as if they were sorry for me, and one of them said, 'Why, I understand Mr M. paid the yearly subscription of five guineas, last week.'

Sir William then asked, in a very rude, coarse manner, when I expected to be confined.

I said, 'The latter end of the month.'

'Oh! plenty of time,' said he; 'here, take it back to Mr M., and tell him to send it into the north, and have it signed by the lady in a proper manner, and bring it back next week.'

Here another gentleman interposed, saying, that as Mr M. paid the money, and the lady was so far away, they might, without any impropriety, accept his signature. But he was inexorable, and I left Brownlow Street very much vexed.[22]

The dream rehearses and foregrounds the meeting with the cross, ugly face of that porcupine with the unlikely but somehow appropriate name ('or something like it') of Knatchbull. These comic touches manage a predicament which is characterized by feelings of oppression – annoyance, fright, tiredness, trembling, confusion, vexation. The attempt at reference to those in high places ('His Royal Highness's [of all people] medical attendant'), recognized as soon as it is begun ('I stammered') as pathetically failing to impress, draws attention to prefigured power relations. The class and gender confrontation here (five gentlemen face the woman), though not articulated as such, inscribes the conditions of oppression in gender consciousness (from all those feelings which characterize female impotence to censure of the enemy as cross, ugly, coarse, rude, and with quills which go off like squibs).

Florence White also voices a gender consciousness which gives priority to a concern with women. She takes as her particular notion of advancement the project of giving credit to domestic service as a 'vocation', and although this attachment can appear to be a reactionary placement ('what fun Victorian girls and women got out of their homely housewifely tasks'), it is informed by a more convincing concern with the relationship between women and waged labour (and job opportunities in general) in late Victorian Britain. 'One of the objects I have in writing this autobiography is to present a correct impression of a woman's opportunities for earning a living in those days.'[23] This type of interest, prefaced in that particular chapter by a quotation from Rebecca West, is part of and symptomatic of a gender consciousness in particular kinds of late Victorian discourse, my inference being that changes in the structure of labour and the development of the women's suffrage campaigns have produced and are produced by a particular gender consciousness in writing. The quotation from Rebecca West utilized by Florence White is as follows:

> It is the habit of the unintelligent to talk of the achievements of women in the modern world as if they represented a sudden sport of nature, comparable to, let us say, the development of the fifth leg in the rabbit species. Such things do not happen, rabbits have four legs, and always have had. Women have the ordinary human faculties connected with the use of reason, and always have had; but the fact that they are also responsible for the human race prevents any but a small proportion of them developing these faculties to any conspicuous degree, and handicaps to which they are subjected by that responsibility prevent even that small proportion from working unhampered.

In defence of 'splendid Victorian women', Florence White reiterates her concern with job opportunities ('My special interest was the employment of girls and women'), and eventually connects her project, in part, with feminism:

> With some of the feminist ideas I was, and am, in full sympathy. I hated the pocket-money wage, and always have believed that it would have paid the men's unions to have admitted qualified women on the same terms as men, that is, equal wages for equal work. When it has fallen to me to employ people, I have tried conscientiously to act upon this principle. It is, I have always insisted, the work for which I have paid, not the sex of the worker. I believe that if working men had had the foresight – the vision – forty years ago to realize this, and had acted on this principle, much of our present labour and unemployment trouble would never have existed.

In this autobiography, of later date than most referred to in my account, it is thus no historical accident, no anomaly, that Florence White can parallel a narrative progress in her own social 'progress' through occupation (from domestic servant to employer of domestic servants), and that she makes explicit reference to feminism and feminist ideas as having contemporary currency.

The autobiographers mentioned so far in this section thus attach significance to rights and to women's rights in the spheres of family or of labour. While these do not constitute holistic political positions (attachments to the family or to the job under capitalism can produce reactionary politics), the importance of such gender consciousness for radicalism should not be underestimated.

It remains to mention those autobiographers whose commitment to feminism as political activism is more direct.

Annie Kenney identifies the history of the fight for female suffrage as largely inseparable from her personal history. Believing that that struggle is her signal autobiographical experience, she proceeds to give 'a clear description . . . however brief, of certain but important parts of the Militant Movement for Women's Suffrage.'[24] This is how she typifies the movement in relation to the issue of independence;

> No home-life, no one to say what we should do or what we should not do, no family ties, we were free and alone in a great brilliant city, scores of young women scarcely out of their teens met together in a revolutionary movement, outlaws or breakers of laws, independent of everything and everybody, fearless and self-confident.

The rhetoric of independence inscribes the necessary rejection of 'home-life', of 'family', also a rejection of that kind of self-definition. Elsewhere, the wit of the account and the wit of the suffragists and suffragettes in their campaigning strategies, is a reminder of that line of feminist wit, gender-specific, which is also glimpsed in Mary Ashford's porcupine.

> Some of the meetings were really amusing. Incident after incident would happen, especially on Saturday night when

money had been spent more freely than usual. At one meeting I was addressing on Clifton Downs, Bristol, with Miss Mary Gawthorpe, a most irate man, who had been doing the week-end shopping, was continually interrupting. He got furious with the speaker, who to his annoyance turned all his remarks to good account, and at last in exasperation flung the Sunday cabbage at her. She caught it neatly, with the remark, 'I was afraid that man would lose his head before the meeting was over!'

At another meeting in Somerset, an elderly man kept repeating the same statement every few minutes: 'If you were my wife I'd give you poison!' Loud laughter greeted the statement each time. At last the speaker, tired of his repeated interruption, replied, 'Yes, and were I your wife I'd take it!'

This counter-humour, though, is feminism of a particularly secure variety. Mary Smith is more typical than Annie Kenney of the working women autobiographers in arriving at feminism only after a difficult working life. She retains too some of those representations from dominant discourse which signal (in comparison, say, with Annie Kenney's account) that uneasy straddling between the particular rhetoric of late nineteenth-century feminist militancy and the dramatization of women as martyred, suffering. In her account, she increasingly generalizes from her particular experience to 'the helplessness of women in the great battle of life'. Later, as a member of the Woman's Suffrage Society, she extends the generalization, the vision. 'The inequality of the sexes in privilege and power, was a great cause of the dreadful hardships which women, especially in the lower classes, had to suffer.'[25] Her poetry also calls upon both discourses. Perhaps, for this section of my account, it should have the last word.

Woman's Claims
'Women's Rights' are not her's only, they are all
        the world's beside,
And the whole world faints and suffers, while these
        are scorn'd, denied.
Childhood, with its mighty questions, Manhood
        with its restless heart,

Life in all its varied phases, standing class from
    class apart,
Need the voice, the thought of woman, woman wise
    as she shall be,
When at last the erring ages shall in all things make
    her Free.[26]

If we had a keen vision and feeling of all ordinary human life, it would be like hearing the grass grow and the squirrel's heart beat, and we should die of that roar which lies on the other side of silence.

George Eliot, *Middlemarch*, 1872

I don't quite know why I should put this all down. I suppose because George Eliot's life has, as I said above, stirred me up to an involuntary confession. How I have been handicapped in life! Should I have done better if I had been kept, like her, in a mental greenhouse and taken care of?

Autobiography and Letters of Mrs Margaret Oliphant, 1899

An itch for scribbling impelled her to write for any generation but her own - for her inclinations and aspirations had been effectually thwarted from early infancy by a disdainful and dully apprehensive circle of relations and acquaintances, by no means disposed to foster talent in their midst.

Edward Hall, Introduction to *Miss Weeton's Journal of a Governess*, 1969

7

An Itch for Scribbling

THE LITERARY

I am employing this category, 'the literary', as a metaphor for those genres which the professional production process in the nineteenth century inscribes as most important in relation to that writing which relies upon the priority of symbolization processes, giving primacy to the novel (increasingly in the nineteenth century), but significance to poetry as well, to drama (particularly melodrama), and, more recently, as might be the case in what I have shown from Florence White, that social history which calls explicitly upon various kinds of fictional or symbolic narrative. What I am suggesting is that it is these forms, and the novel in particular, which largely determine (text determining lived practice) the ways in which working women autobiographers write about ways of life.

But in utilizing this category, 'the literary', I am not referring only to content, to a collation of genres, but additionally to Literature (capital L) as that which has been judged good of these genres and their artefacts. I am arguing therefore that 'the literary' (and from now I shall abandon these inverted commas) exists as a moral category in relation to those genres, artefacts, each with its own kinds of representation, which have been judged good. It is this category of the literary upon which the autobiographers rely as the chief sanction of their tastes, judgements and experiences.[1]

I am arguing therefore that the literary as the moral is crucial to autobiographical subjectivity in the nineteenth century and for those autobiographers living in the twentieth century writing about nineteenth-century lives. These constructions of subjectivity, which have clear representational terms in class and in gender, exist in tension with other gender and class interests of working women.

To attempt elucidation of the way the literary functions in some of the autobiographies and of the tensions it produces, I now take the particular example of Ellen Johnston.

In entering into an artistic persona (factory girl poet from weaver in the aptly named Verdant Works) Ellen Johnston takes on, assumes, the literary as her autobiographical subjectivity. This is in her narrative mode (repeatedly addressing her 'dear reader'), and also directly in self-presentation. 'Mine were not the common trials of every day life, but like those strange romantic ordeals attributed to the imaginary heroines of 'Inglewood Forest'.'[2] The rhetoric of realism ('common trials of every day life') is in tension with that of romance ('strange romantic ordeals attributed to. . . imaginary heroines'), to produce an autobiographical subject *in* the literary. In a similar tension, she repeatedly invokes 'evidence' and 'veracity' (Mary Ashford also commits herself to 'the real truth', Ellen Weeton writes 'the simple and entire truth', Mary Barber's editor proclaims her autobiography as 'truth'), whilst believing that her account is out to present 'the romance of real life'.

The articulation of autobiographical subject as heroine is common. In narrating how she became 'the factory girl', Ellen Johnston writes: 'I had read many of Sir Walter Scott's novels, and fancied I was a heroine of the modern style.'[3] Mary Barber, though with some irony, utilizes these same terms: distressed heroines.

Where the autobiographical subject is not herself a heroine, there often appears a need to create one elsewhere. Even Florence White, in her realistic intentions, nevertheless introduces a 'character' for whom she makes the claim 'real heroine' of the piece. Ida Rose is invoked and afterwards scarcely mentioned. 'Ida Rose Lovering, a pretty little dark-haired girl with cheeks like damask roses.'[4] (In *Jipping Street*, an autobiography published recently by Virago, one of the central figures is treated in similar terms.[5] Jessica Mourn is a heroine who has 'a poetry in her brooding presence'. On

this occasion, though, the autobiographer (Kathleen Woodward) utilizes romance as illusion. Jessica Mourn finds her
'airy heroes' replaced by 'a stocky little man of the "bruiser"
type' who does indeed soon begin to deal out bruises. Jessica
is 'shocked into an almost unbroken silence'.)

This creation of heroines, which may be seen as 'a retreat
from reality', is the signification of an entry by the autobiographers into literary values.[6] One of the means by which this
is manifested and sustained, in addition to utilizing terms like
heroine, which are particularly evocative of fiction, myth,
epic, is in the claim of the autobiographical subject to be
special, unique. The autobiographical voice on these occasions differentiates itself, in individualism, from that voice
struggling to represent a common experience of gender and
class. This voice of the unique (which is also that of an
individual, as distinct from a collective, class aspiration)
frequently takes its form from the terminology of high art.
The ways of life of working women (social group) are thus
brought into tension with the individual woman having
recourse to art and Literature (as the 'high' categories of
culture) in self-perception.

In Mary Barber's autobiography, this tension is a literal
dualism, in the binary construction (Meta and Mary) of the
autobiographical subject. The relationship between Meta
and Mary, alter egos, is characterized by disturbances,
conflicts, differences between them in relation to literary
aspiration and in relation to Meta's artistic sensibility. Much
of this disturbance centres upon the term 'genius'.

> Mary feared, wavered, doubted. To have genius was, in her
> eyes, *not* to have common sense. The ability Meta showed was
> not the sort of ability she desired. She wanted an ordinary
> woman, – she dreaded a genius; she wanted music and French,
> – she looked suspiciously upon Greek and poetry.[7]

'Genius' is here precisely in tension with 'ordinary woman':
individualism in tension with the social group. In other
autobiographies, the self-perception of genius or thwarted
genius coexists quite flagrantly (and without even the sceptic-

ism of Mary Barber's position) with a quite different kind of experience. Ellen Weeton writes of her 'repressed' genius and talents in relation to the literary.[8] Even Mary Smith, who is very well aware, through her experience of poverty, of the material constraints on such notions as ability, upholds in the zone of the literary a similar special pleading, inscribing an attachment to individual intellect as a possible means of transcending class barriers. In believing that 'intellect knows no rank', she is able to privilege herself with the rhetoric of 'a lady', though she is a working woman and has no money. These slippages between 'genius' and 'intellect' occur frequently in the autobiographies in the realm of the pursuit of books, of learning and of the literary, from artistic codes to meritocratic codes which are also artistic codes. Elizabeth Ham, like Ellen Weeton, believes it is no great 'vanity' to perceive herself as mentally superior to most of her kind:

> Whilst living with Ralph at Holy Well I was enjoying a certain degree of independence, and plenty of society, such as it was. I had access to but very few books, and no improving conversation, for it would be no great vanity to say that my mind, little as it had been cultivated, was yet superior to those with whom I associated.[9]

Most of the autobiographers have, at some point, what might be described as, to different extents, the art thing. Indeed, it seems to be inseparable from the act of writing autobiographically. At its most flagrant, as in Elizabeth Ham's autobiography, it collapses the aesthetic into the moral and into the meritocratic, but more frequently it exists as a gentle aesthetic, delicately pointing a social aspiration which has no bearing on materiality. 'I confess that the *sense* of these books was often uncomprehended by me – only the *sound* was not lost – and there was nothing that brought sweeter music to my soul than the sound of beautiful words.'[10] Beautiful words.

Literary values are thus encoded (heroines, geniuses, beautiful words) as significations of particular kinds of subjectivity: individualistic, socially aspiring – though, as I will show in relation to the desire to be a writer, that aspiration has more bearing on an ideal subjectivity than on any materially available. It is these kinds of values, as much as the wish to enter into the professional, literary production process, which prompt Mary Smith, for instance, to make contact with members of literary circles.

That Mary Smith is successful in attracting a modicum of attention from the professional literary world serves only to emphasize her distance and the distance of the other auto-biographers from its internal mechanisms and class assump-tions. The connection which she succeeds in making, which is in one way merely vicarious (all she knows about the would-be correspondent is that she is the wife of Thomas Carlyle), is with Jane Carlyle.

This attempt to approach the 'great men' of Literature (why else write to Jane Carlyle, knowing nothing about her except who her husband is?) has interesting consequences for Mary Smith. I will return more precisely to what these consequences are, but the first thing to be said about them is that they are not really the consequences to which Mary Smith aspires, although they may be those of the process she has put into action, a comment itself on what is possible for the autobiographers, and on the relative determination of their remaining in the margins. Mary Smith, that is, does not find herself taken up as the acolyte of Thomas Carlyle. He does write one letter about her poems, but in approaching 'the wife', Mary Smith had not even, in that sense, aspired to approaching the man. It is her class position in gender which prescribes these limitations. The very strategy of adopting an indirect approach is significant in relation to this gender and class formation when set against the attempts of other aspiring writers to acquire patrons or literary correspondents. The working man, John Overs, for instance, although he demonstrates a similar deference in attitude to that of Mary Smith, contacts his literary man, Charles Dickens, directly, without mediating connection. The man can at least contact the man. Class difference complicates that connection (and indeed ultimately the connection is not of much use to John Overs[11]) but the route between classes is nominally open via gender, male. Charlotte Brontë is also confident enough as a literary *ingénue* to correspond directly with Robert Southey.[12] On this occasion, the woman can write to the man because class provides a route which mediates gender.

Mary Smith, working woman, has access to neither of these routes. She marginalizes her own position by not feeling that she is able to correspond directly with Thomas Carlyle, but it is a failure of nerve which is in keeping with her low social status and her distance from the mechanisms of literary power. The actual consequences of Mary Smith's initiation of a correspondence with Jane Carlyle are also revealing in relation to class and gender formulations in their bearing on the literary. Jane Carlyle's first letter in reply to Mary Smith responds to the latter's voicing of literary aspirations.

> Meanwhile, believe a woman older than yourself, who has seen, and *seen thro!* all you are now longing after. There is as little *nourishing* for an aspiring soul in literary society as in any civilized society one could name! And, between ourselves, . . . you would find yourself – or I am greatly mistaken – no nearer, if so near, to 'clear ideas' and 'broad knowledge' than you are now – teaching a school.[13] (Her emphases.)

This is clear in its demystifications of the literary ideal: as we always suspected 'literary society' is no nearer to 'clear ideas' and 'broad knowledge' (Mary Smith's requirements) than is school-teaching. Nevertheless, the welcome explosion of a myth or two is somewhat soured by the condescension (patronage indeed), keeping Mary Smith firmly in her place: 'a woman older than yourself, who has seen, and seen thro' [with emphasis], all [all!] you are now longing after'. But perhaps the 'between ourselves', the signal of potential intimacy, can be recuperated as that which is potentially productive between Mary Smith and Jane Carlyle. This intimacy does not prove to be an enemy of promise; a friendship is developed to a limited extent. Increasingly, in the correspondence (and it is significant in itself that that correspondence does not end with those two letters), the 'between ourselves' gathers a revealing sort of momentum.

Jane Carlyle writes:

I had gone with my husband to live on a little estate of *peat bog*, that had descended to me, all the way down from John Welsh, the Covenanter, who married a daughter of John Knox. That didn't, I am ashamed to say, make me feel Craigenputtock a whit less of a peat bog, and most dreary, untoward place to live at! In fact, it was sixteen miles distant on every side from all the conveniences of life – shops and even post office!

Further, we were very poor; and further and worse, being an only child, and brought up to 'great prospects', I was sublimely ignorant of every branch of useful knowledge, though a capital Latin scholar and a very fair mathematician!! It behoved me in these astonishing circumstances to learn – to *sew*! Husbands, I was shocked to find, wore their stockings into holes! and were always losing buttons! and *I* was expected to 'look to all that!' Also, it behoved me to learn to *cook*! No *capable* servant choosing to live at 'such an out of the way place,' and my husband having 'bad digestion', which complicated my difficulties dreadfully. The bread, above all, brought from Dumfries, 'soured on his stomach,' (Oh Heavens!) and it was plainly my duty as a christian wife to bake at home!

So I sent for Cobbett's 'Cottage Economy', and fell to work at a loaf of bread. But knowing nothing about the process of fermentation or the heat of ovens, it came to pass that my loaf got put into the oven at the time *myself* ought to have put into bed, and I remained the only person not asleep, in a house in the middle of a desert! *One* o'clock struck, and then *two*, and then *three*; and still I was sitting there in an intense solitude, my whole body aching with weariness, my heart aching with a sense of forlornness and degradation. That I who had been so petted at home, whose comfort had been studied by everybody in the house, who had never been required to do anything but *cultivate my mind*, should have to pass all those hours of the night in watching *a loaf of bread*! which mightn't turn out bread after all![14]

Jane Carlyle shares with Mary Smith the 'horrors' (repeated exclamation) of those activities which culture constructs as work appropriate to woman's sphere, as defining woman's separate sphere: to sew! to cook! to bake at home! Like Mary Smith, if from a different class position, her personal history takes her in the direction of a set of conflicts: the requirements ('it behoved me') of that sphere as against being brought up with 'great prospects', as against being a Latin scholar and a mathematician (through class having made, at some stage, entry into that man's world of a liberal education), and as against the cultivation of the mind. Even in learning to bake, she turns to the literary *Cottage Economy*.

She also shares with Mary Smith the intimacy ('between ourselves' as women) of the perception of domestic man. Thomas Carlyle, 'great man', is, after all, mere husband, has holes in his socks, suffers bad digestion (which requires, it seems, his wife to suffer too), and expects to be serviced by his wife, particularly in the absence of capable servants.

From a different position in class, Jane Carlyle responds, not as a member (though by marriage) of a literary circle who can facilitate social and professional connections for an aspiring writer, but as a woman who recognizes, from experience, some experiences of a working woman. She responds, not to the writer as would-be professional, but to that definition of work (working woman) from which Mary Smith is attempting to escape. Jane Carlyle responds not to writer, but to writing. She replies to the autobiographer with autobiography. She replies to the woman with the woman.

The correspondence proves most interesting (perhaps for Mary Smith too) in the illustrations it produces of women's experiences (loneliness, aching weariness, degradation and their particularities), but it is signally less than useful in furthering Mary Smith's literary ambitions. What was intended as a work strategy becomes a friendship, producing its own literary category (perhaps gender-orientated) of the intimate letter. While this, in the great scale of human values, may prove preferable (intimacy, shared experience, sympathy, understanding), it is no answer to Mary Smith's material problems. We might indeed have expected that such an individualistic strategy might be unreliable.

The reflexivity which emerges in the correspondence between Mary Smith and Jane Carlyle is not, therefore, an entry for Mary Smith into literary circles, nor, more significantly, is that reflexivity a feature of those circles.[15] The literary is, after all, about heroines, geniuses, beautiful words, not the shared experiences of an oppressed social group.

WORKING, WRITING

It is time to turn, after some hints and promises in earlier chapters, explicitly to the issue of work, of what it means to some of the autobiographers, and of what it means in my constituting the social group, working women.

It is important, at this stage of the account, to reiterate an attachment to methodologies which construct gender in class, and class in gender, without displacing one by the other. In chapter five I referred to some of the ways in which autobiographers identify their origins in class according to paternal occupation, and how others experience particular circumstances (deaths of parents, 'losing caste') which over-bear those definitions with a common experience of oppression. I now wish to extend this latter point to an exploration of some of the structures and practices of work which define, for women, a common position.

Writing in the 1930s, Florence White looks back to the late nineteenth century and endeavours to show the opportunities which women had for earning a living. She wishes to correct the impression that all women were governesses.[16] In instancing available types of employment, she lists running hotels (three of her unmarried aunts kept the Red Lion, Fareham), dressmaking, running businesses, painting, journalism, nursing and running schools.

Reading that list now, it might appear to show restriction rather that diversity of opportunity for women in employment. There is not only a problem with the particular illustrations Florence White gives to her instances. (The business woman she cites is a needleworker, and her son takes over the business. The journalist edits the household, cookery and fasion pages of her husband's journal.) The whole inventory is characterized by sex segregation, separate spheres and the sexually stereotypical. (Dressmaking, nursing and running schools were, in the nineteenth century, for the most part, sex-segregated employment peculiar to women, or employment performed particularly with women, whether other women workers or women clients.)

Indeed, what characterizes the work of the women autobiographers is sex segregation and separate spheres (household skills, including needlework, cookery, nursing, performed at home, and the extension of these skills to define the type of employment outside home available to women) in a particular pattern of work. This pattern consists of a combination of home work (housework and work taken into the home, paid by the hour or by item) and, frequently, large numbers of short-term jobs, largely within the categories of Florence White's inventory. Florence White does not specify, significantly enough, the two largest employers of women in the nineteenth century: the factory and domestic service. This neglect of hers does not derive from ignorance (she spent most of her life as a domestic servant), but presumably from her idealistic mission to represent the achievements of women.[17]

What characterizes the work of the women autobiographers, then, is a common experience of gender-specific work which tends to override the distinctions in class which might apply to analogous men's work. Many of the autobiographers, that is, work in jobs from both working- and middle-class categories, for instance, a short-term job in a factory or taking needlework into the home might be followed by a short-term one as a governess. What is most significant in women's work is the separate sphere (sexual ideology determining sex segregation and type of work available) and, most typically, a pattern of work characterized by the short term, by interruption, by low pay, by intervening demands from all kinds of structures of kin (by no means confined to marriage and children) and, most signally, by the absence of any kind of predictable or secure route.

From the age of fifteen, working chronologically, Florence White's working life moves through the following categories: helping her immediate family, 'very poor', doing a bit of teaching, moving away from home to care for relatives, running a school, various jobs in service, helping her own family, journalism, teaching English, return to domestic service, return to Fareham (where she had cared for relatives), governessing, housekeeping (in Cambridge, where she had had ambitions to study), studying cookery. Between 1884 and 1922, she has twenty-eight different jobs. Despite hers being an autobiography of a cook, it is not until part four (of five) in a chronological narrative that she finds work as a cook.[18]

This kind of work pattern, with a multiplicity of low-paid jobs interrupted by unpaid work, with paid and unpaid work frequently performed contemporaneously, is by no means unique to Florence White. Mary Smith sells groceries, does dressmaking, keeps poultry, tries schoolteaching, goes home to relatives, is unemployed, runs a school, tries journalism, tries teaching again, combines journalism and teaching with lecturing for the Woman's Suffrage Society.[19] Elizabeth Ham works for her relatives, does dairy work for them, is a home-worker ('dreary' work of shirt-making), does some governessing.[20] Rose Allen and Mary Ashford each works through a quantity of jobs in domestic service, with interruptions for family.[21] Ellen Johnston and Annie Kenney begin their working lives as factory workers, Ellen Johnston becoming a popular poet, Annie Kenney becoming a full-time militant, and having acute financial problems after the winning of the vote. There is a certain irony in that.[22]

These kinds of work practices, with their fragmentations, discontinuities, are found in the autobiographies in tension with that ideology or mythology of labour which bears on the complete, the coherent, the importance of work to meaningful subjectivity – which still, now, has a close bearing, particularly on the construction of masculinity. Florence White's studying cookery, in her spare time in Cambridge, when she had wanted to be a student at Girton, is an example of such a tension. The waged labour available to women is, in quality and duration, uncertain, sex-specific, low-paid, and mostly 'miserable' and 'monotonous'.[23] As with marriage, the possibility of work which is economically or materially stable, emotionally reflexive, a route, turns out to be part of a pure fiction.[24]

It is into these tensions, these contradictions, that the

possibility of writing, of being a professional writer, enters as the prospective or preferable subjectivity in relation to work. The activity of writing enters as a set of possible subjectivities available to women as ideals in an extension from learning, the arts, the literary, being a writer. They were generally not available (as I tried to show earlier in relation to learning) as anything other than ideals, available, that is, in self-construction, but not in the material (formal, institutional) production process. This is something like seeing oneself as a writer, a preferable subjectivity to that of a working woman, but remaining aeons away from being a writer in the sense of being a professional.[25]

Writing autobiography is frequently itself part of a more general expression of the desire to write, to be a writer. This is a class formation in which the working woman shares with the working-class man a particular attachment to the metaphor, the writer, as an expression of class aspiration and of subjectivity.[26] It is also a particularly concentrated aspiration in its gender formations in that the profession, Literature, was the only one of the professions in the nineteenth century to admit women in any numbers.

In the autobiographies, an attachment to the significance of a subjectivity constructed around writing coexists with a sense of being distanced from (frequently, failing in) the professional literary production process. Mary Smith describes her persistence in her ambition to write books, but concludes that 'There is not much in a struggling life like mine to interest the general reader.'[27] And despite her eventual success in publishing verse, she cannot attain or maintain the demeanour of a literary professional.

> I took no interest at all in the volume; hardly thought it right to offer if for sale, though I knew that no one need be ashamed of the most part of the poems it contained. Thomas Carlyle and his wife had commended them as full of thought, and one of the pieces as like *singing*; but to promote the sale of them by any means, with so many imperfections, I never could – nor did – do.[28]

Even when she becomes a journalist (which is, in her

perception, distinctly 'settling for less'), she must write under a pseudonym in order to publish articles about issues which are not supposed to be fit subjects for women writers. And, ultimately, it is the problem of gender which she locates as the crucial restriction in realizing literary aims. 'My object has been to show the inner cravings of my soul after literary pursuits, which, being a woman, I failed to attain, despite of all my self-denial and persistent endeavours.'[29] 'Being a woman' here brings together the gender constraint in class. Abandoning am ambition to write books is axiomatic with pursuing 'the harder and narrower fortunes of meaner women'.[30]

Ellen Weeton also makes much of the rhetoric of literary aspiration. She blames her education (or more accurately, her mother) for what she perceives as a failure to achieve.

> If I did write, I must be merely your amanuensis; for my own genius has been so strongly repressed, has so long lain dormant, that now I fear it could produce nothing. There was a time, when I think (may I say it without vanity?) something might have been done; I feel confident I could have risen to something higher, something greater, but such pains were taken by my mother to repress my too great ardour for literature, that any talents I then possessed as a child, have been nearly extinguished, and it is too late now to blow them into flame.[31]

In Mary Barber's autobiography, attempts to earn a living as a poet founder in fruitless visits to publishers, impending financial ruin, and an overwhelming sense of futility and despondency.

> We read of women supporting their aged mothers or infant children, or sisters and brothers by the elegant productions of their pencil, their needle, or their pen; but should any distressed heroine, suddenly thrown on the world by adverse circumstances, look to any such channel for her daily bread, she would find, that without friends, without connexions, without *the habit of labour*, that it was a means of earning a livelihood peculiar to romances, even if she possessed what few do possess – genius.[32]

This signally demonstrates that bread-winning and literary career are incompatible for working women, an idea which is sustained as the central construction of the narrative, indicated in the title, *Bread-Winning or, The Ledger and the Lute*, and in the binary representation of the autobiographical subject as the sisters, Mary and Meta. The latter connects with 'the lute' of the title, absorbed by the aesthetic and spiritual, a lover of books and an aspiring writer. The other sister, Mary (not even veiled as autobiographical subject, except in the twinning), has 'moderate abilities', distinguished from the 'great talents' of Meta, and is thereby better qualified to pursue 'the important art of bread-winning'. The quotation from Mary Barber is more signal still in what it demonstrates about the class basis of literary representation. Despite the recognition that earning a living from writing is an idea 'peculiar to romances', the appeal to the reader who may aspire to write or to earn a living from some other form of artistry is still an appeal to the 'distressed heroine'. And 'the ledger' as a metaphor of hard graft barely works. Even 'bread-winning' is an 'important *art*' (my emphasis). Hard graft here, in its representations, has no bearing on what the working woman experiences as work, but is what the dominant discourse constructs, in class, as the significant representation of that work. I shall return to this issue of what the literary makes of the representation of work.

Ellen Johnston is unusual in perceiving herself as a successful writer, but there is a revealing discrepancy between how she articulates her literary aspirations (an acolyte of Walter Scott) and the fame she achieves, which is local to her particular area of the north-west and which, more significantly, is firmly located in the working class. Ellen Johnston, 'the factory poet', is part of a cult of the popular made possible by local journalism, where she prints her poems and is able to read responses of local people. Working women, when they do 'achieve' (gain a readership, make some money) as writers, do so in relation to a class- and/or gender-specific readership of their own sphere. Thus, Ellen Johnston writes for the locals and Annie Kenney for the women's movement.

Florence White is more typical than Ellen Johnston in perceiving herself as someone who has failed to write books. 'Instead of witing a book of English everyday life I have had to live it. And this has set me thinking.'[33]

WRITING, WORKING

Not all working women autobiographers produce a rationale of writing autobiographically in terms of the aspiration to be a writer. Elizabeth Ham, in her initial premises at least, shares with some working-class men the desire to review from old age the relationship between versions of 'herself' in the past-present relation, which is also to review the relations between the personal and the social in the past-present relation.

> I shall now endeavour, at the age of sixty-six, to recall the history of my past life, in order to try if I can to trace out the influences that were most active in forming the present individual *me* out of the little neglected girl of my earliest remembrance.[34]

Women who write in old age tend to produce the same rationales of adopting the genre autobiography as do many men autobiographers, accounting for the present in the past, or imaging a way of life they see receding.

This kind of rationale has its more gendered aspect when something like it is produced at an earlier stage in the life of a working woman. For instance, getting married can prompt a similar review of personal changes. Rose Allen, after a series of positions in domestic service, takes to writing after marrying Edward, 'to beguile some of the long afternoons, while waiting for Edward.'[35] It is possible to locate in those women who marry in their twenties or thirties a marital state which is, especially for those women who do not quickly produce children or continue with their previous pattern in relation to paid work, a period of redundancy or obsolescence.[36] It is not that they have no work to do (Rose

Allen is exceptional – and that autobiography is, as I have suggested, close to fiction – in having long afternoons to beguile), but that getting married can be a retirement from the resources of the 'public' world. Ellen Weeton represents the logical extremity of this in finding herself imprisoned in the marital home.

The argument could go that women, in the act of marrying, particularly if required to conform to that ideology which requires women to abstain from paid work, become desocialized or decontextualized in relation to received understandings of labour power. This, while it may be welcome in old age, is yet another disruption to working life when it represents a withdrawal against the grain of relative youth and energy. In Rose Allen's life, and more particularly in that of Ellen Weeton, the prospect of material comfort and the time for reflection in the period directly after marriage soon collapses in a powerful sense of discontinuity, disruption, which is, politically and socially, a bit like the prospect of death which retirement brings. I am thinking here of those women who, in the act of marrying, are no longer regarded as serious contestants in the labour market. Many working women, of course, are required to continue in waged labour after marriage, but usually they are not then writing autobiographies. After separating from her husband, Ellen Weeton soon returns to that pattern of work cited earlier in my account, which is yet a preferable set of disruptions, for her, to those of marriage.

Other autobiographies which produce rationales of writing autobiographically do so in relation to the gendered category of motherhood, as I described in the previous chapter in relation to Ellen Weeton (Ellen Johnston also uses this appeal, even though her daughter is illegitimate), or, more commonly, in relation to a gendered conception of work.

If I return, for a moment, to Florence White's proposition that, 'instead of writing a book of English everyday life I have had to live it', I can begin to tease out some of the ways in which, in the autobiographies, working functions in writing. What seems to be happening is that certain ways of life, and in particular certain types of work as ways of life, are constructed in particular ways in the class terms of representation. This is as if dominant representations construct in certain fixed categories of work – domestic service, the factory – the genres or types of genre available to working women when they come to write. For instance, Florence White, in inscribing her autobiography as that of a cook, conforms to a notion of subjectivity (created in genre) which, as we have seen, has little bearing on that aspect of her narrative which suggests a particular pattern of work, disrupted, discontinuous (twenty-eight jobs in thirty-eight years). In writing, it is the category of 'the cook', as the literary, which is primarily available to her. Similarly, it is the genre or category of 'the factory girl' which is available to Ellen Johnston, 'the governess' which is available to Ellen Weeton (and in the naming and renaming of her journal, this category appears to harden over time, from *Miss Weeton* to *Miss Weeton: Journal of a Governess* to *Miss Weeton's Journal of a Governess*), and 'the schoolmistress' which is available to Mary Smith. And all these categories are from or in that separate sphere culturally constructed as 'women's work'. The genre itself thus inscribes that sexual ideology which sustains not only the ways in which women autobiographers write about their work, but the actual types of labour they perform.

In producing her explanation of writing autobiographically, Mary Ashford begins by expressing her disappointment that a work she sees advertised as *Susan Hopley, or the Life of a Maid Servant* turns out to be a work of fiction. She concludes that her way of life has not been accounted for in writing. The terms she employs in describing what she believes ought to be achieved by way of that kind of account set up some interesting tensions. What is needed, she states, is an account which does justice to 'the real truth', and yet she carries no illusions about being able to relay 'the facts' unmediated, rather believing that autobiography can be a process more telling than 'fact' which can yet appeal to the 'matter-of-fact' reader.[37] The rationale produced is thus noticeably close to the kind of appeal the realism of the nineteenth-century novel was making to its readership. Mary Ashford argues that while autobiography is preferable to fiction, it is nevertheless its 'novel' aspect which characterizes it. Again, it appears to be the category of the literary which largely constructs the means of writing about domestic service, about work.

Ultimately, in the twentieth century, it appears to be the category 'working woman' itself which becomes the genre. This, in one way, can allow for a greater range of subjectivities than the more prescriptive, partial, 'factory girl' or 'maidservant'. Mrs Layton finds some of this flexibility:

> One day I went with a girl to take home some match-boxes. The match factory was at the back of a large old-fashioned mansion. At one time the neighbourhood was a very aristocratic part of the suburbs of London, but as the town grew the gentlefolk had gone farther out, so it came about that what was once a fine family mansion was now used for the family of the owner of the match factory, and what had been a coach-house and stables had been converted into a factory. The front of the house was beautifully kept. The windows always took my fancy because they looked clean and had nice curtains, the upper ones with brass bars on top of the short curtains, and the bottom ones with long lace ones. There was a large old-fashioned garden with bright flowers in the front of the house, with a large mulberry tree in the centre of a well-kept lawn, with seats under the lovely old tree. As we went past we saw three ladies sitting in the shade doing some kind of fancy work. We were rude enough to look through the fence to admire their pretty dresses, and were told to go about our business. What a contrast the back was to the front! It was a very hot day and the sun was shining just as much there as in the front, but there was no shelter from the sun's rays for the workers who had to stand there and wait their turn. There seemed to be a good many women and children waiting for some more work to be given out and their paltry earnings paid to them. Some were getting into trouble because they had only brought part of their work

back. The girl I went with was one of the unfortunate ones.
They all made reasonable excuses, but what was quite clear
to my childish mind was that they all wanted the money for
the work they had done to buy food for their dinners. Some
had to plead very hard for their pay, and when it was given to
them it was given with a rough word of warning that if the
rest of their work was not done and brought in that night
there would be no more work for them the next day, and that
if they could not do the work there were plenty who could.
While all this was going on in the yard I could see a servant
who was very busy preparing dinner in the kitchen, and the
delicious smell of roast meat came to the waiting workers.
Several women passed remarks regarding the smell and
wished they could be invited to dine off that joint. But that
was too good for matchbox makers. Their diet consisted of
fried fish and potatoes, or pease pudding and faggots, if they
had earned enough to pay for such dinners; if not, bread and
dripping with a glass of the cheapest beer. As I write this, I
can see that house as I saw it on the day I am describing – the
handsome old house with the garden with bright flowers and
well-kept lawn and fine old mulberry tree on one side; on the
other the hard-faced man giving out work and handing the
small sums of money due to the sad-faced women and
children, some of whom had scarcely any boots to their feet
and very little clothing to cover them.[38]

There is a discourse of contrast, of class conflict here, of
mansion and match factory, which is sustained in the realist
detail (roast meat/faggots, pretty dresses/very little clothing)
and in images of shelter and exposure. This is the child
viewing class difference and gender difference – 'hard-faced
man . . . sad-faced women' – but it is also Mrs Layton,
autobiographical subject, identifying subjectivity in the social group, working women.

In Mrs Layton's account, there is a call upon a greater
variety of discourse than that available to some of the early
nineteenth-century autobiographers. This greater flexibility
in the construction of subjectivity (available in 'the working
woman') has been shadowed in some of those earlier
accounts, as in Mary Ashford's concern to write of an actual

way of life of a working woman, 'the truth' about being a domestic servant. Part of the same concern is that type of rationale produced in relation to 'the ordinary': ordinary people addressing ordinary people about ordinary matters. This can be a challenge to fiction (as in the case of Mary Ashford's preface) from the individual constituted in the social group (in this case, working women), from, that is, those people who have actually *lived* certain practices as ways of work, ways of life.

> There are many biographies and autobiographies of the great and good filled with anecdotes of the greater and better amongst the aristocracy of life and letters. But when the social historian seeks similar human documents describing the ordinary life of the middle classes of some bygone age he will probably find insufficient material as far as autobiographies are concerned. He has to get his facts, or local colour, chiefly from fiction and to separate the two - if he can! The poets Langland, Tusser, Herrick, and Clare are the best sources of inspiration for country customs, with perhaps a not too dull manuscript diary such as may be discovered from time to time.
>
> Ordinary people do not consider their lives of sufficient importance to spend time in writing them down, even if they have a flair for scribbling, and they are probably right.
>
> Mine alone most certainly would not be.
>
> The year 1937, however, was the centenary of the accession of Queen Victoria, and during these hundred years so much has happened, and so many interesting changes have taken place, and so many wrong impressions have been given of social life and character during the Victorian era and later, that it seemed to me worth while to supplement the general information concerning customs and ways of living . . . by the story of some happenings, and of a few people. After all seventy-four years is long enough to see the beginning and end of many a story, grave and gay.[39]

The sense of lived practice is here in significant tension, utilizing 'the ordinary' with the literary. Florence White seeks to counter those writings by and about 'the aristocracy of life and letters' with accounts of 'the ordinary life of the middle classes'. (It is typical of the autobiographers to locate 'the ordinary' in terms of 'the middle classes'. This in itself has implications for nineteenth-century representation. 'The working classes' does not appear to be a piece of rhetoric available in the construction of female subjectivity.) The problem, though, as Florence White articulates it, is that 'ordinary people' do not consider their lives worth writing down, and, she thinks, 'they are probably right'. Social history must then turn to the literary, to the poets, for its sources, as Florence White turns to social history – the year 1937 as centenary – to provide her justification of writing as the ordinary about the ordinary. And, ultimately, her rationale is a conventional one of autobiography: being old enough (sheer age) to have seen 'the beginning and end of many a story, grave and gay'. The uncertainty about whether 'ordinary people', including herself, can legitimately write autobiographically thus connects repeatedly with perceived categories of dominant discourse, poets, social historians, as if, again, the text is the more certain measure than lived practice of what can most legitimately be represented as 'ordinary human life'.[40]

I have not written this book for professional historians. The past belongs to us all and we are entitled to find out about it. Why should an investigation of your grandmother's lifestyle be left to some university don, who probably would never bother with it anyway?

Deirdre Beddoe, *Discovering Women's History*, 1983

Professional historians (even socialist ones) may regret the entry of vast numbers of lay people into the business of history-making and recording - 'amateur brain-surgeons', they've been called – but that's their problem.

Ken Worpole, 'The History Lark', *New Socialist*, number 17, May/June, 1984

We have stressed throughout that epistemological and theoretical problems rest, in the end, upon certain social conditions, especially the position of authors of different kinds in the social relations of intellectual production. We have been especially concerned with the role of 'the historian' as a professional monopolist, or would-be monopolist of historical knowledge production. How can these forms of monopoly (and the professional ideologies which they tend to reproduce) be broken down?

Popular Memory Group, Centre for Contemporary Cultural Studies, *Making Histories*, 1982

8

Professional Historians, Amateur Brain Surgeons

In 1936, a hundred years after they were written, Edward Hall found the hand-copied letters and autobiographical sketches in a Wigan bookshop, and presented *Miss Weeton* for publication, with a foreword by himself. In 1939, the book became *Miss Weeton: Journal of a Governess*, and Edward Hall added an epilogue to his original foreword. In 1969, a new edition of the book appeared in two volumes. This time, it was *Miss Weeton's Journal of a Governess*, and it appeared with foreword, epilogue and introduction by Edward Hall, and with an additional new introduction by one J. J. Bagley of the University of Liverpool.

This accumulation around Ellen Weeton (added to now by me) of the paraphernalia of the professional literary production process, this rallying of commentators, raises questions about editorial interventions, supports and appropriations, in relation to working women's autobiographies. The central focus of these questions will not so much be on how these particular autobiographies come to be published and in what circumstances (though all this is of interest), but on some theory and some speculation about what such presences (witnesses, commentators, editors) do to our reading of the autobiographies and, in affecting our readings, what the implications are of such interventions. To elicit reponses to some of these questions, one might, for instance, take the case of the process mentioned above in relation to Ellen Weeton's writing, and pose the initial question in these terms: what is Edward Hall doing with Ellen Weeton?

Before addressing Edward Hall, however, I shall take

some space to refer briefly to two of those nineteenth-century autobiographers who have not yet been seized by the twentieth century as ripe or right for republication. In relation to Rose Allen's autobiography, it is the low profile of the editorial presence which is telling. The editor is not quite anonymous (as is the case, for instance, with Mary Smith's), but is an inscription in gender and class terms: simply, 'A Lady'.[1] The only words which she attributes to herself are those of the short preface:

> If the language or sentiments of Rose Allen should sometimes appear rather above the position in which she is represented by peculiar circumstances to have been placed, the defect must rest on the Editor, who, in the endeavour to avoid one extreme, may perhaps unintentionally have fallen into the other. It is hoped, however, that the story may help to induce a more general recognition of the reciprocal dependence of Master and Servant, and a more conscientious appreciation of the responsibilities of their respective stations.[2]

The class inflections of this tend to corroborate the impression which I wrote about earlier, that Rose Allen's autobiography is fiction, that Rose Allen is indeed 'A lady', that 'A Lady' is indeed Rose Allen. This 'discovery', though, is not very important, for most of the autobiographies, as I have endeavoured to show, rely on fictional modes. Rose Allen is the logical extension of the literary, constructing 'working woman' through middle-class representation. What is important is that editor and autobiographical subject are here subsumed in the moralizing, polemical intention: to cross class barriers, to improve relations between Master and Servant. From this, it appears that, even where the paraphernalia of literary production is less overt (as it is in these autobiographies only available in their nineteenth-century editions as compared with those published more recently), it bears the burden of a mediating ideology which is strongly influential both in the construction of that autobiography and in our reading of it.

If Rose Allen's editor reveals the intention of accommodating class conflict, the Reverend John Garwood is even more explicit in his purposes *vis-à-vis* Mary Barber.[3] He writes the introduction after Mary Barber's death, with the primary intention of displaying a life which is 'an illustration of the wondrous manner in which the Lord provides for them who trust in Him.'[4] This kind of rhetoric, which situates Mary Barber within that convention of spiritual autobiography in which the life is a religious exemplum, reads rather against the grain of her self-perceptions of failed endeavour.[5] Mary Barber's own utilization of religious discourse, while it is certainly there, is not quite so confident. Doubts remain at the end: 'I fear to die. I have loved Thee, though feebly and faintly. I trust I have lived to Thee, but can I die to Thee? I fear! – I fear!'[6] Nevertheless, it is religious experience which sets out here to accommodate the experience of a working woman. Mary Barber and Rose Allen speak through these accommodating voices.

To return, however, to Ellen Weeton and Edward Hall. What is the effect of the accumulation of introductions, epilogues, forewords, commentaries? What is the effect of all this support? What, to push the implications a little further, is the effect of this male support (for I think we can assume, somehow, that J. J. Bagley, The University, Liverpool, is also male)? And, to return to the initial question: what is Edward Hall doing with Ellen Weeton?

In his introduction, Edward Hall produces his version of the social history which is the context of Ellen Weeton's writing. She was writing at a time which was a 'turning-point' in 'world history', when the population in the north (where she was living) was increasing 'alarmingly', and the towns were 'seething'.

> Lancashire miners were a byword; droves of vicious children from the southern workhouses arrived to mix and work 16 hours a day with still more vicious native-born children; weavers were breaking up their own looms for firewood, or breaking those in the factories out of spite or desperation.[7]

Into this drama of seething towns, vicious children, spiteful weavers and unspeakable miners, Edward Hall introduces our heroine, Nelly Weeton. 'Here we have the story of a woman who dared to protest.' Writing in the 1930s, Edward Hall thus enters into that research interest in 'feminism' (articulated as such in the 1930s) and in the lives of nineteenth-century women. As his reading of social history develops, it transpires that he wishes to locate Ellen Weeton as unique (literary value),[8] not only in relation to a troubled class history (vicious children, seething towns, etc.), but also in relation to a troubled gender history.

> The blue-stockings were dead, and who was there to take their place in defence of women's rights? Never had women been more suppressed. The history of that period at almost every point demonstrates the impotence of that sex – for the most part the silly mothers of a mighty race to follow.[9]

In this scenario, the woman who dares to protest, our heroine, is the celebrated unique voice, against the tide of 'dead blue-stockings', 'silly mothers', and an 'impotence' of the sex which has been part of the suppression of women's rights.

Edward Hall continues, throughout his introduction and his commentary, to be wildly partisan on Ellen Weeton's behalf. The terms of melodrama which surround the presentation of her as the literary heroine are extended to the other 'characters' in her life. Her brother is vindictive. Her husband is a villain. And although these are only the terms which Ellen Weeton presents herself, their being taken up by 'the man' constructs an additional set of gender relations for the text (the letters and the autobiographical sketches). I shall return to some of the effects of this relationship on our reading of some of Ellen Weeton's autobiographical utterances.

In these ways, in the 1930s, Edward Hall constructs a reading of Ellen Weeton which has its attachments to feminism, and to this extent, it is possible to be glad that he is sufficiently interested in 'the woman' to rescue her writings from the Wigan bookshop and to research them meticulously and thoroughly. But it is an attachment of the professional historian whose assumptions are about individuals, about rescuing the lone voice, though a woman from a sick class and gender history. While this reading might be seen to corroborate some of the self-perceptions of the autobiographers themselves (literary heroines, unique voices), it is nevertheless a reading which all too easily obscures, in that confederacy, those seams in the autobiographies from which it is possible to read off a less simplistic gender and class history.[10]

In the 1940s, Eric Gillett, the editor of Elizabeth Ham's autobiography, also attaches significance to feminism. 'The most acute anti-feminist will not read it without being convinced that every girl should be taught how to earn her living.'[11] Again, there seems to be some reason to be glad of this interest in women's experiences. But, just as Edward Hall presents us with a reductive social history, so it is possible to doubt (indeed almost impossible to do otherwise) some of Eric Gillett's capacity to make much of his researches into women's history when he tells us that, in presenting Elizabeth Ham's autobiography, he has omitted fifty thousand words of what he takes to be 'almost maudlin self-pity and inconsequential gossip'.[12] It is just possible, though this may be utopian or rash, to speculate that, in that fifty thousand words, in that 'self-pity' and 'gossip', there might have been some women's history of possible interest. Eric Gillett is not so much the academic historian, as a researcher for broadcasting, looking for material for the Home Service. Although the pragmatic 'cut' of broadcasting might explain in part the extent of the fifty-thousand-word omission, Eric Gillett is no less attached than academics to the literary value of the unique voice.

Life As We Have Known It, in which Mrs Layton's autobiography appears, is published in the 1930s (and again in the 1970s). Like Ellen Weeton's autobiographical writings, it is surrounded by commentators and editorial rationales. On this occasion, the interest is *of* women *in* women, which might make the gender relations less immediately suspect than the interest of men – Edward Hall, Eric Gillett – in espousing (apt term) women. There remains, however, a problem of class mediation. In the 1930s edition, Margaret Llewelyn Davies, as editor, writes an introductory note about the Women's Co-operative Guild from which the writings have emerged. Virginia Woolf writes an introductory letter (to Margaret Llewelyn Davies) after having been requested to write a preface. She explains in the letter that she is not writing a preface because books do not need prefaces.

The introductory note, albeit by Margaret Llewelyn Davies, is written from within the women's movement, about the Women's Guild from within the Women's Guild. 'Besides being primarily a record of individual experiences, the following Memories of Cooperative Women bring out the part that is played by the workers' own Movements in their everyday life.'[13] The introductory letter, from Virginia Woolf, who is also in the Guild, presents more significant difficulties. Virginia Woolf's initial judgement, as a professional writer, is that books should not need 'shoring up' with prefaces. She explains when she sees the material of the book, however, that she *will* write in response (not a preface, but a private letter). She thus responds as a woman to women's experiences (rather like Jane Carlyle to Mary Smith), with the clever extrication that the private letter can, with her permission, be presented as a preface. This 'having it both ways' is characteristic not only of that initial strategy – but of the letter itself. It requires more explication because it has a bearing in itself on the question of the gender relations of the literary production process.

Virginia Woolf is able to respond as a professional writer (albeit in a private letter) precisely because she does not take the women autobiographers to be professional writers. She responds because 'this book is not a book'. Books are only written by professional writers, and should not need prefaces. It is not only, furthermore, that the book is not a book, that the women are not professional writers, but also that professional criticism is not applicable to them. The application of what Virginia Woolf describes as 'professional' criteria of literary evaluation would be mistaken.

It cannot be denied that the chapters here put together do not make a book - that as literature they have many limitations. The writing, a literary critic might say, lacks detachment and imaginative breadth, even as the women themselves lacked variety and play of feature. Here are no reflections, he might object, no view of life as a whole, and no attempt to enter into the lives of other people.[14]

Women's autobiography here, it appears, does not constitute a book, does not constitute literature. A book would not need a preface. These writings do need a preface, because without the intervention of a professional writer, they do not add up to a book. The knot (double or triple bind) twists again, for it is in writing the preface that the book can be judged not to be a book.

These twists and turns, it transpires, are precisely because of Virginia Woolf's beliefs about art (about writing, about the professional writer and critic) in its class formations. 'Writing is a complex art, much infected by life.'[15] Art is of the middle classes, 'life' is of the workers:

Because the baker calls and we pay our bills with cheques, and our clothes are washed for us and we do not know the liver from the lights we are condemned to remain forever shut up in the confines of the middle classes, wearing tail coats and silk stockings, and called Sir or Madam as the case may be, when we are all, in truth, simply Johns and Susans. And they remain equally deprived. For we have as much to give them as they to give us – wit and detachment, learning and poetry, and all those good gifts which those who have never answered bells or minded machines enjoy by right.[16]

'We', the middle classes, are 'deprived' because of the limitations of our experience, because of our lack of 'life'. They, the workers, are 'deprived' because of their lack of art: 'wit and detachment, learning and poetry'. Virginia Woolf knows what privilege is ('good gifts' enjoyed 'by right'), but the class terms of art remain intact. Life, that infection, gives to art some qualities 'that the literate and instructed might envy', but art and professionalism remain the province of the middle classes. It should be possible for the middle classes to give art to the workers ('we have as much to give them as they to give us'), but that time has not yet arrived. 'The barrier is impassable'.

In revealing the class terms of the working women autobiographers' relations with literary production, Virginia Woolf accounts for the differences in class which explain her position as professional and their position as amateurs, while retaining a sense of the literary, and the professional, as criteria of evaluation superior to the writings. Virginia Woolf thus reveals her stake in professionalism in the very process of attempting to give credit to working women's lives and the restrictions of their class position.

For all that, Virginia Woolf does at least explicate the differentiated status in class between herself and the working women autobiographers, and she takes it to be important that any judgements she might make from this position in difference will have to be tempered and complicated by that understanding of difference. This is rather closer to an apt response, therefore, than the largely unexplicated position of Edward Hall, to whom I now return.

It is the academic historian, J. J. Bagley, who in the new introduction to *Miss Weeton's Journal of a Governess*, written in the 1960s, cements the critical relations between Ellen Weeton and Edward Hall, and the gender relations of woman autobiographer and professional historian. The literary terminology recurs. Ellen Weeton is again, for J. J. Bagley, the heroine, but on this occasion treated ironically. If the story, argues J. J. Bagley, were reconstructed by a 'lady novelist', it would make for stock melodrama, after which the reader ('he, or probably she') would repress a 'tear-stained smile' at 'a heroine' finding comfort in her final years. J. J. Bagley has got it, has found the literary in the life, has exposed fiction in autobiography. Ellen Weeton, he knows, was not just a heroine, but was a 'tough fighter', who 'could give as good as she was given'. Given that J. J. Bagley had sussed this plot, it is interesting that he then proceeds to reinscribe Ellen Weeton as heroine, because he is at pains to inscribe Edward Hall as hero. Edward Hall (not Ellen Weeton, note) is the 'true historian' of the piece and therefore the true hero. 'The fates . . . allowed the editorial prince to discover and give new life to his sleeping authoress exactly one hundred years after she had written the last extant page.'[17] The entry is from melodrama into another genre. The fairy tale constructs our hero, Edward Hall, the prince rescuing the sleeping princess. The true historian (now aided and abetted by that other true historian, J. J. Bagley himself: the men together) is the true hero.

J.J. Bagley, true historian of the 1960s, proceeds to develop his commitment to men as true historians. Now that he knows the truth (that Ellen Weeton was not a simple stereotype of melodramatic femininity, but may well have been rather 'a trial to her friends and relations'), he calls upon the corroborative evidence of other male witnesses in their capacities as true historians. What we really need, he proceeds to argue, is the view of the brother (who Edward Hall had found vindictive) and/or of the husband (who Edward Hall had found the villain). Ellen Weeton cannot quite be trusted. Edward Hall, however, can be trusted:

> With the instinct of a true historian, he has continued to search for more material – he comments upon this in the Epilogue to this present edition – and he has generously handed over the original manuscripts to Wigan Public Library, so that any future researcher can study the primary sources for himself.[18]

The men together (the himselves) set out in their search for that holy grail, woman: our heroine, Nelly Weeton.

These gender relations (such as those between Edward Hall and Ellen Weeton, between J. J. Bagley and Ellen Weeton, between J. J. Bagley and Edward Hall) are not confined, in their implications, to self-contained appurtenances (forewords, introductions, etc.) which can be ignored in a turn towards the 'text itself' in all its innocence. They are part of an editorial, research, and literary production process which constructs the text in particular ways. This can be seen clearly in Eric Gillett's treatment of Elizabeth Ham, precisely because he has admitted the omissions (fifty thousand words) and thereby explicated a certain kind of editorial process (the cut) which has clearly altered the original text, although we are teased by not knowing the quality of those alterations. Eric Gillett, however, is unusual only in his obviousness as a certain kind of editor. With Edward Hall and J. J. Bagley, it is possible to observe the same kind of process in their commentaries in the fabric of the text and, again, it is virtually impossible to read the text innocent of these mediating and constructing presences.

Density of commentary in *Miss Weeton's Journal of a Governess* nearly always occurs at moments of vulnerability. By that, I mean that on occasions when Ellen Weeton is venturing into subjects of social and sexual (in particular) delicacy or possible impropriety, the male commentators make their most forceful and sustained interventions. When Ellen Weeton is writing about a problematic marriage, characterized by domestic violence, her text can hardly move without encountering an explanatory, mediatory remark in the commentary.

> [Commentary] Aaron Stock was a dyspeptic; and there were then no front-page advertisements to speed him to immediate relief. To her infant daughter Miss Weeton was to write (in the course of a letter penned during her subsequent exile and loneliness)
> [Ellen Weeton] Your father, my love, had always better health when he had no supper; for when he had, he would be seized with vomiting, violent head-aches, could sleep but little, and no appetite for breakfast; yet became bloatedly fat, and was in danger of apoplexy.
> [Commentary] The 'danger of apoplexy' was, alas, more apparent than real. He had 'nervous irritations, he wriggled and twitched', and he had a blind partiality for walnuts; with the best intentions in the world, Miss Weeton would send him a small peace-offering of these, from her lonely lodgings, some years hence.
>   This, then, was the man of her choice; this, the consummation of her dreams.[19]

This is characteristic of the kind and quantity of intervention throughout this section of the text, where autobiographical experience is repeatedly at its most transparent in relation to that which is socially and sexually delicate. The commentary, it seems, is motivated by a desire to support the woman which includes explicating, on her behalf, the problem husband, and justifying ('with the best intentions in the world') *her* behaviour, (although Edward Hall does mention on one occasion that he himself, in a revealing identification with the imagined readership, is disturbed by some indelicacies, some 'nasty ideas' of Ellen Weeton's). As such, the commentary, again, constructs those gender relations which begin to seem so characteristic of the literary production process: the hero rescuing the heroine, protecting her virtue, defending her honour.

With a move towards some of the editorial processes of the 1970s and 1980s, particularly in those areas of literary production where the women's movement has begun to have some influence, it is possible to find some working women's autobiographies which have escaped some of the worst aspects of this treatment.

Anna Davin, who writes the new introduction, in 1977, to *Life As We Have Known It*, is rather more preoccupied with Virginia Woolf than with the autobiographers (the art thing), but she does locate interest in the autobiographies as being about significance in 'the history of ordinary people' (though the problems with 'ordinary' remain), in 'working class life' and 'the lives of women'.[20] Our interest is set against that of 'outsiders' ('clergymen, teachers, doctors, employers, charity workers'). Gaby Weiner, who writes the introduction, in 1983, to Harriet Martineau's *Autobiography*, takes as its starting-point a location in 'the long struggle for political equality which was to characterise the nineteenth century women's movement'.[21] Carolyn Steedman, who writes the introduction to *Jipping Street*, is also interested in the women's movement and 'working-class womanhood', though she is also rather concerned with dismissing descriptive categories – feminism, sociology, and even genre (autobiography itself) – in the attempt to place the text as 'underground literature'.[22]

To prefer these kinds of interventions, by women in the 1970s and 1980s, to those of Edward Hall and J. J. Bagley is, of course, to have an attachment to a particular history which gives significance to gender and class, to working-class lives in the nineteenth century and to the women's movement. That attachment has not, I hope, been veiled in my account. In explicitly signalling that preference and that attachment again, it seems impossible, now, in my account, to avoid (much as I would like to) some questions about my own interest in working women's autobiography and about the effects here, in this account, of my own constructions and reconstructions of the particular autobiographies quoted throughout my account.

Given that I have attached more than a little significance to some of the subjectivities and social relations, not least, gender relations, of epistemology and of the literary production process, it should at least be clear that I am not about to disclaim my own partialities or the limitations of my own account in a dramatic act of revelation, such as: will the real (THE REAL) Nelly Weeton now stand forth? Indeed, in having claimed and in continuing to claim a particular interest in the women's movement and in working-class history, my appropriations of the autobiographical texts may, for some people and by some criteria, be less acceptable than those, for instance, of Edward Hall. It is just possible to imagine, for instance, that Ellen Weeton herself might be happier with the gallant rescue of her individualism and of her literary uniqueness by that true historian, than she would be with an account which places her as a working woman (with particular sexual and social concerns and experience of employment patterns) alongside other nineteenth-century working women.

It might also be said, that I, afforded time by Jesus College, Cambridge, to do the research for this book, am the last person to point a finger at J. J. Bagley, The University, Liverpool, even though I have the excuse, in focusing on his gender attitudes, of surmising some influences of 'masculinity' on women writers and writers in general in the literary production process. It might even be thought (and this, of course, would be much more acceptable than an allegiance with J. J. Bagley) that I am, by virtue of my position, closer to Virginia Woolf in the professional, literary, production process than any of the autobiographers ever were, and that I am even more compromised by the art thing than Virginia Woolf in having gained access, though temporary, to an academic establishment.[23]

Having acknowledged, indeed confessed all this, I do not propose to leave the question (reluctant as I am to continue responding to autobiography with autobiography – I have tried to show how that is not always enough[24]) without producing some legitimations, by the criteria to which I attach significance, of my use in this book of working women's autobiographies.

The first of these is that I speak from a particular position in the women's movement, which has a particular interest in and investment in the history of that movement and in the gender and class terms of women's experiences in history. That investment, as I argue in my first chapter about the autobiographies, is about past-present relations, about memory (we are our memories) and about particular strategies for the survival of the women's movement. This investment is also, of course, about my own subjectivity (as woman, as writer, whatever) in the context of those concerns, in the contemporary and in history.

I make no excuse, therefore, for having thought of myself as a working woman. My sexual and social concerns and my employment patterns have been those of a working woman, which may be to say that the condition of twentieth-century working woman is a continuity, despite material improvements, from the nineteenth century. Both are characterized by sexual and marital ideologies which separate 'work' and 'home', which leave to women low-paid, short-term, part-time jobs, in employment patterns (with separate spheres, sex-segregated) not so very different from those of the nineteenth century. The fragmentations, discontinuities, insecurities, continue. And if I can indulge this special pleading, it is because I have had the help from women (perhaps there are beginning to be enough of us) and the luck (in the form of a DES grant) to be able to enter into the literary production process.

With that, it is time to lead back to nineteenth-century working women's autobiographies, and to some conclusions and implications about what has gone before, with reference to that same issue, the process of literary production.

AMATEURS

Virginia Woolf, in believing that *Life As We Have Known It* is not 'a book', not 'literature', inscribes herself as a professional writer and the autobiographers as amateurs who write, but do not write 'literature'. The autobiographies which constitute the collection *Life As We Have Known It* are not characterized, she argues, by literary merit. She thus enters, in a similar fashion to Edward Hall, Eric Gillett, J. J. Bagley, though somewhat more self-critically, as a professional writer (in her case a critic, in theirs, historians and broadcasters) in a self-consciously different relationship from that of the autobiographers, to the social relations of literary production and 'the social relations of intellectual production'.[25]

As a critic distinct from a social historian, Virginia Woolf gives significance to what she describes as the professional criteria of literary evaluation, and proceeds to find the autobiographers, by those criteria, lacking 'breadth', lacking 'detachment', and failing to be the producers of 'literature'. It is these judgements which sustain, in her account, Virginia Woolf as a professional, and the autobiographers as amateurs. And in being a critic (writer self-consciously assessing writers) it is in Virginia Woolf's response that qualities of the literary are particularly explicit.

It would be possible, now, to apply these professional criteria of literary evaluation to working women's autobiographies. A very brief outline of the kind of case which might be sustained for the autobiographies as 'literature' might be as follows. Mary Smith's metaphoric 'air castles' are at once poignant and ironic, utilized in the narrative as signifiers of recurringly thwarted aspirations against a background of material constraint. Her propensity for generalizing from the particular shows the 'imaginative breadth' which Virginia Woolf requires of 'literature'. Elizabeth Ham's images of childhood are strikingly modern in defying notions of narrative chronology. Mrs Layton, as in her juxtaposition of mansion and factory, utilizes resonant symbolization processes to produce an account of the tension between social classes which equals, in imaginative breadth, in literary merit, that kind of writing by Gaskell and Dickens. It would not be difficult to add to this list. Nor would it be difficult to present extensive, supportive illustration from the autobiographies.

To undertake this detailed exercise in literary evaluation would be, however, as indeed Virginia Woolf finds, somewhat spurious if not damaging. For what is important to the argument is not an assessment of the literary according to the professional criteria of literary evaluation (as Virginia Woolf, again, eventually finds), but a structural, cultural and political reading of why working women autobiographers have a different relationship to the conditions of literary production from professionals, and why they are seen as amateurs, which may amount to the same thing.

Mary Smith's editor, in attempting to describe the social, historical conditions in which her work is produced, places her as one of a number of 'clever amateurs'. As critical judgement by an editor (though he is anonymous, he is a professional), this is intended as a compliment, an enhancement of her position as writer – just as Edward Hall and others, in falling in love with their heroine writers, seek to compliment them (via gender: the man loves the woman) as writers.[26] To be complimented on being an 'amateur' is at least to be taken seriously as a *producer* (as if to say: she has done it, if not professionally) and to be described as 'clever' is also complimentary in a context of gender and class where sexual and social ideologies construct women, because of breeding, and working women in particular, as incapable of mental labour.

The problems, though, of being constructed as amateur, however clever, begin to show themselves as problems of sexual ideology and of the sexual division of labour. The mid-nineteenth century, as I have shown, is characterized by an enormous growth of the professional classes, an expansion of that work describing itself as professional. To be constructed as an amateur in a society which increasingly gives value to the professional, is either to be privileged above the need to work (the gentlemen and the players) or to be replaced firmly in the working class as not achieving, not being characterized by 'mental' work, professional work. To be an amateur, in relation to the hierarchy of labour in the nineteenth century, is thus to be privileged or to be working-class or a woman, to be thought to be characterized by something other than the particular activity in hand. Mary Smith, her editor seems to say, is a working woman who writes (little hobby, secondary activity).

It is an easy slide, in this scenario, to take amateur to connote inferiority. But, again, it will be seen that this is a class and gender judgement. When gentlemen produce as amateurs, they produce, it seems, quality. When working women produce as amateurs, they do not produce 'books' or 'literature'.

Virginia Woolf is therefore right when she begins to eschew the professional criteria of literary evaluation (even though she has somewhat spuriously defended her own position as writer by applying criteria of literary merit), not because the autobiographies cannot take a literary reading, but because she is approaching the real problem of gender differences produced in class. These are the real distinctions between her position as a writer and that of the working women autobiographers.

I have not yet detailed the peculiarly sexual or gender-linked aspect of the description, 'amateur', except in so far as I have hinted that gentlemen historians like to fall in love with, indeed make capital out of, working women: heroes and heroines; professionals and amateurs. There are fairly complex ramifications in the utilization of the term in relation to the sexual division of labour. The cultural construction of women's work, as I have shown, is such that it is characterized by part-time, low-paid, disrupted, discontinuous, coexisting jobs in a particular kind of perpetually fragmented, non-linear working life, in contrast with male occupational routes. I have also shown that what women take to be their work is not always sanctioned as their work by other judges. Genre sustains this process: women who think they are writers turn out to be cooks.[27] A notorious modern equivalent of this is how, when women enter into post-school education, even where this is full-time, it is taken by others to be the woman's hobby, not her work. This is the tautology which the sexual division of labour has created, that women cannot enter into the division of labour except as women (sex-segregated, separate sphere). Women cannot enter into professional work, except as amateurs. Class may at some point mediate this process (George Eliot and Virginia Woolf are professionals), but working women are too firmly fixed in class and gender categories to escape restriction. And, as I have said, the working classes are supposed to be manual not mental labourers, in a formation which compounds a sexual ideology which works against a capacity for mental activity in women.

It can be seen, then, that the definition of working women autobiographers as amateurs is about gender and class prejudice (of professionals) and about gender and class restriction. The literary functions, again, to sanction the class and gender attitudes of professionals. 'Imaginative breadth', that terminology, is the expression, but not the explication, of class difference. In other words, the artistic or literary judgement presents class differences as natural (with 'natural' differentiations in merit), as given, not to be questioned. The professional's judgement that, for instance, the writing lacks 'detachment', can therefore be seen as a judgement on a particular class or social group. It is *the life* of, for instance, the working woman (the lived practices as much as the text) which, for the professional, lacks detachment, lacks variety, lacks imaginative breadth. But this judgement is concealed in the literary one, that the failing is in the imagination, in the text, in the writing.

I have probably said enough, though, about how the professional criteria of writing (of the literary, of the professional writer, critic, historian) mediate class prejudices and assumptions. What is important, now, for feminists and socialists, is not only an exposure of these veiled assumptions, but an understanding of how sexual ideology and the sexual division of labour have structured, in the past, and continue to structure the ways in which people write and are read.

Perhaps it is time, therefore, to turn again to the working women autobiographers and to reassess or construct the space they occupy in relation to professional historians and other professional writers. I have argued in previous chapters that, in the narrating of particularly difficult areas of experience such as the sexual and the marital, working women autobiographers call upon a range of dominant discourses to find moral force and self-protection in the literary. I have also argued that the women's movement introduces and is part of the development of new discourses which are useful in finding, in writing, a greater flexibility of subjectivity than is possible from dominant discourses. And I have argued that, while working women share much with working men (in understandings of childhood, some of the family relations which centre upon the child, and experiences of schooling) their relationship to the literary production process is even more fraught, because of the double restriction of class and gender. Literature (to be a professional writer acclaimed for literary merit) remains largely an ideal unattained and unattainable, available to the gender (there are women writers, professionals), but not to the social group. It remains clear, too, that Literature is an incorporation of a number of features of individualism and class prejudice which is, at some moment, in tension with and possible contradiction to the intentions of working people's autobiographies to further the interests of a social group in ways which do not sacrifice that group to the individual.

While it does not seem possible to argue for working women a counter or oppositional culture in autobiography, it is possible to read from their writing something of the material and ideological detail often operating as restrictions in their lives and to find something of a basis from which to challenge some hierarchies in labour and in writing. In this sense, working women's autobiography, as a genre, is in tension with certain dominant literary modes in the historical production of writing and of knowledge. This tension resonates the latent oppositions of dominant and marginal versions of experience, secure and insecure cultural modes, fiction and autobiography itself, the professional and the amateur.

It is with that reminder of the autobiographers' supposed amateurism that it is necessary to turn back to some original questions about women and our supposed silences in history. It does seem to be the case that women of all classes have, in history, managed to write, despite all the material and ideological constraints on doing so.[28] What seems nearer to the issue of 'silence' is that, while women have managed to write, we have not necessarily been read. That is indeed a kind of silence. It is necessary, therefore, to glimpse the beginnings of a theory about why working women's writings have not been read. Some readers will be content with arguments about the failure of these writings to achieve literary merit. Others may argue that in writing autobiography (that particular genre[29]), working women have 'doomed' themselves to be the unread.[30] Others will be content, with justice, to itemize, as I have tried to do, some of the reasons why women, except from certain classes at certain historical moments, have been unlikely to enter into the professional literary production process as publishing writers.

It is necessary, however, to attempt to take the argument further by raising more questions. Why have working women's autobiographies been infrequently read even where they have been published? Why have working women's autobiographies, in the case of some texts, been left to accumulate dust on library shelves? Why is it only recently that a number of nineteenth-century working women's autobiographies have been published? And will the 1970s and 1980s be seen as a time when, rather like the 1840s and 1850s, it was temporarily and ephemerally (a passing fashion, as some would have it) possible to publish some working women's autobiography?[31]

I would hazard the theory that an important reason for this neglect is precisely that the experience of working women, our lives, our writing, remains categorized in culture as amateur. Our subjectivities remain constructed in culture as amateur to professional, as relative, as dependent, as secondary, as second-rate; the second sex.

Rather than finish with that bleak thought, however, I will turn to some thoughts about what the autobiographies achieve, despite restrictions, despite limitation, in a cultural and political frame.

> [Here, in] Sir Winston Churchill's extended autobiographical account of the Second World War . . . . a sense of personal significance and 'historic role' is asserted in almost megalomaniac proportions, but the accounts that follow, though certainly personally revealing, are rarely self-consciously so, and remain locked up within an upper-class military and high-political culture and a highly mythical Conservative version of national character and history.
>
> 'Representativeness' in our sense, is *more* likely to be found in popular autobiographical forms where dominant social relations are viewed from the typical subject position: that of daily oppressions and of the struggle against them. Representativeness, moreover, is a feature of social positions that are understood to be *shared* and *collective*: the main feature of much autobiographical writing is to *distinguish* the author from the people and the determinations that surround him. Such accounts belong not to the construction of 'popular memory', but to the reproduction and dissemination of 'dominant memory', of which the Churchillian myth is indeed a salient and persistent modern feature.[32]

While some of this is too simple (that which is shared and collective is not always given, not always obvious, but has to be fought for and most autobiographical writing is 'compromised' at some point by 'dominant memory' in the literary), it captures the centrality of the political arguments to our readings of working women's autobiographies.

'Representativeness' *is* a characteristic of the autobiographies, emerging from 'daily oppressions and . . . the struggle against them'. This 'representativeness' is available to be read out from particular features: a transparency in matters sexually and socially delicate, a description of work which subscribes to the genre (the domestic servant, the cook, etc.) while living a more complex subjectivity, a repetition and incantation of self-destruction, of attempted suicide, of sickness, which threatens the narrative direction with entropy, an intense preoccupation (even in the metonym, 'losing caste') with exigency and insecurity.

Perhaps it is now possible to allow the autobiographers some of their individuality, that which 'distinguishes' as well as that which is 'representative'. Perhaps it is possible to allow Mary Smith her 'air castles' and her particular dislike of needlework, to allow Ellen Weeton the distinguishing characteristic of playing the flageolet when low-spirited, to allow Elizabeth Ham her midnight walks, half-dressed and wrapped in a cloak. After all, why separate 'personal significance' from the 'shared and collective'? Why leave all the 'distinguished' authors to 'dominant memory'? There is no need to diminish subjectivity in representativeness. It is the Right's mythologies about the Left which do that.[33]

To retain subjectivity in representativeness, I now make the cultural leap to the contemporary twentieth century and present Diane Harpwood, diarist rather than autobiographer, but working woman. The historical continuity with nineteenth-century working women's autobiography, in experience, in form, is there. The leap is not such a leap. The 'progress' is not always as much as we think it. Those judgements, though, are not really for me alone to make in conclusion. I therefore leave a working woman autobiographer the last word.

Decided to leave David before lunch today. I mean that. Before lunch today I decided that I would leave David at some time in the future when the children are old enough not to be affected by the split. I'm dying to tell him. I was seething, he made me furious, laying about in bed till past eleven then lolling around on the settee with a book till twelve by which time I'd fed and dressed the children, put the dinner on, washed the kitchen floor, washed mine and Lucy's hair, got steaming mad and finally accepted that there is no way he is going to change. All the things I did this morning aren't considered as work, they're just things that get done. His mother never complained so why should I? I'm not supposed to object to doing them, I'm supposed to subdue my spirit and rebellion at the unfairness of it all, subdue the bits that aren't already numbed by Valium, that is. I'm not even supposed to think it's unfair that I work and he rests. This weekend he is supposed to be laying the bathroom carpet. It's a wonder the children haven't got splinters in their feet. We've had it for six months. I was hoping he'd fill the holes in the dining room walls as well so that I could start decorating. We've had the paint longer than we've had the bathroom carpet.

If I tell him how I feel I'm accused of nagging and he looks innocent as if I was at fault and he was forgiving me.

I am a bad-tempered cow on Sundays and he did lay the carpet eventually, you can't see the joins. And if I did leave him, where would I go?

I feel trapped and I rail against my captivity and against the fact that there's never enough of anything from coffee to time off, and against the trivia that makes up my life. Oceans of anger and resentment will not change anything except me. I think maybe it's better left below the surface, admitting it serves no useful purpose. I don't want to be a crabbed bitter unhappy woman. It's important that I'm not. On me hangs the responsibility for building our family and that's a highly valued construction.

But cooking and cleaning things can't be important. No one pays them any attention except other women, and women in general aren't important, no one really gives what they do any attention, except other women.[34]

Notes

INTRODUCTION

1. Cynthia Cockburn, 'The Material of Male Power', *Feminist Review,* 9 (Autumn, 1981), p. 84.
2. Geoff Esland, 'Professions and Professionalism' in *The Politics of Work and Occupations*, edited by Geoff Esland and Graeme Salaman (Milton Keynes: Open University Press, 1980), p. 216.
3. Raymond Williams, 'Ideology' in *Marxism and Literature* (Oxford: Oxford University Press, 1977), chapter 4.
4. Catherine Belsey, *Critical Practice* (London: Methuen, 1980), chapters 2 and 3.

1 OUTRAGEOUS CLAIMS

1. Ivan Illich, *Gender* (London and New York: Marion Boyars, 1983), p. 79 quotes Burton S. Bledstein, *The Culture of Professionalism* (New York: Norton, 1976).
2. Illich, p. 79 quotes Christopher Lasch, *The New York Review of Books*, 24 November 1977, pp. 15-18.
3. Illich, p. 79 quotes John L. McKnight, *The Mask of Love: Professional Care in the Service Economy* (New York, London: Marion Boyars, 1983).
4. Illich, p. 79.
5. E. H. Hunt, *British Labour History 1815-1914*, London: Weidenfeld and Nicolson, 1981), p. 30:

    Most of the contraction in agriculture's share of employment after 1850 was taken up by expansion in the service, or 'tertiary', sector . . . civil servants and local

government workers and those helping to provide
professional, administrative, and commercial services to
British Industry and to much of the rest of the world.

6.   *OED* entries for nineteenth century for 'professional'
     and 'professionalism' reflect that emphasis.
7.   Alfred Sohn-Rethel, editorial introduction to 'Science
     as alienated consciousness', *Radical Science Journal*,
     2/3, p. 65 (1975) quotes E. P. Thompson.
8.   Antonio Gramsci, 'The Intellectuals' in *Selections from
     the Prison Notebooks*, edited by Geoffrey Nowell Smith
     and Quintin Hoare (London: Lawrence and Wishart,
     1971.)
9.   Gramsci, 'On Education', pp. 42 and 43.
10. Raymond Williams, 'Danger: Intellectuals!', *Guardian*,
     Thursday 1 July 1982 'Guardian Books:

         Most modern English complaints about intellectuals are
         based precisely on their habit of intervening in public
         affairs in which they have no official standing or practical
         experience. It is different when they are perceived as
         what they usually also are: professional people, who can
         give an informed opinion on some matter in dispute.
         Indeed, in orthodox English life, respect for profession-
         al opinions coexists with disrespect for merely intellec-
         tual opinions.

11. Bob Young, 'Science *is* social relations', *Radical Science
     Journal*, 5, 1977.
12. Gramsci, 'On Education', p. 36.
13. James Robertson, *Power, Money and Sex* (London:
     Marion Boyars, 1976), p. 74.
14. Virginia Olesen and Elvi W. Whittaker, 'Critical notes
     on sociological studies of professional socialization', in
     J. A. Jackson, editor, *Professions and Professionaliza-
     tion* (Cambridge: Cambridge University Press, 1970), p.
     181.
15. J. D. Milne, *Industrial and Social Position of Women, in
     the Middle and Lower Ranks* (London: Chapman and
     Hall, 1857), p. 105, quotes G. M. J. B. Legouvé,

Histoire des Femmes translated in *Westminster Review*, July 1850.

16. The archaic form, 'being female', may be a useful way of understanding 'femininity' here.
17. Legouvé.
18. Milne, pp. 9, and 8 to 19.
19. Barbara Ehrenreich and Deirdre English, *For Her Own Good* (New York, London: Pluto Press, 1978 and 1979), chapter 4.
20. Virginia Woolf, 'Professions for Women' in *The Death of the Moth*, posthumous publication edited by Leonard Woolf (London: Hogarth Press, 1942), pp. 149-54.
21. Woolf, p. 153.
22. A. M. Carr-Saunders and P. A. Wilson, *The Professions* (London: Clarendon Press, 1933), voice this idealism, p. 491:

    > Professional associations are stabilizing elements in society. They engender modes of life, habits of thought, and standards of judgement which render them centres of resistance to crude forces which threaten steady and peaceful evolution.

23. Woolf, p. 153.
24. Anna Coote and Beatrix Campbell, *Sweet Freedom* (London: Pan, 1982), p. 48.
25. To describe Margaret Thatcher as a man, which some people do, may be misplaced, but signifies (from feminists) that she has known when to camouflage gender in the interest of individualism. (This does not mean that she does not also utilize certain representations of 'femininity', being female.) This study has begun. For an example see Angela Carter, 'Masochism for the Masses', *New Statesman*, 3 June 1983.
26. T. J. Johnson, *Professions and Power* (London: Papermac, 1972). Johnson argues that nineteenth-century professionalism has its basis in social class rather than specialism and that it 'followed the rise to power of an urban middle class'. See chapter 3, about occupational control.

27. Ivan Waddington, 'General Practitioners and Consultants in early 19th Century England', in John Woodward and David Richards, editors *Health Care and Popular Medicine in 19th-Century England* (London: Croom Helm, 1977), p. 164.

28. Waddington.

29. 'divinity, law and medicine' ('the military' appears in *OED* as a possible fourth 'learned profession'): education in the learned professions was preparation for Government: the professionals *were* the governors.

30. Cecil Woodham-Smith, *Florence Nightingale* (Harmondsworth: Penguin, second edition, 1955), p. 113.

31. George Dawson, *Lancet*, I, 1855, p. 250.

32. *Lancet*, p. 250.

33. 'Ideological capital' introduced to me by Susanne Kappeler, Senior Lecturer in English at the University of Rabat, in lengthy correspondence about the professions, about Cambridge University and many other matters of ideology.

34. Karl Figlio, 'Chlorosis and chronic disease in nineteenth-century Britain: the social constitution of somatic illness in a capitalist society', *Social History*, vol. 3, no. 2, May 1978, pp. 167-70.

35. See my article, 'Falling Short With Marx', in *LTP* (journal of literature teaching politics) no. 3, 1984.

36. Figlio, pp. 167-70.

37. W. J. Reader, *Professional Men: the Rise of the Professional Classes in 19th-Century England* (London: Weidenfeld and Nicolson), 1966), quotes H. Byerley Thomson (1857), preface to chapter 1.

38. Karl Figlio, 'Sinister Medicine? A Critique of Left Approaches to Medicine', *Radical Science Journal*, 9, 1979, raises the issue of Medicine under socialism, pp. 65-6.

39. Stuart Hall, 'Culture and the state' in 'The State and Popular Culture', *Popular Culture U203* (Milton Keynes: Open University Press, 1982) p. 19.

40. Barbara Taylor, *Eve and the New Jerusalem* (London: Virago, 1983), p. 146.

41. Virginia Woolf, *A Room of One's Own,* first published 1929 (London: Granada, 1980), p. 27.
42. A. S. Collins, *The Profession of Letters 1780-1832* (London: G. Routledge & Sons, 1928), p. 22.
43. Collins, p. 128, and 'The condition of authors in England, Germany and France', *Fraser's Magazine*, 35, 1847, p. 285.
44. Robert L. Patten, *Charles Dickens and his Publishers* (Oxford: Clarendon Press, 1978), quotes *Boswell's Life of Johnson*, 1776, chapter 1.
45. Patten, p. 55.
46. Rachel Harrison, '*Shirley*: relations of reproduction and the ideology of romance', in *Women Take Issue* (Women's Studies Group, Centre for Contemporary Cultural Studies) (London: Hutchinson, 1978), p. 178.
47. Cynthia Cockburn, 'The Material of Male Power', *Feminist Review*, 9, Autumn 1981, for more on 'the material aspect'.
48. Fraser, p. 285.
49. Virginia Woolf, *Orlando*, (London: Granada, 1977) first published 1928, p. 175.

2 GEORGE ELIOT: MAN AT WORK AND THE MASCULINE PROFESSIONAL

1. Raymond Williams, *Keywords* (Glasgow: Fontana, 1976), pp. 32-5.
2. Charles Kingsley, *Alton Locke*, first published 1850 (London: Cassell, 1967), p. 323.
3. George Eliot, *Adam Bede*, first published 1859 (London: J. M. Dent, 1906) p. 8.
4. *Adam Bede*, p. 174.
5. *Adam Bede*, p. 43.
6. *Adam Bede*, pp. 149-50.
7. *Adam Bede*, p. 232-3.
8. As in *Janet's Repentance*, *Scenes of Clerical Life*, first published 1858 (London: J. M. Dent, 1910).
9. *Adam Bede*, p. 146.
10. *Adam Bede*, p. 153.

11.   *Adam Bede*, p. 433.
12.   George Eliot, *Middlemarch,* first published 1871-2, (Harmondsworth: Penguin, 1965), p. 853.
13.   It is important to note, though, that the 'bad' woman is still in attachment with the 'good' man, one mediating the other (each mediation with its gender-specific aspect): tolerance of Lydgate depends on intolerance of Rosamond.
14.   *Middlemarch*, p. 179.
15.   *Middlemarch*, p. 810.
16.   George Eliot, *Romola*, first published 1863 (London: J. M. Dent, 1907), p. 50.
17.   *Romola*, p. 62.
18.   Ruby Redinger, *George Eliot: the Emergent Self* (New York: 1975; Bodley Head, London: 1976), quoting John W. Cross, p. 361.

3   Representational Responsibilities in Dickens

1.   *Fraser's Magazine*, 'The condition of authors in England, Germany and France', vol. 35, April 1847, p. 285.
2.   Gordon N. Ray, editor, *The Letters and Private Papers of W. M. Thackeray*, I (London: Oxford University Press, 1945), p. cxx. Thackeray, among others, found Dickens 'vulgar'.
3.   See *Fraser's Magazine* and chapter 1, 'Outrageous Claims'.
4.   Robert L. Patten, *Charles Dickens and his Publishers* (Oxford: Clarendon Press, 1978), chapter 1.
5.   See chapter 1, 'Outrageous Claim'.
6.   Patten, chapter 1.
7.   Patten, p. 12: from a letter of Dickens to Thackeray in 1843.
8.   Dickens editions used in this piece:
     David Copperfield (1850) (London: Ballantyne Press, Waverley, 1912).
     Bleak House (1853) (Harmondsworth: Penguin, 1971).
     Dombey and Son (1848) (Harmondsworth: Penguin, 1970).

Martin Chuzzlewit (1843) (London: Ballantyne, Waverley, *c.* 1912).

Gradgrind in *Hard Times* (1854) (Harmondsworth: Penguin, 1969)

Headstone in *Our Mutual Friend* (1865) (London: Ballantyne, Waverley, *c.* 1912).

Circumlocution Office in *Little Dorrit* (1857) (Harmondsworth: Penguin, 1967).

9. *Chuzzlewit*, I, pp. 222-3.
10. *Chuzzlewit*, I, p. 203.
11. *Chuzzlewit*, I, p. 208.
12. *Chuzzlewit*, II, p. 20.
13. *Dombey*, pp. 53-4.
14. Kate Millett, 'The Debate over Women' in Martha Vicinus, editor, *Suffer and Be Still*, 1980 (London: Methuen, Indiana: Indiana University Press, 1972), p. 122:

> Dickens, for example, achieved a nearly perfect indictment of both patriarchy and capitalism in *Dombey and Son* – a novel virtually inspired by the phenomenon of prenatal preference, and a superb illustration of Engels' statements on the subordination of women within the system of property.

15. *Dombey*, p. 70.
16. *Dombey*, p. 142.
17. Raymond Williams, *The Country and the City* (London: Chatto & Windus, 1973), chapter 16.
18. *Copperfield*, II, p. 273 and I, p. 7.
19. *Copperfield*, II, p. 276.
20. 'Outrageous Claims', see chapter 1.
21. *Bleak House*, p. 291.
22. 'Outrageous Claims'.
23. 'Outrageous Claims'.
24. Cecil Woodham-Smith, *Florence Nightingale* (Harmondsworth: Penguin, 1955), chapter 4.
25. Woodham-Smith, p. 305.
26. Woodham-Smith, p. 63.
27. Woodham-Smith, p. 62.

28. Woodham-Smith, p. 83, quoting from Florence Nightingales novel *Cassandra*.
29. Woodham-Smith, p. 83.
30. Woodham-Smith, p. 238.
31. The second half of the nineteenth century, often held to be a period of greater stability than the first fifty years, was in many ways a period of greater intractability for women, as it may have been for working men, perhaps because the 1867 Reform Act inscribed the powerlessness of the majority of the population.
32. Woodham-Smith, p. 328.
33. Woodham-Smith, p. 338.
34. John Ruskin, 'Of Queens' Gardens' in *Sesame and Lilies* (London: Nelson, 1865) for 'the sweet approving smile' that is meant to be 'woman': but also, see Dickens.
35. Nightingale's own perception of the feminine ideal was that it made for disastrous working relationships. On the employment of 'ladies' as nurses, she objects: 'It ends in nothing but spiritual flirtation between the ladies and the soldiers.' Woodham-Smith, p. 147.
36. *Chuzzlewit*, I, p. 243.
37. *Chuzzlewit*, II, p. 295.
38. Woodham-Smith, p. 107.
39. *Copperfield*, I, chapter 25: good and bad angels, Agnes and Steerforth.
40. *Copperfield*, II, p. 49.
41. *Dorrit*, p. 111.
42. *Dorrit*, pp. 279-80.
43. *Dorrit*, p. 285.
44. *Dorrit*, p. 288.
45. *Dorrit*, p. 278.
46. *Dorrit*, p. 291.
47. *Dorrit*, p. 291.
48. *Dorrit*, p. 341.

4 THE GENTLEMAN'S CLUB, LITERATURE

1. Lewis Melville, *Some Aspects of Thackeray* (Boston: Little, Brown & Co., 1911), quoting Thackeray in

defence of *Pendennis* (see note 7), p. 5.
2. Melville, p. 13.
3. Melville, p. 5.
4. *Fraser's Magazine*, 'The condition of authors in England, Germany and France', April 1847, p. 285.
5. Melville, pp. 18-19.
6. As distinct from taking Thackeray to be more significant in relation to the eighteenth century than the nineteenth century.
7. William Thackeray, *Pendennis*, first published 1848-50 (Harmondsworth: Penguin, 1972), p. 348.
8. *Pendennis*, p. 349.
9. *Fraser*, p. 285.
10. *Pendennis*, p. 392.
11. *Fraser* as traced in chapter 1, 'Outrageous Claims'.
12. Robert L. Patten, *Charles Dickens and his Publishers* (Oxford: Clarendon Press, 1978), p. 12.
13. Gordon N. Ray, editor, *The Letters and Private Papers of W. M. Thackeray* (London: Oxford University Press, 1945), II (of 4 volumes), letters 394-7.
14. Melville, pp. 19-21.
15. The gender and class meanings of that term in the nineteenth century being signally about aristocratic and bourgeois males developing some community of interest.
16. Gordon Ray, *The Buried Life* (London: Oxford University Press, 1952), chapter 2.
17. *Pendennis*, p. 266.
18. *The Letters and Private Papers*, II, letter 202.
19. John Ruskin, 'Of Queens' Gardens' in *Sesame and Lilies* (London: Nelson, 1865): and Coventry Patmore, *The Angel in the House* (London: George Bell & Sons, 1905).
20. Ruskin, p. 157.
21. Ray, (*The Buried Life*), p. 36.
22. Ray, p. 31.
23. *Pendennis*, pp. 227-8.
24. *Pendennis*, pp. 49, 55.

25. *Pendennis*, p. 552.
26. Chapter 1, 'Outrageous Claims'.
27. *Pendennis*, pp. 170-1.
28. *The Letters and Private Papers*, biographical memoranda, p. cvi.
29. *The Letters and Private Papers*, biographical memoranda, p. xciii.
30. Mrs Trollope made more money from writing fiction than her son Anthony did (an example frequently given by male critics defending Anthony).
31. Although Gaskell does not appear to have utilized her choice of pen-name, Stephen Benwick.
32. Currer Bell, 'Biographical Notice of Ellis and Acton Bell', editor's preface to the new 1850 edition, reprinted with Emily Brontë, *Wuthering Heights* (Harmondsworth: Penguin, 1965), p. 31.
33. This is not to say that all nineteenth-century critics are male, but it does seem to be the case, as might be expected, that women critics adopt the common gender-specific prejudices. It is a woman critic who, for instance, judges *Jane Eyre* the work of a woman who must have forfeited the company of her own sex (see note 42).
34. Patten, p. 21.
35. Mrs Gaskell, *The Life of Charlotte Brontë*, first published 1857 (London: J. M. Dent, 1908), p. 102.
36. Gaskell, p. 104.
37. Gaskell, p. 104.
38. Currer Bell, 'Biographical Notice' etc.
39. Gaskell, p. 104.
40. Gaskell, p. 105 and 106.
41. J. A. V. Chapple, *Elizabeth Gaskell: Portrait in Letters* (Manchester: Manchester University Press, 1980), p. 127.
42. Gaskell, (*The Life of Charlotte Brontë*), p. vii.
43. Gaskell, p. 374.
44. J. A. V. Chapple and A. Pollard, editors, *The Letters of Mrs Gaskell* (Manchester: Manchester University Press, 1966), letter 451.
45. Chapple and Pollard, letter 451.

46. Chapple and Pollard, letter 151.
47. Chapple and Pollard, letter 148.
48. Chapple and Pollard, letter 150.
49. Compare, for instance, reactions to *Mary Barton* and *Ruth* with those to Disraeli's *Sybil* or Dickens' *Hard Times*.
50. Chapple and Pollard, letter 148.
51. Just as to find woman an angel is to deny woman power. See chapter 1 'Outrageous Claims'.
52. Chapple and Pollard, letter 41.
53. Chapple and Pollard, letter 87.
54. Chapple and Pollard, letter 148.
55. Elizabeth Gaskell, *Mary Barton*, first published 1848 (Harmondsworth: Penguin, 1970), preface, p. 38.
56. *Mary Barton*, p. 95.
57. J. A. V. Chapple, *Elizabeth Gaskell*, p. 129.
58. Dickens once professed that if he were Mr Gaskell, he would not be able to resist beating Mrs Gaskell. This was at a time when Dickens was in negotiation with Gaskell about the editing and publishing of some of her work.
59. Chapple and Pollard, letter 451a.

5 WORKING WOMEN AUTOBIOGRAPHERS

1. Mary Smith, *Schoolmistress and Nonconformist*, I (of 2 volumes), *Autobiography* (London and Carlisle: Benrose & Sons, 1892). Mary Smith's editor describes her as one of this number of 'clever amateur writers', p. 302.
2. David Vincent, *Bread, Knowledge and Freedom: a Study of 19th-Century Working Class Autobiography* (London: Methuen, 1982), quotes Roy Pascal, p. 36.
3. David Vincent.
4. David Vincent, p. 40 and p. 8 ('The one major silence is that of women').
5. Raymond Williams, *Writing in Society* (London: Verso, 1983), p. 214, for comment on the problems of working 'from a central base in literary criticism':

    Yet it has been clear from the 1930s, and obvious from

the late 1950s, that many other kinds of knowledge and
analysis have to be drawn on if the work is to be properly
done, and that instead of relatively isolated forays from
some presumed and then increasingly specialized centre, there has to be a more open and equal-standing
convergence of independent disciplines, seeking to
make their evidence and their questions come together
in a common inquiry.

6. Sheila Rowbotham, *Dreams and Dilemmas* (London:
    Virago, 1983), p. 216.
7. Sheila Rowbotham, p. 217.
8. James Cameron, *Witness* (London: Gollancz, 1966), pp.
    26-7.
9. Sheila Rowbotham, p. 216.
10. Sheila Rowbotham, p. 216.
11. Centre for Contemporary Cultural Studies, *Making
    Histories* (London: Hutchinson, 1982). 'Popular mem-
    ory: theory, politics, method', p. 205: 'In this article we
    explore an approach to history-writing which involves
    becoming "historians of the present too".'
12. Barbara Taylor, *Eve and the New Jerusalem* (London:
    Virago, 1983), p. 182.
13. David Vincent, p. 10.
14. Gareth Stedman Jones, *Languages of Class* (Cam-
    bridge: Cambridge University Press, 1983), introduc-
    tion, for some reservations about 'class consciousness' as
    a pre-existing category, p. 12.
15. F. R. Leavis, *How to Teach Reading: Primer for Ezra
    Pound* (Cambridge: Gordon Fraser, 1932), p. 19, also
    pp. 38-41.
16. David Vincent, p. 10.
17. Graham Martin, introduction to Block 4, 'Form and
    meaning', *Popular Culture* (Open University course,
    Milton Keynes, 1981), p. 3, for a refinement of the
    distinction between 'text' and 'lived culture':

    The distinction between 'practices' and 'texts' is, of
    course, far from absolute. 'Going to the movies' would
    have to be called a 'practice', and yet without a

consideration of 'texts' (that is, the films) which are at the centre of the 'practice', analysis wouldn't get far . . . 'Texts', that is, exist within 'practices', and should not be conceived as discrete entities to be considered in isolation. Nevertheless, the distinction is useful both in marking out an important difference between 'practices' wholly independent upon the existence of 'texts', such as reading, watching television, going to the movies, listening to records or going to concerts, and other 'practices' in which 'texts' play a lesser role, or none at all.

18. David Vincent, p. 133.
19. David Vincent, p. 2.
20. David Vincent, p. 8.
21. M. A. S. Barber (Mary Barber), *Bread-Winning or the Ledger and the Lute: an Autobiography* (London: William Macintosh, 1865), p. 4.
22. Mary Barber, p. 4.
23. Rose Allen, *The Autobiography of Rose Allen* (London: Longman & Co., 1847), p. 14.
24. Mary Barber, p. 29.
25. Mary Smith, p. 29 to 32.
26. Elizabeth Ham, *Elizabeth Ham by Herself 1783-1820* (London: Faber, 1945), p. 29.
27. Rose Allen, p. 98.
28. Mrs Layton (no initial), *Memories of Seventy Years (London 1931) in Life as We Have Known it*, edited by Margaret Llewelyn Davies (London, Virago, 1977), pp. 26-7.

6 'WOMEN'S ISSUES'

1. Margery Spring Rice, *Working-Class Wives*, first published 1939 (London: Virago, 1981). *Maternity: Letters from Working Women*, edited by Margaret Llewelyn Davies, first published 1915 (London: Virago, 1978).
2. It might sound like a contradiction to argue that a move towards the gender-specific is a move towards subjectivity, but in a certain kind of gender politics it must be,

which is of course to say that my account has its partialities (and will therefore operate those partialities in the understanding of subjectivity), but is prepared to articulate that partiality and to attach significance to its limitations.

3.   This is to shorthand what is now a whole debate about how far 'experience', in reading history, is constituted in text. For different aspects of the argument, see: Raymond Williams, *Problems in Materialism and Culture* (London: Verso, 1980). Gareth Stedman Jones, *Languages of Class* (Cambridge: Cambridge University Press, 1983).

4.   Mary Smith, *Schoolmistress and Nonconformist*, I (of 2 volumes), *Autobiography* (London and Carlisle: Bemrose & Sons, 1892), p. 196.

5.   Ellen Weeton, *Miss Weeton's Journal of a Governess*, 1969, a reprint of *Miss Weeton: Journal of a Governess*, first published under the title of *Miss Weeton* by the Oxford University Press in 1936, I, p. 3.

6.   Rose Allen, *The Autobiography of Rose Allen* (London: Longman & Co., 1847).

7.   Elizabeth Ham, *Elizabeth Ham by Herself 1783-1820* (London: Faber, 1945), pp. 106-7.

8.   Elizabeth Ham, p. 107.

9.   Elizabeth Ham, p. 212.

10. Elizabeth Ham, p. 187 and 185.

11. Ellen Johnston, *Autobiography of Ellen Johnston, 'The Factory Girl'* (Glasgow: William Love, 1867), p. 8.

12. Ellen Weeton, I, pp. 28-30.

13. Ellen Johnston, p. 62.

14. Ellen Weeton, II (of 2 volumes), p. 140.

15. Mary Ann Ashford, *Life of a Licensed Victualler's Daughter* (London: Saunders & Otley, 1844), pp. 45-6.

16. 'The literary' used throughout to imply an accumulation of genres in a sanctioning morality (deriving from writing of 'right' value). My next chapter elaborates.

17. Mary Smith, p. 65.

18. Instance: Barbara Taylor, *Eve and the New Jerusalem* (London: Virago, 1983).

19. Barbara Taylor.
20. Ellen Johnston, p. 14.
21. In my next chapter about working and writing.
22. Mary Ashford, pp. 64-6.
23. Florence White, *A Fire in the Kitchen: the Autobiography of a Cook* (London: J. M. Dent & Sons, 1938), p. 92.
    Rebecca West, p. 82.
    'feminist ideas', p. 244.
24. Annie Kenney, *Memories of a Militant* (London: E. Arnold & Co., 1924), p. v. 'no home-life', p. 110, 'some of the meetings', p. 103.
25. Mary Smith, p. 257.
26. Mary Smith, II, pp. 156-9.

7 AN ITCH FOR SCRIBBLING

1. This understanding of the literary as the moral has its different inflections, but also its continuities in writings about culture from the mid-nineteenth century until now. Notable in this tradition are:
   Matthew Arnold, *Culture and Anarchy*, 1869 (the literary sustains the civilized in countering anarchy)
   F. R. Leavis, *The Great Tradition*, 1948 and
   The Common Pursuit, 1952 (the 'intelligent' and 'sensitive' decide the literary)
   and for the critique:-
   Raymond Williams, *Culture and Society 1780-1950*, 1958
   Politics and Letters, 1979
   where the literary is 'the court of appeal' for right value and where the literary possesses the same kind of spell as the 'divine' in feudal society.
2. Ellen Johnston, *Autobiography of Ellen Johnston, 'The Factory Girl'* (Glasgow: William Love, 1867), p. 5.
3. Ellen Johnston, p. 7.
4. Florence White, *A Fire in the Kitchen: the Autobiography of a Cook* (London: J. M. Dent & Sons, 1938), p. 17.
5. Kathleen Woodward, *Jipping Street*, first published 1928 (London: Virago, 1983).
6. David Vincent, *Bread, Knowledge and Freedom: a Study of 19th-Century Working Class Autobiography*

(London: Methuen, 1982), pp. 177-93. (The pursuit of knowledge can set up tensions in working men's lives, encouraging 'a retreat from a reality which was becoming increasingly transparent'.)

7.   M. (Mary) A. S. Barber, *Bread-Winning or The Ledger and the Lute: An Autobiography* (London: William Macintosh, 1865), pp. 46-7.

8.   Ellen Weeton, *Miss Weeton's Journal of a Governess*, 1969, a reprint of *Miss Weeton: Journal of a Governess*, first published under the title of *Miss Weeton* by the Oxford University Press in 1936, I (of 2 volumes), p. 9.

9.   Elizabeth Ham, *Elizabeth Ham by Herself 1783-1820*, (London: Faber, 1945), p. 183.

10.   Kathleen Woodward, p. 137.

11.   Sheila M. Smith, 'John Overs to Charles Dickens: A Working-Man's letter and its implications', *Victorian Studies* (1974-1975), 18, number 2.

12.   Mrs Gaskell, *The Life of Charlotte Brontë*, first published 1857 (London: J. M. Dent, 1974), p. 97: from 'So Charlotte, as the eldest, resolved to write to Southey.'

13.   Mary Smith, *Schoolmistress and Nonconformist: Autobiography* (London and Carlisle: Bemrose & Sons, 1892), I (of 2 volumes) Appendix, letter from Jane Welsh Carlyle, p. 308.

14.   Mary Smith, pp. 309-10. The emphases are those of Jane Carlyle.

15.   Ellen Johnston is an example of how reflexivity is class bound. Her 'factory girl' poems are published locally in journals and newspapers, and are presented alongside an invitation to reply, to the column 'poetic responses'. The readers share the culture and class of the writer. The fan mail follows:

> I'm proud tae see a factory lass
> The modern bardies a' surpass;
> I'll buy her book if I have brass
>   Be't cheap or dear,
> An' read it ower a flowing glass
>   My heart to cheer.

16. Florence White, pp. 92-3.
17. There is a difference, that is, in the life which might be represented as an achievement, and the explicit rhetoric of 'work opportunity'. Florence White's autobiography moves between the two, and the two are mutually influential. Though she does uphold domestic service as suitable and satisfying work, it is the unusual and the unique which she upholds when illustrating 'opportunity' for women.
18. In writing, it is that category, that subjectivity of 'the cook' which forms that unity required by 'the literary'. I mention this again (and in relation to Florence White) later in this chapter.
19. Mary Smith, I.
20. Elizabeth Ham.
21. Rose Allen, *The Autobiography of Rose Allen* (London: Longman & Co., 1847), and Mary Ann Ashford, *Life of a Licensed Victualler's Daughter* (London: Saunders & Otley, 1844).
22. Annie Kenney, *Memories of a Militant* (London: E. Arnold & Co., 1924).
23. Elizabeth Ham.
24. A notion of individuality which can derive from a unity called work or waged labour is not available to women. It conflicts materially and ideologically with marriage and the home (which is also work) and is, anyway, in being gender-specific, not a unity for women, but disrupted, discontinuous, etc. (as I have shown). In comparison, most men's lives do not put labour and home in ideological conflict, rather, the role of the male bread-winner depends on both and on reconciling both.
25. See chapter 1, 'Outrageous Claims'.
26. It seems though, that working women are less able than working-class men to further the individual through the social group. Again, the routes and institutions are not available.
    David Vincent, p. 177, for how working-class men 'sought to use book knowledge to enhance the freedom of themselves and their class'.

27. Mary Smith, p. 200.
28. Mary Smith, p. 214.
29. Mary Smith, p. 192.
30. Mary Smith, p. 225.
31. Ellen Weeton, p. 9 of Edward Hall's introduction.
32. Mary Barber, p. 16.
33. Florence White, p. 3.
34. Elizabeth Ham, p. 13.
35. Rose Allen, p. 161.
36. This could account for why the average age of the women autobiographers at the time of writing appears to be lower than that of working-class men. Vincent, p. 203, of working-class autobiography: 'the majority were written in old age'.
37. Mary Ashford, pp. iii-iv.
38. Mrs Layton, *Memories of Seventy Years* (London: 1931) in *Life as We Have Known it*, edited by Margaret Llewelyn Davies (London: Virago, 1977), pp. 12-14.
39. Florence White, pp. ix-x.
40. See chapter epigraph on page 173 from George Eliot, *Middlemarch*, 1872.

8 PROFESSIONAL HISTORIANS, AMATEUR BRAIN SURGEONS

1. Rose Allen, *The Autobiography of Rose Allen* (London: Longman & Co., 1847), title-page.
2. Rose Allen, preface.
3. M. A. S. Barber (Mary Barber), *Bread-Winning or The Ledger and the Lute: an Autobiography* (London: William Macintosh, 1865), introduction.
4. Mary Barber, p. vi.
5. See my previous chapter.
6. Mary Barber, p. 124.
7. Ellen Weeton, *Miss Weeton's Journal of a Governess*, 1969, a reprint of *Miss Weeton: Journal of a Governess*, first published under the title of *Miss Weeton* by the Oxford University Press in 1936, I (of 2 volumes), Hall introduction.

8. My previous chapter.
9. Ellen Weeton, I, Hall introduction.
10. See the issue of 'work' in my previous chapter.
11. Elizabeth Ham, *Elizabeth Ham by Herself 1783-1820* (London: Faber, 1945), introduction, p. 12.
12. Elizabeth Ham, introduction, p. 7.
13. *Life as We Have Known it*, edited by Margaret Llewelyn Davies (London: Virago, 1977). Virginia Woolf (introductory letter), p. xi.
14. *Life as We Have Known it*, introductory Letter, p. xxix.
15. *Life as We Have Known it*, p. xxix.
16. *Life as We Have Known it*, p. xxx.
17. Ellen Weeton, I, Bagley introduction.
18. Ellen Weeton, I, Bagley introduction.
19. Ellen Weeton, II, p. 138.
20. *Life as We Have Known it*, p. vii.
21. *Harriet Martineau's Autobiography: Volume 1,* 1877 (Virago, 1983), p. ix.
22. Kathleen Woodward, *Jipping Street*, first published 1928 (London: Virago, 1983), p. xiv.
23. Which Virginia Woolf could not gain access to: Virginia Woolf, *A Room of One's Own*, first published 1929 (London: Granada, 1977).
24. As with Mary Smith and Jane Carlyle: see my previous chapter.
25. To make reference back to the title-page of this chapter: Popular Memory Group, Centre for Contemporary Cultural Studies, *Making Histories* (London, Hutchinson, 1982).
26. Susanne Kappeler, 'Falling in Love with Milly Theale: Patriarchal Criticism and Henry James' *The Wings of the Dove*', *Feminist Review*, Spring 1983, pp. 17: introduced me to critics who fall in love with heroines.
27. My previous chapter.
28. David Vincent, *Bread, Knowledge and Freedom*: *a Study of 19th-Century Working Class Autobiography* (London: Methuen 1982), pp. 8-9.

The one major silence is that of women. When I began to collect these works I expected to find at least a sizeable minority of autobiographies by working women covering the first half of the century: I have located just those of the cotton weaver Catherine Horne, the domestic servant Janet Bathgate, the Fen child worker Mrs Burrows, the 97 year old widow Elspeth Clark, the straw-plait worker Lucy Luck and the servant and teacher Mary Smith. There is a scattering of works by humble eighteenth century poetesses, and an increasing volume of material from later in the nineteenth century, but for this period the composition of autobiographies seems to have been very largely a male prerogative. Why this should be the case is an interesting question. It cannot be explained merely by differentials in literacy, and there was a relative equality of opportunity within the very low levels of education open to working class children at this time. The answer must lie, in general terms, in the absence among women of the self-confidence required to undertake the unusual act of writing an autobiography, and in particular from the increasing exclusion of women from most forms of the working class organizations, especially self-improvement societies, which provided the training and stimulus for self-expression for so many of the male autobiographers. The silence may also be a reflection of the subordinate position of women within the family: the husband was the head of the family and as such thought to be responsible for communicating its history to future generations. The consequence of the silence is that here, as in so much of written history, women can rarely be seen, except through the eyes of the fathers, husbands, lovers and sons.

29. Autobiography as genre is low in the hierarchy of literary genres. It is, in a sense, the 'amateur' genre, dependent on a fame achieved in some other sphere or in some other genre, or precisely a bid for recognition for lives characterized by lack of fame or social status (particularly in the literary sphere). In the nineteenth century, realism creates some space for self-

representations by working women. The existence of representations (in fiction) of domestic servants, factory workers, etc. allows working women, though within the constraints of genre, to answer back.

30. A male member of Cambridge English Faculty announced recently that nineteenth-century autobiography is 'doomed'. As Edward Hall to blue-stockings (and miners), so the Cambridge English Faculty to nineteenth-century working women.

31. I prefer to think that the women's presses who have rescued some nineteenth-century working women's autobiographies are here to stay.

32. *Making Histories*, p. 239.

33. The sort of argument that says socialism is a levelling to the lowest common denominator, a colourless uniformity.

34. Diane Harpwood, *Tea and Tranquillisers* (London: Virago, 1981), pp. 42-3.

Index